# TRINITARIAN LETTERS

## YOUR ADOPTION AND INCLUSION IN THE LIFE OF GOD

Paul Kurts

WestBow
PRESS
A DIVISION OF THOMAS NELSON

WestBow Press books may be ordered through booksellers or by contacting:

WestBow Press
A Division of Thomas Nelson
1663 Liberty Drive
Bloomington, IN 47403
www.westbowpress.com
1-(866) 928-1240

ISBN: 978-1-4497-0940-2 (sc)
ISBN: 978-1-4497-0941-9 (e)

Library of Congress Control Number: 2010941846

Printed in the United States of America

WestBow Press rev. date: 04/19/2012

DEDICATION

"ONLY GOD KNOWS HOW MUCH I LOVE MY FAMILY TO
WHOM I DEDICATE THIS BOOK. MAY YOU ALWAYS SHARE
THIS GOOD NEWS."

www.trinitarianletters.com

# AUTHOR BIOGRAPHY

Paul was born, along with a twin sister, Pattie, in Philadelphia, Mississippi in 1944. The family soon moved to Jackson, Mississippi where the children grew up.

Over the years Paul had many varied interests in his life. Participating in music, choir, band, symphony and many youth sports of baseball, basketball, tennis and collegiate golf. He later coached baseball, basketball and instructed golf professionally for over 40 years.

Paul graduated from Mississippi State University in 1966 with majors in Political Science (pre-law) and Psychology. He graduated from Ambassador University in 1972 with a Theology degree. Paul has an honorable discharge from the United States Air Force and still maintains an interest in flying with a private pilot's license. Other interests include writing poetry and a love of learning.

With his wife, Pat, the Kurts have pastored Grace Communion International churches around the eastern United States for over 40 years. Now retired from full time pastoring Paul devotes much spare time to studying and writing on Trinitarian, Adoption and Inclusion Theology— an understanding of God's Love for all of humanity and His plan to have mankind live inside of His life forever made a reality for all by Jesus Christ.

The Kurts have three grown children, Pastor Paul David, Michael Shane and Dr. Allison K. Kurts and two grandsons, James Paul Kurts and Michael David Kurts.

Paul continues speaking engagements around the country sharing God's Love for all people. The Kurts reside in Madison, Alabama.

# FOREWORD

Why this book? Why at this time? Why YOU need to know this Truth. Christians and non-Christians alike deep down are not happy or filled with joy. Many Christians have their church clothes, faces, and actions but realize something is missing and they feel like hypocrites when they know full well they are not measuring up to standards they or the Church has set for them. Non-Christians feel miserable not knowing why they are living in this physical world and knowing something is missing in their life but they don't know what it is.

This book comes along on the heels of ancient great church leaders who knew the truth of why God created man in the first place! Men like Irenaus and Athenasius, and later theologians like Karl Barth, T.F. Torrance, J.B. Torrance, C. Baxter Kruger, Colin Gunton, Michael Jinkins, Robert Capon and others knew the real reason God made humanity and why Jesus came to the earth and why Jesus had to die and what Jesus' life, death, resurrection, and ascension meant for All mankind. These great Theologians mentioned here, as do most Theologians, write from an erudite and professorial standpoint. One almost has to be a theologian himself in order to understand what these very learned men write. This book is different. It speaks in layman's language. Clearly. Plainly. Understandably. Written in short and concise revealing chapters or letters.

Why NOW this book? Most of the Christian world and the world as a whole have wandered around the complete truth of the Gospel mainly focusing on the Cross and the forgiveness of our sins rather than on the ORIGINAL purpose God made man in the first place. And make no mistake, the forgiveness of our sins was critical. This book brings the complete Gospel to light.

The really amazing thing about this truth is that it is SO PLAINLY revealed throughout scripture that we could ask ourselves how has it been pushed aside by so many churches and Christians over the centuries?

You need to know this truth!! We have wallowed around in Greek Philosophy long enough. False philosophies which crept into the church over the ages have caused much anguish and unneeded suffering. You will see where they came from and how they have remained in the Western Christian church. We have NOT been set free because we have only had part of the truth that is in Jesus, only part of the Gospel.

Get ready. Your are about to read in easily read short chapters the Greatest Good News you will ever hear in your life. You will see it in step by step fashion. You are going to see just how much God the Father LOVES YOU and get this, He always has even BEFORE you were born!!! You are getting ready to see the Real GOSPEL through new lens, new glasses, and new pagadigms. Come see THE GOSPEL OF JESUS CHRIST.

# CONTENTS

AUTHOR BIOGRAPHY     vii

FOREWORD     ix

ACTS 2 – THE POURING OUT OF THE HOLY SPIRIT     1

ADOPTED AND INCLUDED IN GOD'S LIFE     2

ADVOCATE AND INTERCESSOR…NOW!     4

THE "ALREADY" BUT "NOT YET" REALITY     6

ANNOUNCING THE TRUE GOSPEL OF CHRIST     7

ANOTHER LOOK AT SPIRITUAL GIFTS     9

ANSWERING THE GREATEST QUESTIONS     11

ARE SET FREE CHRISTIANS FREE TO SIN ?     13

ARE THE DEAD CONSCIOUS WITH GOD NOW?     15

BEFORE TIME BEGAN AUGUST 11, 02     16

BELIEVE…BUT BELIEVE WHAT ?     17

SIN, BLASPHEMY/ BLASPHEMY AGAINST GOD     19

CALVANISM'S & ARMENIANISM'S ERROR     20

CAN SOMEONE "FALL FROM GRACE" ?     22

CAN MAN BE SEPARATED FROM GOD ?     24

CAN SINS 'EXCLUDE' ONE FROM INHERITANCE IN THE LIFE OF GOD ?     25

CAN WE BE "TOO" SINFUL TO BE FORGIVEN ?     27

CAN WE DISQUALIFY FOR SALVATION ?     28

CAN WE "LET GOD DOWN" ?     30

CAN WE SEPARATE OURSELVES FROM GOD ?     32

CAN CHRISTIANS FORFEIT THEIR SALVATION?     33

CONDEMNATION--"HELL" OR UNBELIEF?     35

DO SCRIPTURES CONTRADICT THE GOSPEL? Pt.2     36

DO SCRIPTURES CONTRADICT THE GOSPEL ?     38

DO SOME 'NOT' BELONG TO CHRIST ?     41

DOES CREATION PRECEDE COVENANT ?     43

DOES SCRIPTURE ADDRESS US ALL ?     44

EVERYONE IS A THEOLOGIAN !!!     46

EZEKIEL CHAPTER 37 DRY BONES AND RESURRECTION     47

FAITH VS. SCIENCE     49

GOD HAS FULLY BLESSED US ALL IN JESUS     50

GOD LIKES YOU! REALLY !!!     52

GOD SEES IN THE PRESENT     53

GOD'S ORIGINAL PLAN STANDS FIRM FOREVER     54

GOD'S PLAN     56

GOD'S PLAN ASSURED FROM THE START     57

GOD'S PLAN INCLUDES EVERYONE !     58

GOD'S PLAN OR YOURS ?                                   59
GOD'S REALITY AND OUR EXPERIENCE                       60
GOOD NEWS FOR......YOU !!!                              62
GROWING SPIRITUALLY FOREVER                            62
GROWING UP IN JESUS—FOREVER !                          64
THE HEALING OF THE PRODIGAL SON                        65
HEAVEN-- MORE THAN GOLD AND PEARLS !                   67
HEBREWS 6:4-6—FALLING AWAY FOREVER?                    68
HELL IS GOING TO BE " HELL"                            70
HELL. NOT WHAT YOU MAY HAVE THOUGHT                    72
HOLINESS AND HOW WE GET IT                             73
HOW GOD SEES                                           74
HOW LONG UNTILL CHRIST RETURNS ?                       75
" I HAVE OVERCOME THE WORLD ! "                        77
"I NEVER KNEW YOU!" MATTHEW 7:21-24                    79
"I WILL MAKE YOU FISHERS OF MEN !"                     80
IMMANUEL IS NOT JUST FOR CHRISTIANS                    81
IMMANUEL—MORE THAN GOD "WITH" US !                     83
IN THE IMAGE OF GOD                                    84
IN WHAT "TENSE" DO WE READ SCRIPTURE?                  86
INCARNATIONAL THEOLOGY- GOD ACCEPTS US!                88
INSTINCT ? OR GOD ?                                    90
IS GOD BIG ENOUGH ?                                    91
IS GOD DISTANT AND UNINVOLVED                          93
IS GOD FAIR ?                                          95
IS IT FINISHED OR IS IT DONE ???                       96
IS JEREMIAH 10 ABOUT CHRISTMAS TREES ?                 98
IS JESUS' RESURRECTION ALL INCLUSIVE?                  99
IS THE GOOD NEWS FOR "EVERYONE" ?                     101
IS THE HOLY SPIRIT GOD OR A POWER?                    102
IS THE HOLY SPIRIT IN ALL HUMANS ?                    104
IS THIS YOUR VIEW OF HELL—REALLY?                     105
JESUS AND NICODEMUS-WHAT'S GOING ON?                  108
JESUS CAME TO SAVE WHAT WAS LOST                      109
JESUS IS THE RESURRECTION FOR ALL--NOW                110
JESUS REVEALS OUR INCLUSION                           112
JESUS THE SAVIOUR OF THE WHOLE WORLD                  114
JESUS...THE ULTIMATE SURROGATE !                      115
JESUS, THE VICARIOUS HUMAN                            116
THE RESURRECTED BODY                                  118
JESUS—THE EVER PRESENT GOD !                          120
JUST HOW BIG IS OUR CREATOR ?                         122
"LET GO AND LET GOD"                                  124

LIVING INSIDE THE KINGDOM OF GOD—NOW! 125
LOOKING DOWN ON THE ENEMIES OF GOD 126
MALACHI 4:3 AND TREADING THE WICKED 128
MORE GOOD NEWS ABOUT SALVATION 129
NO MORE PRICE TO PAY….EVER ! 130
OLD COVENANT FEAST DAYS 132
OUR VIEW AND GOD'S VIEW OF SCRIPTURE 133
OUTLINE OF THE GOSPEL OF JESUS CHRIST 134
FOR GOD SO LOVED THE WORLD !!! 137
PAUL INTERPRETS THE GOSPELS !!! 139
PHILOSOPHY OR THEOLOGY—WHICH? 140
RELIGIONS ARE NOT THE WAY TO GOD 142
REPLACING THE 'IF' FACTOR WITH 'SINCE'! 144
REVELATION 'SIMPLY' REVEALED 146
YOUR PERSONAL GOOD NEWS 148
SALVATION, HELL AND UNIVERSALISM 151
SALVATION IS NOT A CONTEST!!! 153
SEEING THE 'REAL' GOD OF CREATION 154
SIMPLICITY OF THE TRUTH 157
THE COMMANDS OF JESUS CHRIST 158
JESUS COMMANDS 159
THE BOOK OF LUKE 160
THE BOOK OF JOHN 161
THE BELIEVERS' UNBELIEF 161
THE "BEST" NEWS YOU WILL EVER HEAR ! 163
THE CHRISTIAN'S HOPE 164
THE GOSPEL FOR CHILDREN 165
THE GOSPEL IS ADOPTION BY GOD 166
THE PAROUSIA OF JESUS 167
THE RESURRECTED BODY 169
THE TRUTH OF GOD MAY NOT BE WHAT YOU'VE HEARD 171
THE TRUTH SHALL SET YOU FREE 173
THE TWO DYNAMICS 174
THE ULTIMATE FUTURE 176
THE "WAGES OF SIN" AND THE "GIFT OF GOD" 177
THE "WHAT IF" FAITH 178
WORSHIPPING GOD AS THE PAGANS DID ? 179
THE WORD AND JESUS MAKE IT SO. 181
TRUTH FOR BELIEVERS AND UNBELIEVERS 182
TRUTH FOR BELIEVERS AND THE "UNPARDONABLE SIN"
WHAT IS IT ? 183
WALKING IN THE FLESH AND SPIRIT 184
WE NEVER DIE IN JESUS 186

WHAT DO CHRISTIANS, JEWS, BUDDHISTS, MUSLIMS, HIN-
DUS, ATHEISTS AND ALL OTHER RELIGIONS HAVE IN COM-
MON?                                                     188
WHAT DO YOU MEAN, "ENDURE TO THE END"?                   189
WHAT DO YOU MEAN INCLUDED ?                              191
WHAT GOD HAS DONE FOR US ALL                             192
WHAT IS THE "HELL" OF II Peter 2:4 ?                     193
WHAT IS YOUR VIEW OF GOD AND HOLY?                       194
WHAT KIND OF THEOLOGY DO YOU WANT ?                      196
WHAT THE LAST JUDGEMENT IS AND IS NOT                    198
WHEN GOD'S TIME CAME                                     200
WHEN WAS / IS MAN ADOPTED BY CHRIST ?                    201
WHERE DO YOU GET YOUR TRUTH ?                            203
WHERE IS JESUS WHEN WE SIN ?                             205
WHERE THE HELL DID THAT COME FROM?                       206
WHO COMES INSIDE THE "PARTY" ?                           208
WHOSE FAITH REALLY MATTERS ?                             209
WHY CHRISTIAN LIVING ?                                   211
WHY IS BELIEVING ENOUGH?                                 212
WHY MAN AND THE INCARNATION?                             214
WHY MANKIND HATES THE TRUTH OF JESUS                     216
WHY TELL SOMEONE THE GOOD NEWS ?                         218
WILL GOD PUNISH THE WICKED FOREVER?                      219
WITH ADAM'S SIN, WHAT WAS GOD TO DO?                     220
"WORK OUT YOUR OWN SALVATION"?                           222
WORSHIPPING GOD AS THE PAGANS DID?                       223
YOU CAN'T HAVE IT BOTH WAYS !                            224
YOUR INCLUSION IN THE LIFE OF GOD                        226
JESUS ACCEPTED US INTO HIS LIFE ORIGINALLY               229
YOUR PERSONAL GOOD NEWS                                  230
RESOURCES  AND RECOMMENDED READING LIST                  233

# ACTS 2 – THE POURING OUT OF THE HOLY SPIRIT

When Joel 2 is fulfilled in Acts 2 on the Day of Pentecost, something happens at that time that was "new and different" than the way things had been since the garden of Eden.

Several questions arise concerning the inclusion of all humans IN Jesus "since before the foundation of the world." Is SALVATION dependent upon one "receiving and having" the Holy Spirit? Did people have the Holy Spirit before the Day of Pentecost in Acts 2?

There are many things that the Great Triune God keeps for Himself in spiritual theological understanding. We can look at this subject here, but we may NOT be able to answer any and all questions concerning this Truth.

We do know that all things were created by, for, in, and through Jesus Christ. ( Colossians Ch.1). We know ALL humans are IN Jesus. ( Jn. 14:20) He sustains all things in creation. In Jesus all humans have lived, moved, and had their being since Adam. ( Acts 17:28). Jesus died for ALL humans, was resurrected for all humans, and ascended and carried all humans to the Father in Heaven. ( Eph.2:6). This is objectively the Truth even before Pentecost in Acts 2.

On occasion in the Old Testament some are mentioned as having the Holy Spirit, ie., David ( Psalm 51) and others. But, Acts 2 points out that this phenomenon was a fulfillment to occur "at the last day". Remember that last days began with the ministry of Jesus. Not the 20th Century.

The Greatest event of all of Created time was the Incarnation of God as a human being in Jesus. After the resurrection of Jesus God fulfills His prophecy of Joel 2 and on the Day of Pentecost in Acts 2 "Pours out His Holy Spirit" on ALL humans. Powerful signs accompanying the miracle.

Man had always been IN Jesus, reconciled in Jesus, saved in Jesus, and included in the life of God. But now, the Holy Spirit would be AVAILABLE to humans to allow for ACTIVE PARTICIPATION in the relationship of God and man. The Holy Spirit would be there to go along side with man. Teach man and lead man into All Truth. Teach man more and more about the Great Triune God—Father, Son, and Holy Spirit, and become more Christ-like. A new day dawned in the history of mankind, the Savior had come, the Holy Spirit had now come being "poured out" or MAGNIFIED in humans' minds to see and understand the truth of the

1

Gospel when revealed to them. The Truth of Jesus would grow to cover the earth as the oceans do, and that continues to this day!

The intimate life of the Holy Spirit IN ALL flesh would allow humanness to be changed from the inside out. To "grow in the Spirit."

To become more and more like Jesus Christ. To have more and more of the mind of Christ. To experience more of the LIFE of Christ in us. The Spirit is now available for all of this and He was POURED OUT ON PENTECOST in Acts 2 on ALL Flesh.

The Holy Spirit allows us to EXPERIENCE and LIVE in the New Covenant of Jesus Christ. He generates in us and empowers in us the ABUNDANT LIFE Jesus gives. He is POWERFUL. He is WONDERFUL.

We see most in the world who do not know or believe that the Holy Spirit has been "poured out" on them as well. He is ready to help them understand the Gospel when it is presented to them. When they come to know and understand who they are in Jesus and believe it, then the RELATIONSHIP, security, peace, joy, assurance, and abundant life begins to start bearing the fruit of the Holy Spirit that was poured out on all humans since Pentecost in Acts 2.

The key factor is that although the Holy Spirit has been poured out on everyone, they must come to see, understand, and believe who they are in Jesus, otherwise the Holy Spirit will not be experienced in their life like He wants to be experienced.

He IS there ready to be appreciated more fully when they come to belief. That is why sharing the Gospel with these people is important. It helps grow the Kingdom and helps people come to the Joy of the Lord and live in that ABUNDANCE and ASSURANCE.

May we be bearers of the Truth of the Holy Spirit to others as we share the GREATEST NEWS EVER, The GOSPEL OF JESUS CHRIST.


# ADOPTED AND INCLUDED IN GOD'S LIFE

The god of this world has deceived it so completely that the truth of God and His love for us as demonstrated from His original plan to take humanity into His very life and live forever with all of us has been all but lost in the religions of the world. ( II Cor.4:4).

The Father, Son, and Holy Spirit destined us to be adopted ( Ephesians 1:3-5) into the very life of God through the incarnation of the Word which became flesh—Jesus Christ. Whether man ever sinned or not, the plan was going to be completed in Jesus. However, when man did sin all of the sin of the world was taken away in the ultimate sacrifice of the life of Jesus Christ. Sin no longer would factor into the salvation equation for man. Through the one man Jesus life was granted to all humanity. ( Romans 5:18; I Cor.15:22-23).

With the incarnation of the Word, God connected humanity and created the necessary UNION to take humanity into God's existence and very life through the Spirit. Jesus talks about this in John 14:20 when He says that, "…in that day you will realize that I am in the Father, you are in me, and I am in you." Later we see in Acts 2 the Holy Spirit being poured out on all people to allow us all to begin to see this reality.

With the life, death, resurrection and ascension of Jesus and His being seated at the right hand of the Father, we were taken by Jesus and seated with Him at the Father's right hand as well. ( Spiritually and Objectively speaking, Ephesians 2:6).

What this means is that every blessing God the Father has blessed Jesus with WE are blessed with as well in the Heavenly realms. ( Ephesians 1:3).

The radical truth of this means that in Christ the fullness of the Deity lives in bodily form and that we have been given fullness in Christ. (Colossians 2:9-10). Another way of saying this is to say that The Triune God has taken us INTO His very Triune life by and through Jesus Christ in and by the Spirit. This is WHO we really are and WHERE we really are. FOREVER.

Notice the " Past tense" application of all of this for us. This is not something that is going to happen in the future, this has already happened in Jesus Christ. The Holy Spirit is just revealing it to us more and more and one of these days we will see it in its fullness when we "see Jesus as He is." We will be "like" Him with His likeness. ( I John 3:2).

We often mistake I Corinthians 2:9 as being fulfilled in the future. This verse says that no eye has seen, no ear heard, no mind conceived what God has prepared for those who love Him. But verse 10 clearly says that by the Holy Spirit of God He has revealed these things to us NOW.! This is what we are discussing here in this paper. It can't get any better for us all than what you read here. How could you ever add to what God has already done for us, to us, in us, and blessed us with in Jesus and even included us into His very life forever? We just wait for it ALL to be revealed to us in His "time".

Lord I believe, help my unbelief.

AMEN


# ADVOCATE AND INTERCESSOR...NOW!


It is a wrong concept to think that Jesus was the eternal sacrifice at the Cross for all sins and then just went off to Heaven to be back with the Father as they had always existed. Far from it. If that were true then Jesus would be no more than a payment for sins and with that job done return to the Father in Heaven with nothing left to do. But Jesus is far more than a payment for our sins—which He is.!!!

Jesus Christ is a human being at the right hand of the Father in Heaven! He is the continual incarnate Son of God. His Incarnation continues on and His humanity continues on as He takes our humanity upon Himself perpetually.

It is Jesus Christ who is at the right hand of the Father who has a powerful continuing job to do as our Saviour. Jesus is our Saviour, to be sure, but that job was not over at the Cross and resurrection . Jesus continues to be our Saviour, redeemer and deliverer,

Jesus performs a continuing special job at the Father's right hand. He is our ADVOCATE. ( I John 2:1). He is our spokes person. He is, in legal terms, our Lawyer, or our attorney. He knows what it is to be human since He was and STILL is. ( He is also God.) He knows the weaknesses and sins of humanity since He took all of them on and into Himself and became that sin for us all. ( II Cor. 5:19-21). He obviously knows we still sin and will continue to do so.

Jesus does not work a 9 to 5 job at the Father's right hand. He is there 24/7. He is there all the time. He is there on our behalf interceding for us always to see to it that we forever stand in forgiveness and righteousness before the Father. It is His declaration and will to do so. It is His job. He is Advocate ( Lawyer) and Intercessor for us ALL THE TIME. (Hebrews 7:25).

It does not catch Jesus by surprise when we sin. Sins do not shock Him. In our humanity we live in the fallenness of Adam. The evils and sins of human beings do not catch Jesus off guard. He is fully aware of them. He takes them ON and INTO Himself and forgives them and reminds the Father that they are all forgiven in Himself.

Not only is Jesus our Advocate, or Lawyer, He is also the JUDGE. John 5:22 shows that all judgement has been given to the Son and that the Father judges no man. This is a pretty good deal for us humans. Jesus is the "lawyer" for us and He is also the Judge. A little "home cooking" if you ask me.

So, when Jesus tells us that He has overcome the world and to be of good cheer, ( John 16:33), He is aware of the sins that so easily befall all of us, He is aware of all the trials of dealing with our personal inadequacies and weaknesses that we see so often in ourselves, and He knows we look at ourselves as unworthy often times. So, He says , " I have overcome these things of the world," so be of good cheer. Be Happy. Rejoice. It does not depend on you, it depends on ME!

Again in Matt:11:27-29, He tells us all who are weary and heavy laden and burdened by our personal humanity and sinfullness to come to Him and realize we can rest in Him. REST. He says He has done it all for us. Realize it and REST.

Jesus continues to be incarnate. It is in His eternal humanity that He is our Advocate and Intercessor at all times. There are no sins of mind or physical sins we can possibly commit that Jesus has not already taken care of. This is what it means to have a "living sacrifice and Saviour" always at the Father's right hand as Advocate and Intercessor.

So what can we do? Nothing. Nothing but be thankful, rejoice, celebrate, appreciate, and love the one who loved us before we were ever born. Rejoice that Jesus has taken all of us to the Father's right hand with Himself and seated us there. ( Ephesians 2:6).

You may be disappointed to know that there is NOTHING you can do to aid in your salvation process. Get over it. Deal with it. But by all means , BELIEVE IT.!!!

Thank you, Jesus.

AMEN

# THE "ALREADY" BUT "NOT YET" REALITY
## ( OBJECTIVE AND SUBJECTIVE UNDERSTANDING )

In understanding the TRUTH of Jesus, there are several areas when viewed from the human perspective seem either too good to be true, or impossible.

The Good News is really quite simple. "God is Love and He created mankind to live in and with Him always, and He made all the arrangements for that to take place in Jesus Christ. PERIOD.

When we look at God's Plan from our "subjective" viewpoint, we see through our own lens of interpretations with all kinds of machinations and hoops and ladders through which to jump or crawl. Do's, Don'ts, standards, laws, morality, deeds, overcoming, qualifying, and attaining eternal life based on what we bring to the experience. Salvation becomes a challenge to the human life and a contest to see if one can "make" it. We do not see ourselves in the present reality of living in salvation and eternal life NOW. Everything is "conditional". Maybe we'll experience it and maybe we won't.

When we look at God's Plan from His "objective" perspective we see the picture quite differently. Adoption and salvation by God along with all the spiritual implications which this includes are not something to be "gained" or waited for or hoped for, but these are a present reality which God has declared by His Sovereignty in our life NOW secured in Jesus Christ.

Said another way, what God has done in humans in Jesus Christ has an "already done" aspect and also a "not yet" aspect as well. For example, in Rom.6:1-4, we see that we have been raised with Christ. We have been resurrected with Him. We walk in His newness of Life. All this already a reality. However, we await the literal change of our bodies into immortal bodies at Christ's Second Coming for that has not yet happened. Again in Eph.1, we see our Adoption by God from the foundation of the world. Yet in Rom.8:22-23, we see our "waiting" for our adoption as sons by the final exercise in the "redemption" or CHANGE of our physical BODIES.

In Rom.8:30, we see the already aspect in the fact that God predestined, called, justified, and glorified those He foreknew. From God's OBJECTIVE PERSPECTIVE this is a present reality. Yet, from our subjective view, we are waiting for our bodily change into Glory when Christ returns.

The question then is this: What is TRUTH? Whose viewpoint or perspective are we going to trust and have faith in? God's Objective and "already" eternal view, or our subjective and present view based on our personal experience. Is our view based on what God KNOWS or on what we THINK and FEEL?

We read scripture and view it through a linear or time and space understanding. We experience the present, relate to the past, and expect and look to the future.

God, however, is much different than this. He is the Great "I AM". He created time and space. He dwells in eternity. He also exists outside of time and space and sees everything in the PRESENT. He sees the ultimate finished "product" of our faith. He sees us in His presence forever NOW.

God simply makes the declarations that we are loved , adopted, redeemed, reconciled, justified, saved, and glorified because that is the way it IS with Him and the way He sees it. He then says that no one or nothing can change that FACT. ( Rom.8:37-39). Jesus says in John 10:29-30, that no one can snatch God's children out of the Father's hand . And, that He and the Father are one.

When the "already" but "not yet" revelation of scripture presents itself to us, let's always remember Who it is Who is in charge. Who has designed this wonderful plan to stand the test of all time and stands the test against ALL powers of the Universe.

God says, " I have declared it, I WILL DO IT.!!!"

And that is good enough for me!

AMEN

# ANNOUNCING THE TRUE GOSPEL OF CHRIST

The Gospel of Jesus Christ is a truth that goes back to 'before the creation of time, space, or the cosmos"! God's original plan included humanity being taken into the life of God. Jesus made it happen by becoming a human, fully human, yet still being fully God as well. Let's notice scriptures which speak to this.

Rev.13:8; I Pet.1:18-20, Jesus was chosen and slain before the foundation of the world to be Savior of mankind. All of mankind was "elected" by God at that time to be given eternal life, Titus 1:1. God simply foreknew us and predestined us to be conformed to the likeness of His Son. Rom.8:28-34.

II Timothy 1:8-10, shows that this Grace of God was given to us in Christ before the beginning of time, and NOW is revealed to us. It is God's time to reveal it! II Thes.2:13, from the beginning God chose us all to be saved through the sanctifying work of the Spirit and through belief in the Truth.

Ephesians 1:3-14, God Adopted us and chose us in Christ before the creation of the world to **BE** ( not become) Holy and Blameless IN His sight, and done so by His Glorious Grace and by HIS WILL and for HIS Good Pleasure. This is what God did because He WANTED to.

Jesus came to make it happen and He did. "It is Finished", Jesus proclaims in John 19:30. Jesus is the Author and Finisher of our faith. Heb.12:2. We are promised in Philippians 1:6, that He who began a good work in you will finish it. And God gives us the Victory through Jesus, I Cor.15:57.

What we see here in this revealing of the Plan of God is that God's Plan and the Good News—The Gospel of Jesus Christ and Salvation in Christ—is NOT something to be attained by whatever means, NOT some opportunity to be saved by God, NOT some challenge to "make it" into God's Good Graces and thereby become Saved. NO, the Good News is an ANNOUNCEMENT. It is a PROCLAMATION of what God has done in Jesus for His creation.

The problem we have seeing all of this is that we all come from a background of Western Theological Philosophy dealing with Christianity which is bound up in legalism and Plato's philosophy dealing with 'rewards and punishment' that we can not see the Amazing Love of God for all of His creation and for His children, all of His children,

Satan wants us desperately to believe that God chose some to be saved and in relationship with Him forever, and chose others to be tormented and tortured forever in the eternal flames of 'hell fire'—i.e. that God Damned those children from the very beginning. What a terrible lie. It causes humans to look at God as some Cosmic, Capricious, Callused, Caustic, Clandestine, and Confused Ogre God that we find hard, if not impossible, to honor and love. This false concept of a loving Heavenly

Father does NOT come from God. It should be obvious where it comes from. Satan does not want any of us loving our Dad in Heaven.

Satan has inspired the idea of a "hell" since the very first world religion called Zorastrianism. (Sp.?) One goes to a Bad place if your evil outweighs your good, and a good place if your good outweighs your evil. Plato refined the concept in the fourth century B.C. when he introduced the idea of "HELL and HELL FIRE". Levels of hell, etc. St. Augustine of Hippo further promulgated the idea in the 5th Century A.D. in the Catholic Church. And it has stayed around in Western Theology ever since. But, note carefully. JESUS NEVER PREACHED ABOUT THE CONCEPT OF TORTURING ANYONE IN A FIERY EVER BURNING HELL FIRE. That simply violates God's love for His children.

God is LOVE. He loves all of us and has provided a wonderful future in His eternity with Him and each other to all who believe. Believe who we are in Jesus and what Jesus has done for us and to us. It really is Good News , or as Karl Barth said, "the Best News"!

Finally, let me just say that YOU are Adopted by God, Included in the life of God, Wanted by God, Loved by God, and Secure in His loving embrace and have been since the very beginning. Jesus has made it so.

Can we believe? Lord, I believe, help my unbelief.

AMEN


# ANOTHER LOOK AT SPIRITUAL GIFTS


Spiritual gifts can be and have been a much-debated subject over the years. The question as to who has which gift and how much of it and who does not have which gift has been discussed many times.

To be sure I Corinthians 12:4-11 and I Peter 4:7-11 mention Spiritual gifts. So we definitely have scriptural backing for the reality of Spiritual gifts. The problem arises when we try to assess who has which one or ones and how many a person may have.

Often thought is the idea that each one of us has at least one and sometimes two or three, maybe more. Also often as not some who have the manifestation of a particular gift have become puffed up over the gift or vain about it or somehow have allowed self aggrandizement, self adulation and self exaltation to be manifested as well. Sadly this is not the purpose of Spiritual gifts. ( Tongues and healing could be sited here.)

I Corinthians 12 shows that there are differing Spiritual gifts but all from the same Spirit from the One Lord who works ALL of them in ALL men! This being done for the common good of all. All of the gifts are the work of one and the same Spirit and God exercises them in each person just as He determines at the time each gift needs to be applied for the benefit of others.

But if Spiritual gifts are only given and parceled out to specific individuals by one or two or even three Spiritual gifts, then what if God were to need a person with the gift of healing, or the gift of tongues or any other gift and NO one is around with that particular gift? Oops, is God now up a creek?

Could it be that since all humans live and move and have their being in Jesus Christ by the same Spirit (Acts 17:28) and since there is only one Holy Spirit that ALL people possess through and by Christ, could it be that ALL have all of the Gifts of the Spirit inherent within? By the Spirit Christ can call forth any of the gifts at any time as He sees the need. And if this is the case then any use of any one of these gifts inspired by God at a particular time is for God's glory and praise through Jesus Christ -- not the individual's. ( See I Peter 4:9-11).

The Spiritual gifts are for the general good and well being of God's children. James 1:17 says that EVERY good gift is from the Father. We might conclude that Spiritual Gifts only are given to Christians. But let us allow God the privilege to call forth the Spiritual gifts from ANYONE He so chooses. Can any of us deny Him that privilege?

The main point to be made here is that for us all Christians possess All the Spiritual gifts inherent within each by the Spirit of Christ living in each and can be called to be exercised at anytime by the power of Christ.

It is also true that some individuals have more of a propensity to be naturally gifted in certain areas as well as the personality that enhances the giftedness. For these individuals to manifest a particular Spiritual gift in an area they are naturally gifted in would then be a plus as God calls forth that particular Spiritual gift to action in that person.

With this particular understanding there should be no personal exaltation by the individual being used by God to share His giftedness. God gets all the glory. God is exalted and to be praised for His love and kindness expressed through the Spiritual gifts He calls forth out of His love and grace.

In the final analysis it is God, Father, Son and Holy Spirit who get all Praise, honor and glory. The Good News is that He shares His Divine Nature and Gifts WITH all of us.

# ANSWERING THE GREATEST QUESTIONS

ANSWERING THE GREATEST QUESTIONS OF LIFE

Why am I here and where am I going? Who am I? Really, who am I? Is there a secret to life and human existence? No religion or philosophy has EVER answered these questions!! The TRUTH of WHO IS JESUS does!! When Jesus says in Jn.14:6, that "He is the way, the truth, and the life", what does that really mean? Where do you personally and individually fit into the grand design of God? Read on.

God, the Father, Son, and Holy Spirit, the Triune God, has always existed in a face to face relationship with each other, enmeshed one in the other that these three actually are just one God. ( The Greek word for this is 'Perichoresis'.)

This God decided to create a cosmos, universe, and humans in order to share His Great love with others and to invite and involve this creation of humans INTO His very life and existence. This plan to include man into the life of God by adopting man and creating union with God Himself was planned for in the coming of God to man in the form of a human being named Jesus who was the Word of God from all Eternity. So before anything was created in the cosmos God's plan for humans individually and personally—you included—was in place. ( See Eph.1:3-14). This was God's plan and purpose originally. And no matter what this plan would Never change!

With Adam sinning and bringing the death penalty on all humans, i.e. all dying in Adam- I Cor.15:22, the payment for man's sins now would take place in the life, death, and resurrection of Jesus. This life of Jesus would give all mankind who was dead in Adam, life now in Jesus. (See Rom.5:18) And not only life, but Jesus' life living in man and man being accounted sinless and guiltless and righteous in Jesus. What Jesus did to the cosmos, to the creation, to humanity, and to ALL things was to reconcile all to Himself through His shed blood on the cross. ( Col. 1:19-20). In practical fact, Jesus UNDID what Adam had done and through His life, death, resurrection and ascension establishes a NEW CREATION which is now new in Himself—New in Jesus. We all participate in this New Creation.

Further, Jesus enters our darkness with us, is MADE Sin for us and in our place, ( II Cor.5:21), reconciles us to Himself and does not ever count our sins against us, vs.19. Jesus even tastes our death for us, (Heb.2:9), and raises us up with Him in resurrection to live in this New Life—now—and seats us With Him at the Father's right hand. ( Eph.2:6).

When God devised this plan originally He was absolutely intent on NOTHING coming between Himself, His creation and man with nothing thwarting that plan of His.

Remember God has all power and can accomplish what He planned. And He has. "It is finished" Jesus said in Jn 19:30.

When we consider that Almighty God is a LOVING FATHER and we are his children who He desires to share His glorious life with we can begin to look at our Father with the love, appreciation, worship, and thankfulness He deserves.

Unfortunately religion and Western Christianity has not portrayed our Father in Heaven in this light in the past. God has been viewed as some type of 'judge and executioner' who would just as soon cast His kids into a fiery furnace as not. Religion has not pictured God as one with whom we would love and enjoy an INTIMATE relationship. God is seen as distant, unknowable, austere, demanding, punishing, vindictive, unapproachable, judgmental, and angry with us. Even so called 'Great Sermons' have been preached in the past on sinners being the hands of an ANGRY GOD. People have been scared off from Christianity because of the fear of following that type of God. Jesus reveals a far different Father. Jesus says that He knows the Father and that the Father and He have loved each other from eternity with a love so beautiful that it is hard to describe. And, here is the really good news--that God the Father loves each of us JUST LIKE HE LOVES JESUS!!!!!!!!! That means YOU too!!!

In answering the questions posed here at the start, Jesus is God!! The Father, Son, and Holy Spirit are ONE. You are the son or daughter the Father has ALWAYS loved and wanted to be with Him forever. You are adopted into the life and family of God and were from BEFORE THE CREATION. ( Ephesians 1:3-14). You were in the original 'blue print' of God.

So, you are Special. Special to God. You are not outside, but inside! Here is some more really good news, you didn't do anything to get yourself in this relationship any more than you did anything to get yourself born of your physical mother, and you can't do anything to get yourself OUT of this relationship you are in with God the Father now.

The benefits of this truth are STAGGERING! What God has planned for you and all mankind is INDESCRIBEABLE. No human terms can begin to paint the picture of the joy, happiness, fun and pleasure God has for His children for all eternity. (Psalm 16:11). Some even call this Heaven. A good term, I think!

Does this sound like something you would like to know more about? We have only scratched the surface here. Would you like to know more of this Truth? Do you want to get rid of the guilt, the angst, the discouragement, depression, fear, insecurity, and lack of assurance in your life? The Real Jesus is the answer. Jesus said in Jn.8:31-32, "you shall know the Truth and the truth shall set you free." And it does!

You are probably thinking this sounds too good to be true and you are RIGHT if you use human reasoning influenced by the 'father of lies', but in our Heavenly Father's thinking it is as good as He could make it that is why it is called, THE GOOD NEWS!

# ARE SET FREE CHRISTIANS FREE TO SIN ?

"You shall know the truth and the truth shall set you free." So said Jesus in John 8:32. But when you look around at many Christians who carry guilt, shame, resentments, bitterness, anxiety, insecurity, lack of assurance, and fear, we have to ask ourself what kind of 'truth' is it that they are experiencing? Jesus' words are true to be sure.

Some people see Jesus' words of being set free as a blank check to go out and sin all they want. Free to do whatever whenever they want. They see it as being set free to live under grace in any way they carnally desire. But Jesus gives no one such license to sin freely by being set free. Living under Grace is no permission to sin.

As the offspring of Adam we all live and experience life in the fallen condition bequeathed to us by Adam due to his disobedience. With the influence of Satan the Devil who is the prince of the power of the air and the god of this present world we constantly are bombarded by his spiritual arrows of sin and rebellion. We live with our minds ever telling us that we are weak, sinful, immoral, not spiritual enough, not good enough, not righteous enough, not humble enough, not liked and not loved by God and condemned. And that we probably are going to "hell" since we realize how unworthy we are. We say we are a pretty sorry lot as a whole. And we buy into this. We are literally held in a state of 'captivity' by the sway and influence and power of the Devil. We are Captives. We are NOT FREE!!!

When Jesus says in John 10:10, that 'He came that we might have life and have it more abundantly', He is referencing the freedom of life in knowing Him and what He gives.

Isaiah had prophesied of this freeing of the captivity of humans who were held captive. Isaiah says it this way in Isaiah 61:1, " The Spirit of the Sovereign Lord is on me, because the Lord has anointed me to preach good news to the poor. He has sent me to bind up the broken hearted, to proclaim FREEDOM for the captives and release from darkness for the prisoners, to proclaim the year of the Lord's favor." Jesus quotes this passage of Isaiah in Luke 4:16 word for word. Jesus says that this prophecy is fulfilled at that day and time! The prison was not a physical one but a MENTAL/SPIRITUAL one.!

But, the TRUTH is in Jesus. (Ephesians 4:21). That TRUTH tells us that we were chosen in Christ and Adopted as His children even 'Before the foundation of the world'. Or, before ANYTHING was ever created in the first place!!! (Ephesians 1:3-14). This truth tells us that while we were yet and still sinners Christ died for us. (Romans 5:8). That all of our sins are forgiven in Christ who is the payment-propitiation-the atoning sacrifice- for our sins and for the sins of the whole world. (I John 2:2). That for those in Christ Jesus there is NO MORE CONDEMNATION. (Romans 8:1). Romans 8:2, goes on to say that through Christ the law of the Spirit of life set me free from the law of sin and death! Christ releases all of us from ANY claim the law ever had on us! We are set free.

Far from giving license to sin all one wants the Christian living chapters of Ephesians 4, Colossians 3, and Romans 12, give guidance as to how one should be living once he or she sees that their life is hidden in Christ and that He is their life. ( Colossians 3:4).

But we are STILL sinners. We still sin. Yes, we live in a body of sin and death waiting to be changed from mortal to immortal in the bodily resurrection. (I Corinthians 15 ). But while we wait we live by the Faith of Jesus Christ in a perpetual state of forgiveness --always clean, always righteous( Romans 3:21), always saved and always loved by our Father in Heaven.

The person who is set FREE through the Truth, WHO is JESUS, now lives in peace, joy, security, assurance, hope, abundance, and in the love relationship with Jesus Christ. The Father, Holy Spirit and Jesus, The Triune God lives in the individual and the individual LIVES IN the Father, Holy Spirit, and Jesus. ( John 17:20-26).

The individual has been freed, set free from all the lies the Devil has devoured him with. The eyes are opened. He sees through the eyes of Faith. The individual is now free to experience the life of God on a personal and loving basis. And this will grow throughout the individuals life by allowing more and more of the mind of Christ to be active in him. (Philippians 2:5).

One final thought. When we sin and we will, we always have a Savior who never counts those sins against us. Never takes note of them. Never remembers them and removes them from us as far as the East is from the West. We just stay forever clean in His eyes through the Word which He has spoken. (John 15:3). We are forever forgiven!

What a FRIEND we have in Jesus Who is the Way, the TRUTH, and the LIFE. Once we know the Truth we are forever set FREE.

AMEN

# ARE THE DEAD CONSCIOUS WITH GOD NOW?

Are deceased loved ones consciously alive and with God now? Or, are they "soul sleeping" and waiting on the resurrection to be "awake" and with God then? Of course the only ones who are concerned with this question are those of us who are still ALIVE.

Scripture can be taken supporting both perspectives mentioned here. However, most all of the time when this is questioned the perspective is one which involves linear time. Time which is confined to the parameters of time and space—the dimension we live in as humans.

God is not confined to time and space and linear time. God is eternal and in one sense views all things in the present from his vantage point outside of time and space. One theologian said, " God gives us linear time and space so everything doesn't happen at once!"

We know when an individual dies that the spirit goes to God. Some would say that this spirit is immediately conscious with God. Others would say that this spirit is NOT conscious and is awaiting the resurrection to become conscious. One is now, the other is later—however how much later this later is.

But think about it from the deceased person's stance. He or she is dead not knowing anything UNTIL they realize they are in God's presence and loving arms I might add. But, whether that length of time is a nano second at death, or 1000 years or a million years, to the individual it is INSTANTLY. It is like one going to sleep at night then waking up not knowing if he has slept one or two hours or six or seven!

There can be philosophical arguments as to why one way or the other would be more appropriate and many do argue those perspectives.

If the individual enters God's heavenly presence not confined to linear time and space, then no matter how much "time" elapses the individual is immediately conscious and with God at death and therefore how we "calculate" it has no bearing in the matter.

The answer as to how God does this is to say that He does it for the very best of all concerned based on His Unconditional Love for all people.

# BEFORE TIME BEGAN
# AUGUST 11, 02

God establishes His Devine Master Plan for His building of His family with no POSSIBILITY OF FAILURE!

1.) Jesus Christ was chosen and slain before the foundation of the world!

I Pt.1:18-21 Christ was chosen before the creation of the world as saviour.

Rev. 13:8 Christ was slain FROM the creation of the world.

Heb. 2:9 Christ tasted death for every man (from the foundation of the World.)

2.) God CHOSE us INDIVIDUALLY AND PERSONALLY IN CHRIST before the CREATION of the world.

Eph. 1: 4-14 …He chose us IN Him before the creation of the world to BE ( Not BECOME ) Holy and Blameless IN His sight, and done so by His glorious Grace and by His Will and for His good pleasure!

II Tim.1:8-10 God's Grace was given to us in Christ before the beginning Of time. And now is revealed to us.

II Thes.2:13 …from the beginning God chose you(me) (by personal name) To be saved through the sanctifying work of the Spirit and through be-Lief in the truth.

Titus 1:1 God's elect promised eternal life before the beginning of time.

Rom.8: 28-34 God FOREKNEW us and PREDESTINED us to be Conformed to the likeness of His Son.

For Christians Salvation is a done deal. And was so from the Foundation of the world.

Jesus said in Mt.25:34 to those on His right, " Come inherit the Kingdom prepared for you SINCE THE CREATION OF THE WORLD.

The concept of our Individual predestination by God from the beginning is somewhat foreign to us since we used to say that God only predestined a "family", but not individuals. God did predestinate a Family, and we were chosen to be in it from the foundation of the world.

We truly are a chosen people, I Pt.2: 4-10. Not chosen in the 20th Century by any of our merits, but by God's love and Grace from the beginning.

# BELIEVE…BUT BELIEVE WHAT ?

Why don't some people see and grasp the Truth of Trinitarian Theology –The Gospel--and who we are in Jesus? Well, shoot, Jesus faced the same dilemma in 30 AD. Paul faced it in his ministry 25 years later. We can get some clues from scripture as to why even today some don't "get it".

In Jesus' day it usually was the religious pundits, religious leaders, the Pharisees, and Sadducees who could not see the reality of who Jesus was. They were so steeped in various religious perspectives, that Jesus' announcement of who He was and that Life came through belief in Him only confused them and made them angry. They did not understand.

What Jesus was telling them was WAY TOO SIMPLE for them to give it any credibility and believability at all. No 613 rules and regulations to observe and keep. No legal standards to measure up to. No outline of obedience. No standard to measure righteousness by. Just believe? You gotta be kidding. They were totally blinded by religious perspectives they had had for 1500 years.

Today, we are not so far removed from the same kind of influences. We have inherited much of our beliefs from the false teachings of Plato as well as the influences of Augustine of Hippo who endorsed much of Plato's pagan concepts. Therefore, we have grown up with a Western Theological approach of legalism, works oriented faith, concepts of Heaven for the good people, Hell for the bad people, rewards and punishment, God being Love but burning someone in an ever burning tormenting fire forever if they would not love Him back, and making just payment for anything we have received whether goods, services, or salvation. All too often we really are just a bunch of Pharisees and Saducees clinging "faithfully" to our own ideas and concepts of what it is God is doing. Most of the time we are wrong.

It is hard to see that God is Love—and ONLY LOVE. He doesn't hate anybody, He loves everyone, and He even LIKES all of His children. He accepts us in Christ and makes all provisions for us IN Jesus Christ.

He Planned originally to adopt us into His very life and existence IN Jesus Christ from before the foundation of the world. (Eph.1:3-14). He made us ALIVE IN JESUS after we were made DEAD IN ADAM. (I Cor.15:22).

Our very physical existence only happens because of the fact that we along with all things created exist IN JESUS CHRIST. Our very spiritual existence only happens because of the fact that we live and have our total 100% being IN JESUS CHRIST. We receive our personal inclusion and adoption and salvation through and in Jesus. We participate in Jesus' crucifixion and in Jesus' resurrection and in Jesus' new birth and in Jesus' ascension. We share in everything that He is and has become. He is a New Creation. We are new creations in His being a new creation. He is

EVERYTHING for us. He shares everything He is with us. We are IN HIM. Our life is HIDDEN in Him. ( Col.3).

Jesus is face to face with the Father. We are face to face with the Father in and by and through Jesus. Let me say it again, EVERYTHING we are or ever could possibly be is what we are IN JESUS. He has taken us INTO himself, His life, His relationship with the Father.

Understanding the Trinitarian Theological Adoption and Inclusion life we have in Jesus is a matter of letting go and turning loose of EVERYTHING –100% of EVERTHING— that we are. We don't add anything or carry anything over into our eternal relationship with the Father. Everything is through the life, death, resurrection, ascension, and person of JESUS.

When we understand and BELIEVE this, then we can truly celebrate our life in Jesus. We can truly be thankful and appreciative of what God has done TO us and FOR us. And finally we can grasp just how wonderful the real LOVE OF GOD REALLY IS.

# SIN, BLASPHEMY/ BLASPHEMY AGAINST GOD

We have written previously on the subject of "the unpardonable sin" or blaspheming against the Holy Spirit but, recently I have noticed something definitely worth your study. Matt.12:31-32 tells us that "**every** sin **and** blasphemy ( not the same thing) will be forgiven men, but blasphemy against the Holy Spirit will not be forgiven in this age nor in the age to come."

So we see sin is forgiven--all sin. Blasphemy is forgiven. Speaking against the Son of Man ( blasphemy ) is forgiven. A number of scriptures come to mind which state that All sin is forgiven.. That Jesus forgives the sins of the whole world. Here are a few. I John2:2; I John 1:7; John 1:29; Heb. 7:27; Heb. 10:10; Colossians 1:20; Heb.9:12,26; there are more you can look up.

In understanding all of this one must realize that ALL sin is forgiven in Christ. All sin is pardoned in Christ. No sins are left out. Since this is true then NO sin is "unpardonable."

( Note: "unpardonable sin" is not in the Bible, nor in any manuscripts.) All sins of man including blasphemy have been forgiven in the blood of Christ—I John 1:7.

Speaking of the Holy Spirit in John 16:8-9, Jesus says that when It comes He will convict the world of unbelief. Jesus has done it all. Jesus has paid it all. All things are reconciled in Jesus. What else is there for humans to do but to believe?

Now back to blaspheming the Holy Spirit. In accusing Jesus of performing miracles by the power of the devil the Pharisees demonstrated their unbelief in Jesus and His power. Jesus says to them that it is impossible for God to forgive "unbelief" and thereby turning their unbelief into belief for in doing so that would deny their distinction and their free moral agency. Even if they were forgiven the blaspheming against the Holy Spirit and declared believers by Jesus when in actuality they were still unbelievers where would that leave them? They would still be unbelievers in fact. So blaspheming against the Holy Spirit is a process which is impossible for God to change without denying one's distinction or free choice which He insists upon for all people.

It is possible for one to maintain this unbelief in this age **and** in the age to come thereby continuing in the state of perishing which theoretically could last forever. But, God will never give up on these people. His mercy endures forever. ( Psalm 136). He is not willing that any should perish but that all should come to repentance, or a change of mind –metonoia, GK--and accept and believe what Jesus has done TO and FOR them. ( II Peter 3:9).

The bottom line is this. One can choose to not believe Jesus and as long as that unbelief persists then that person is in the continuing process of blaspheming against the Holy Spirit and this can not be overturned or forgiven since it would make the individual an adjunct believer in "name" only, i.e., a false believer. Not real. And that dog won't hunt.

# CALVANISM'S & ARMENIANISM'S ERROR

What is right and also wrong with Evangelical Protestantism' theology? This is a good question to ask since basically all Protestant denominations adhere to one of the following—either Calvanism on the one hand or Armenianism on the other.

First off let me say that both of these religious philosophies teach atonement in Jesus Christ. That is that Jesus died for sins to save sinners. And this is good, but it is not complete. Further, this is by no means an attack on individual Christians of any denomination since there are many fine Christians in all Christians faiths. This is an attempt to point out certain positions of Evangelical Protestantism which do not stand the test of scripture nor produce the joy, peace and assurance in individuals that God intended.

Calvanism is a teaching which posits "double predestination" and "limited atonement". Double predestination says that God originally predestined some of the human race to be saved and the rest ( reprobates ) to be damned. And that this 'election' took place before the foundation of the world by God's wisdom and all knowing somehow who should be saved and who should be lost or damned. "Limited atonement" declares that the atonement of Christ was 'limited' to only a certain group of individuals and that it did not apply to everyone.

Calvanism is correct in saying that God elected humans to be saved in Christ before the foundation of the world, but wrong in saying that the election did not apply to all humanity. The "once saved, always saved" doctrine springs from this teaching. However ones who thought they were saved and always saved may find out at the time of death that they unfortunately were one of the ones "chosen" by God originally to be in the class of reprobates and there is nothing they can do about it but to suffer eternally because of it!!! The question is, Where is God's love in all of this?

A major problem with this position is that no one "knows" for sure which category one is in. No one can be absolutely sure of his or her standing with God until death and the afterlife unfolds. Therefore there can be no mental peace, assurance and security in knowing one's eternal standing in God's salvation, only a GIANT question ????????

The other Evangelical position is that of Armenianism. This doctrinal understanding says that although one accepts Jesus as saviour by his or her free will choice, the same individual can at sometime in the future by the same choice reject his or her standing in Jesus and thereby become "unsaved", and face the torment of hell once again. With this kind of question looming over one's head it is impossible to completely worship and praise God for His limitless unconditional love and absolute salvation for the individual.

GIANT questions remain. And there again there can be no absolute mental peace, assurance and security in knowing one's eternal standing in God's salvation.

Scripture is filled with the truth of Atonement, salvation, and inclusion for ALL who ever lived. Just to name a few: John 3:16-17 ; I John 2:2 ; I Corinthians 15:22 ; Romans 5:18 ; I Timothy 4:10 ; II Corinthians 5:14-15. And, there are many others as well.

The Great Triune God's original plan and purpose was to share His Father, Son, and Holy Spirit existence with a created human family which He would Adopt and Include into His very life. Here was the reason for creating humanity in the first place. ( Ephesians 1:3-14 ). The idea of "election" is certainly correct, but it is correct for ALL humanity not just a limited few.

The Triune God 'accepted' us into His life long before we ever had a chance to "accept" Jesus into ours. Jesus said on the cross, " It is finished". ( John 19:30). Not it will be finished when man makes it finished by "accepting" me into their life.

In Jesus Christ we have been chosen, redeemed, reconciled, justified, crucified, resurrected, glorified, ascended and SEATED at the right hand of the Father WITH Jesus in the Heavenlies. ( Ephesians 2:6). ALREADY. This from God's Objective viewpoint is true!

Our salvation is secure in Jesus. We have "blessed" Assurance as Fanny Crosby wrote about in her great hymn, " Blessed Assurance". All this because we did not make it happen for Jesus made it happen a long time ago.

Salvation is not a contest but a declaration of FACT of what God has done TO us, FOR us and WITH us IN Jesus. As Jesus said in John 19:30, " IT IS FINISHED." We just wait for the rest of God's plan to come to completion as the future unfolds.

And the Saints all said with one voice,
"AMEN"

# CAN SOMEONE "FALL FROM GRACE" ?

When answering the question, Can one "fall from Grace"?, the place to start is with Who we are IN Jesus. We were chosen in Jesus before the foundation/creation of the world and adopted into the life of God by Jesus.

(Ephesians 1:3-14). Jesus came in the incarnation to make this a reality and to "close the deal". Through Jesus, the Father placed all of us in Jesus as Jesus said in John 14:20 and John 17:20-26.

We need to understand that we did not place ourselves in Jesus nor can we take ourselves out of Jesus. We did not "accept" Jesus into our life, Jesus accepted us into His life and He is not ever going to let us out of His embrace. (John 10:28-30).

Our salvation by Grace is "not **of** ourselves", or we had NO part in the process of what saved us. We were not even there when it happened— Before the foundation of the world. God planned it, Jesus made it happen, we belong forever to the Father and we can not do anything about it. BUT, we don't have to experience it now or forever for that matter!!! How so? Simply by not believing it! But not believing it does not make it NOT so. It is so whether we believe it or not. If we believe it we get to experience it and if we do not believe it we do not get to experience it. In this latter case we would just get to suffer or perish as scripture calls it—at least until we came to believe it and then experience it.

Paul addresses those who are trying to be "justified" by law in Galatians 5:4 and says that they have been alienated from Christ and have **fallen away from grace.** Here in chapter 5 Paul is talking about those being circumcised, keeping the whole law, and trusting in the law to be justified are simply in a different "boat" than those who are completely trusting in Christ in Christ's "boat" of grace. Law and Grace are two **different** boats! Whatever "righteousness" a person had under the Old Covenant was as a result of keeping the Law. ( Which no one did perfectly). However, under the New Covenant of Grace in the blood of Christ, righteousness is given by God **APART** from law through faith in Jesus Christ to all who **believe.** ( See Romans 3:21-22.)

So the Good News really is Good News. God loves us. He has saved us by His love and grace **in, by, and through Christ.** It is not of ourselves— we had nothing to do with it and we did not make it happen and we can't make it un-happen. We can not get out of God's grace and we can not be removed from being under it. But we can suffer now and forever by not believing it. In that case, we have **fallen or distanced ourselves as far from God's Grace as it is possible for us to do. All by unbelief.**

Now maybe we can see why Paul was so adamant about leaving the law behind completely and trusting and believing in Jesus Christ.

# CAN MAN BE SEPARATED FROM GOD ?

Is man separated from God? Has man ever been separated from God? Can man ever be separated from God? Where did this concept come from?

We read in Colossians 1:15-17, that ALL things were created BY Jesus Christ and FOR Him, and that all things are held together—sustained— by Him. It should be obvious to us that if all things are sustained or held together by Jesus Christ then if ANYTHING were to be removed from or disconnected in anyway from Him then that thing or individual would not hold together, not be sustained, and therefore no longer exist. Jesus is the source of all existence. Jesus says it this way referring to man in John 14:20, "...I am in my Father, and you are IN me, and I am in you." Connection! Union !

The Apostle Paul addresses this point in Acts 17:28, where he tells the pagan religious leaders in Athens that , "We live and move and have our being IN Jesus." These pagans were looking in all the wrong places to 'find' God who they called the 'Unknown' God. Paul reveals God to them in this truth that they have their life, movement, and being in Jesus.

Romans 8:28-39, Paul is clear that we can not be separated from the love of Christ. That nothing in all of creation can separate us from the love of God that is in Christ Jesus.

In John 10 Jesus is identified as the Good Shepherd. He says plainly that nothing can take His sheep out of his hand. Psalm 100:3 declares that we—humans—are the sheep of His pasture and that nothing can take us out of his hand.

Some will argue a particular verse, such as Isaiah 59:2, shows that sin SEPARATES man from God and therefore man IS separated from God and must somehow 'get back' to God. Let's understand.

The Old Covenant made at Mt. Sinai was a physical covenant, or agreement, between God and Israel. Leviticus 26 and Deuteronomy 28 list the conditions of the agreement. Physical blessings would follow obedience to the law and curses would follow disobedience to the law. Israel agreed to the covenant and became married to God through this covenant. ( See Jeremiah 3:14; Ezekiel 16; Isaiah 54:5, for a description of the marriage between God and Israel. ) But Israel played 'the harlot' and by violating the agreement was divorced from God. Isaiah 59:2, therefore, is stating that the sins of violating the 'marriage agreement', i.e., the Old Covenant, DID cause a SEPARATION between God and Israel. God removed Himself from the agreement in effect divorcing Israel due to Israel's unfaithfulness.

Ephesians 1:3-14, shows that man was chosen in Christ to be ADOPTED as His sons ( and daughters ) before the creation of the world. Man has ALWAYS belonged to God. Belonged to our Father in Heaven. There is NO 'unbelonging' relevant to anyone who has ever lived. Humanity is simply the offspring of God and we belong to God FOREVER. Man's life IS God's life living in us. ( Colossians 3:4). There is no life apart from God. There is NO existence of any kind apart or separated from God.( John 1:4).

One last scripture we will address is Colossians 1:21. We confuse separation with alienation. This verse says that once we were alienated from God and were enemies in YOUR MINDS because of your evil behavior. We are the ones who felt guilty and condemned in our minds. We were alienated in OUR minds. But, God never separated Himself from us. In fact it is while we were yet sinners that Christ died for us! (Romans 5:8). Colossians 1:22, declares that Christ reconciles us and presents us HOLY in His sight without blemish and free from accusation of any kind.

Separated ? ---- NEVER!!!

# CAN SINS 'EXCLUDE' ONE FROM INHERITANCE IN THE LIFE OF GOD ?

"Gotcha!" Ephesians 5:3-7 shows that these people in these sins and categories do NOT have any inheritance in the kingdom of Christ and of God. So what is going on anyway?

While there are some scriptures which at first seem to mitigate against the Trinitarian Incarnational Adoption and Inclusion Theology scripture shows, upon further inspection, a clearer picture emerges.

Paul had clearly shown in Ephesians that the adoption of humanity into the life of God had occurred 'before the foundation of the world' in chapter 1.

Then in chapter 2, Paul shows that it is by Grace that we have been saved—Already. In chapter 4, Paul shows that we have been 'sealed' with the Spirit ensuring our participation in the eternal life of God. Paul treats all of this in a matter of fact understanding. So, what is going on in chapter 5:3-7 ?

A little history lesson. The city of Ephesus had been founded some 1400 years before by Amazon women who migrated there from northern Africa. They were extremely war-like capable fighters. They considered themselves the stronger sex even killing off weaker men and choosing mates of the stronger men to produce stronger women in the society. They believed the woman was the 'head of the man' and house.

The Temple of Diana of the Ephesians, one of the wonders of the ancient world, stood some 200 feet tall with a statue of Artemis ( Diana) in the middle of it. This 'multi-breasted' goddess was worshipped by individuals coming into the temple to have sex with the temple prostitutes whom they believed 'connected' them to the goddess Diana. Other immoral practices were involved with the temple worship of Diana as well.

Paul is writing from prison in Rome and warns the church at Ephesus not to be practicing the pagan rituals involving the sex worship at the temple of Diana which many of the new converts were touting as proper for the new converts of Christ to continue doing.

Paul had already shown in chapters 1 and 2 that the new Christians were IN Christ. Adopted in Christ and saved by His Grace. In Chapter 5:3-7, Paul is listing immoral practices which are not consistent with WHO these Christians were in Christ. These are NOT sins which 'UNDO' what Christ has already done in these individuals lives. He is just citing things which should not be practiced by Christians once they come to know WHO they are in Jesus Christ.

When Paul uses the term that one who continued in these sins would 'have no inheritance in the kingdom of Christ or God', he is not saying that they have been EXCLUDED from what they were INCLUDED in before the foundation of the world by Grace ( ch.1), but that as long as they continued to practice these licentious activities through unbelief they were not going to 'EXPERIENCE' the abundant life in Christ's Kingdom now nor in the future. They HAD the INHERITANCE, but it would be of no personal benefit to them since they would be opposing that inheritance by their actions in essence denying WHO they were IN Christ.

# CAN WE BE "TOO" SINFUL TO BE FORGIVEN ?

Paul writes in Romans 7 of his life, the good with the bad, with some saying that he could not possibly be all that bad since Paul was the one God used to write fourteen books of the New Testament. Surely Paul almost walked on water!

Jesus gives us another example of how often one should forgive one's brother (anyone). In Matthew 18:21-22, Jesus gives an example of not forgiving 7 times only , or 7 times 7, but seventy times seven, that's 490 times! What Jesus is doing is showing the unending and merciful forgiveness which He extends to all of His children. I think I ran out of my 490 forgives some where along my 2nd year of life !!! A lifetime of being forgiven by Jesus is FAR more sinful and needful for being forgiven than just 490 times!

Often some feel that their sins are too numerous and too egregious for Jesus to stoop low enough to forgive. How foolish. That is just personal vanity on their part. Jesus is in the business of forgiving exceedingly sinful indiscretions. The account in Luke 7:36-50, tells of a "lady of the night", a prostitute, a common whore, and one I might add that all of the Pharisees were familiar with, came to wipe Jesus' feet with her tears. Jesus was the only one who had any compassion or heart for this poor suffering wretch of humanity and took interest in her and demonstrated His unconditional love, and forgave her.

It should be coming clear to all of us who are reading this that no matter what sin or sins we have in our life Jesus meets us right there IN those sins and becomes our sin for us and delivers us from any and all claims sin has over us. We are FREED. Released from sin's claims. Jesus takes the hit for us and He takes it over and over and over AND OVER again and again and again AND AGAIN. ( II Corinthians 5:19-21).

Jesus is our friend. He is FOR us. He never leaves us nor forsakes us and leaves us to our own selves. He is here for us 24/7. He is the propitiation for our sins and for the sins of the whole world 24/7. (I John 2:2).

One of the greatest tools Satan has in his spiritual arsenal is the tool of denigration. He says, " you are not good enough; you are not worthy enough; you are too sinful; God does not like you; God does not love you because—'just look at yourself'; God does not want you and He certainly does not want to live FOREVER with you around!!!! Satan is the accuser of the brethren TO the brethren. It is what he tells all of us that is so destructive. Satan says " You are NOT". And, God says, " Oh yes you ARE."

To make a long story short, God said originally WHATEVER it takes for Me to adopt and include all of humanity into my life forever, In Jesus Christ …I WILL DO IT. God says His purpose will stand. Nothing will ever thwart God's purpose. He has all power in all of the universe to make it happen and He has made it happen in Jesus Christ.

Yes, WHATEVER it takes. And, it took the Son of God, Jesus Christ and He made it happen for all of us sinners who now may claim SAINTHOOD in the life and in the existence of the Triune God forever.

Amen

# CAN WE DISQUALIFY FOR SALVATION ?

## ( Can we become a "castaway" ? )

"Can a person disqualify for their position in the eternal Kingdom of God?" Or, can a person once saved disqualify themselves for their salvation? Or, can a saved person become "unsaved" ? You get the point!

There are a couple of scripture that come to mind which beg this question. One is in I Corinthians 9:27 where Paul says that after he has preached to others he does not want to be ""**disqualified"** for the prize. The KJV says "castaway".

Other verses beg this same question. Without turning to all of them let's set a ground work position to begin to explain all of them.

First let's understand what or should we say WHO "qualifies" us for anything. How are we qualified for eternal life? For service? For anything? And, probably the most important question to ask is WHEN? When were we "qualified" for the blessings we receive from Father, Son, and Holy Spirit, the Great Triune God.

Triune God's original purpose in creating humans was to Adopt them and include them in His eternal relationship He had always had as Father, Son, and Holy Spirit. This was determined by God before the creation of the very universe. ( Ephesians 1:3-14). God has always loved us all and wanted us all with Him in relationship INSIDE of His life, face to face with Him ( Intimate ) enjoying eternity with us His children.

With Jesus being "slain" before the foundation of the world ( Revelation 13:8 ) all sin and anything that could possibly "disqualify" us for eternal life with God was taken care of in Jesus. When you consider what man is, vain, selfish, lustful, greedy, jealous, and all the evil nature which proceed from the inherited "fallenness" from father Adam, the first Adam, how could man with a heart which is deceitful above all things possibly ever "qualify" for life with and in a perfect God. So we see that the "way" is in Jesus. ( John 14:6). And has been all along. Jesus declares His life to us. Jesus declares His righteousness to us. We are crucified with Christ, we are raised with Christ, we ascended with Christ, and we live and exist IN Jesus Christ. We are secured in Christ and assured in Christ. With all of this being said, HOW CAN WE DISQUALIFY SOMETHING WHICH HAS ALREADY BEEN QUALIFIED FOR US IN JESUS **BEFORE WE WERE EVER BORN INTO THIS PHYSICAL WORLD?"** We did not have anything to do with the "qualifying" acts and we can not undo things which we never had a hand in doing originally. But we can accept what Jesus did for us and to us and in us and through us. We can believe it and enjoy it all. We can live it and experience it now and forever.

When you look at it as a done deal, signed, sealed, and delivered for us all **before** we were ever born then there is NO way we could possibly undo it.

Back to the original verse quoted above. I Corinthians 9:27. Paul is here speaking of being disapproved for service to the church. It is from the Gk. "adokimos" meaning, disapproved. He is speaking of being disapproved for service to the church, but not being disallowed his salvation. That was secure. In effect, Paul is saying that when the evil temptations of the world come along on a daily basis, he "beat" his body into subjection and in effect made himself resist those temptations lest he become unqualified to lead the church.

For us to "unqualify" ourselves for all Jesus has QUALIFIED us for would make us more powerful than the Eternal Son of God. How foolish is that?

Grace does not leave any loopholes in its position to allow us to undo anything Jesus has done for us through His Love, Mercy, Forgiveness, Grace and Life.

All of our evil nature, our sins, our weaknesses, our shortcomings, our failures, our problems, and all of our experiences generated from the fallenness we all have from father Adam which brought on death for us all ( I Corinthians 15:22) have been adequately taken care of in Jesus, the Second Adam by His reconciliation and resurrection which give LIFE to all of us.

We must remember, this is God's deal. His Plan. His purpose. His work. His decree. His decision. And He is carrying it out with **ALL OF HIS POWER** to make it all happen exactly the way He wants it to.

We do get the opportunity to **Believe it.**

**Lord I believe, help my unbelief.**

**AMEN**


# CAN WE "LET GOD DOWN" ?


Can we humans "let God down"? When we act out of our humanness or from the fallenness that we exist in from Adam do we let God down? When we sin or act out of selfishness or vanity or greed or lust or envy or jealously or any other sinful action do we "let God down"?

What does God expect from us anyway? God knows our frame and our nature. He knows that we are NOT good and that only He is good. He knows that we are all together Vanity. He knows we have a deceitful heart and that we do not know it. He knows that we live in the inherited life of fallenness coming from Adam. He knows that we are a "bad" tree producing fruit. And bad fruit at that. So WHAT does God expect form us anyway and how can we let God down when He knows full well who and what we are in and of ourselves?

Could it be that those who ask these questions as to whether or not we let God down by our actions are focusing on themselves and not on Jesus Christ and the life we now live in and by His faith? Is it not a type of self-exaltation to assume that we do good things to "please" God on the one hand but when we let down OUR personal guard and do bad things that we let God down? Is God like a yo-yo on a string up one minute with us in OUR good actions and down the next in our bad actions? Who is in charge of our faith, life, eternity, redemption, reconciliation, and salvation anyway?

We don't speak for God. God has already spoken and what He has spoken is Good. Very Good!

God says that all of our sins have been forgiven from the foundation of the world. ( Rev.13:8). He says that the blood of His son has covered all sin. John said that the Lamb of God takes away the SIN of the world. John again says in I John 2 that Jesus is the payment for all sin of all people of the world. Paul says that we have been given a RIGHTEOUSNESS apart from law and apart from sin. (Romans 3:21).

Humanly we often let others down when we default to sin and selfishness. We may let them down due to their High expectations they may have of us. Our sins do affect and hurt others and ourselves but they do not let God down. He has "gone to the trouble" to take care of all of mankind's sin in the life, death, resurrection and ascension of Jesus Christ. How could we let God down when He realistically does not expect anything good out of us in the first place?

II Corinthians 5:19-21 points out that Jesus Himself enters into our existence and becomes sin in place of our sins. He now is our sin and has paid the price for them all.

Maybe what we need to do is to focus on the Greatness of our loving Father in Heaven, the Loving kindness our older brother, Jesus Christ, extends to us and the power of the Holy Spirit to ultimately transform us into the fullness of the life we all share in Jesus.

Maybe we need to realize that it is God who is the author and finisher and perfector of our faith. Maybe we need to realize that there is not any "work" we personally can do good or bad to please God. All good works we may do are only done in and by and through Jesus Christ living in us. The old man is dead crucified with Christ.

The more we come to see WHO we really are in Jesus Christ, the more we are going to come to see who we are NOT in ourselves. And we will begin to live like it and behave like who we really are.

It is not a matter of us letting God down, it is a matter of God always loving us and accepting us UNCONDITIONALLY!

Thank you Jesus.

AMEN

# CAN WE SEPARATE OURSELVES FROM GOD ?

Often times various things 'seem' to indicate that we humans who live in and share in the life of the Father, Son, and Spirit can be 'separated' from God. Maybe a play, or skit, or maybe the wrong choices and decisions we make can be the cause.

Some basics are in order here. First, God is LOVE and His love is unconditional based on His abundant Grace. Second, God's Plan, decision, to Adopt us and include us humans in His life was sealed from before creation. This Adopting and including by God from the very (a) beginning was never planned to be conditional or could it be altered in any way.

With these concepts in mind let us look at wrong choices we all make from time to time. Where is God, Jesus, when we are in the midst of these trials brought on ourselves by our actions.

Romans 8 tells us that Nothing can separate us from God's Love. II Cor. 5:21, tells us that Jesus was made sin for us, being with us in our darkest hour. It is when and while we are sinners that Christ died for us all. He takes our weaknesses and makes us stronger.

Jesus says in John 14:20, that He is in the Father, and we are in Him and He is in us. Notice He does not say that this is any way conditional based on our sins or our victories. Actually ALL of our human goodness and human victories were destroyed at the Cross anyway.

Romans 8 again addresses the point that God foreknew us, predestined us to be conformed to the likeness of His Son, called us, justified us, and glorified us and will not hear of any charge being brought against us from any source.

We don't live our Christian life under the dilemma of conditional Grace. Or, conditional justification, or conditional glorification-- these being given when we are close to God and removed when we stray in our humanness. Sin has NO claim on us whatsoever!

We can't separate ourselves from Jesus anymore than we can separate ourselves from our shadow. Besides, if we are in His hands, John 10, and nothing can take us out, then how is it possible to be separated from Him ?

The same goes for 'Inclusion' in His life. We have been made partakers of His divine nature and it is not conditional. We don't become non-partakers of His divine nature and separated because of some human foible we wrong-headedly choose to exercise.

Bottom line. We are ALWAYS ADOPTED. We are ALWAYS INCLUDED in God's life. And Nothing can change that FACT.

# CAN CHRISTIANS FORFEIT THEIR SALVATION?

( A Study paper for your information only )
September 7, 2002

( There are two study papers which need to be read before one goes into depth in this present discussion of " Can a Christian give up his/her Salvation by their choice?" They are, " MORE GOOD NEWS ABOUT SALVATION", and, " BEFORE TIME BEGAN" both papers by Paul Kurt's , deal with Our Predestination and Salvation)

Once a person accepts and believes in Jesus Christ as their personal Savior by their choice from their free moral agency, can that person by their own choice choose to renounce that salvation and give it up and become unsaved and lost again? This paper will present the argument from certain scriptures and personal understanding and belief that that is not a viable possibility for the Christian.

Before going to certain scriptures, let's state some givens concerning God ( Father , Son, and Holy Spirit ) and Jesus Christ who IS God.

Jesus Christ has All POWER in heaven and earth. He is NOT WILLING for anyone to perish, but for all to come to repentance— "metanoia" in the Greek meaning a change of mind to understanding and belief. He said he came to SEEK AND TO SAVE WHAT WAS LOST. Lk.19:10. God's ORIGINAL PURPOSE was to send His Son into the world to Adopt mankind not to condemn. ( Jn.3:16-17 and Ephesians 1:3-14. ) The whole world is RECONCILLED to God by the Blood of Jesus Christ. Col.1:19-20.

## CAN A CHRISTIAN CHOOSE TO BECOME UNSAVED?

Christ literally TASTES DEATH for the Christian and takes their second death upon himself on the Cross and the Christian's OLD SELF,

OLD MAN OR WOMAN DIES.!!! Paul puts it this way in Gal.2:20, " I have been crucified with Christ and I NO LONGER LIVE, but Christ lives in me. The life I now live in the body, I live by faith **OF** the Son of God, who loved me and GAVE HIMSELF FOR ME.!" Rom.6:1-8, again Paul shows that we were BURIED with Christ through baptism INTO DEATH that we may have a NEW LIFE also. :6, ...our old self was crucified WITH HIM so that the body of sin might be DONE AWAY WITH....:7,...because anyone who HAS DIED has been freed from sin.! :8,...now if we DIED WITH CHRIST we believe we will ( and do now ) live with Him and we also live in Him and He lives in us. (John 14:20; Colossians 3:4).

THEREFORE: God does not count sin against us because all of our sins are forgiven in the Blood of Christ.( Rom.4:7-8 ; II Cor.5:19). ALL !!!! Past, Present, and ALL Future sins are also Forgiven. God simply accounts us as Righteous in Christ.

We were bought and paid for with the precious Blood of Jesus Christ and we BELONG TO HIM PERMANENTLY, ( I Cor.6:20, I Cor.7:23, Rom.3:24 ); and remember this NEW US is a NEW CREATION who walks in a newness of LIFE in Jesus and we are raised with Christ and seated with Him in Heavenly Realms NOW. (Eph.2:6)

Paul can declare in Eph.2:8 , that we HAVE BEEN SAVED, ( past perfect tense) our Salvation has already been accomplished BY JESUS CHRIST!!! NOT BY US OR ANYTHING WE CAN DO OR NOT DO, OR......UN-DO!!! And actually it was before we were ever born! We can choose to believe it or not.

We have been sealed by and with the Holy Spirit for the Day of Redemption at which time Jesus returns and we are changed from mortal into Immortal beings.(Eph.4:30). As human beings we have received a "new spiritual DNA", if you will, that CAN NOT BE ALTERED OR CHANGED. IT IS PERMANENT IN GOD AND CHRIST. Rom.8:28-39, show NOTHING CAN CHANGE THIS. NO POWER, NO ANYTHING IN ALL OF CREATION---INCLUCING WE OURSELVES—CAN CHANGE THIS!!!

Rom.8:30, is very encouraging and positive: " And those He predestined, He also called; those He called, He ALSO Justified; those He justified, He ALSO GLORIFIED!!! We are Glorified in Christ NOW. ( Our bodies are changed into Glorified bodies when Christ returns, but we are, in Christ , GLORIFIED NOW.)

All of this is done by Christ, for Christ, by His will and for His Good Pleasure because He LOVES US!

A comment concerning the subject of **FREE MORAL AGENCY.**

God gives humans the free moral agency in their distinction to choose to accept and believe or not accept and not believe Jesus Christ's Salvation at this time if and when it is presented to them. If the DECISION is made to accept and believe that GREAT SALVATION in Christ, then it is non-negotiable from that point on. Not only can they not make a later decision to rescind their Salvation, they no longer even have a right to make such a decision. One's free moral agency to obey, disobey, sin or not sin is not affected. They still have a mind and can make choices. Paul says to choose to not continue sinning because we are under GRACE! ( Rom.6:12-14). However, their PERMANENT SALVATION REMAINS FOREVER. What Christ has DECLARED, we can NOT by our puny human power UN-DECLARE.

# CONDEMNATION--"HELL" OR UNBELIEF?

What is **CONDEMNATON?** Does scripture give the definition of condemnation? This question relates to one of the scriptures which seems to mitigate against the Truth of Trinitarian Theology of salvation, adoption and inclusion of **ALL** humanity. John says, "that some will face the resurrection of Condemnation" in John 5:28. " That does it, they are going to Hell. There's your proof!" But is it?

John 5:19-45 is about the **honor of the Father** and the **validation of the Son- Jesus.**

Jesus here is showing where life comes from. Where eternal life comes from. And **how** it comes through the Son. The two dynamics discussed are **Abundant Life** (John 10:10) and **Condemnation.**

John 5:24-25, "I tell you the truth, the one who hears my word and **BELIEVES** the one who sent me has eternal life and will **not be condemned,** but has crossed over from **death** to life. I tell you the truth, a time is coming--and is **NOW** here—when the dead will hear the voice of the Son of God, and those who hear will **live.**" Here we see that hearing and **BELIEVING** Jesus moves a person from DEATH to life. This is true for a person who hears this and believes it **NOW** as well as a person who hears it and believes it " in the time that is coming." What this is saying is that EVERYONE is DEAD until each hears **THE WORD** and believes it. It is all about hearing and believing Jesus and Who we are in Jesus! So what is CONDEMNATION ? Maybe we can find a Bible definition! ⊠ Let's go to John Chapter 3.

John 3 is talking about salvation and eternal life where Jesus says in verse 18 referring to Jesus the Son, " Whoever **BELIEVES** in Him is **NOT CONDEMNED,** but whoever does not believe **STANDS CONDEMNED ALREADY** because he has not believed in the name of God's one and only Son." Condemnation is simply remaining in one's current state of DEATH by continuing to exist in a state of perishing and alienation through **UNBELIEF.** This happens in this life and can also happen in life after earthly physical death and scripture here calls that rising to the resurrection of condemnation—continuing on for however long in that state of unbelief. We could just as easily call it the Resurrection of Unbelief or the Resurrection of Unbelievers. Scripture calls it the Resurrection of Condemnation". Now back to John Chapter 5.

John 5:28-29, "Do not be amazed at this, because the hour is coming when all who are in the graves will hear His voice and will come out— those who have done good ( ie, heard and believed ) will rise to live, and those who have done evil (ie, did Not believe ) will rise to remain in condemnation **AS LONG AS THEY REFUSE TO BELIEVE!!!** In so doing they will remain in that state of condemnation in resurrection **UNTIL** such time as they come to believe—if they hopefully EVER do.

The Triune God is not after retribution. He wants all to **Believe.** He wants all to be with Him forever in joyful abundant life. Anything short of that is **CONDEMNATION!**

# DO SCRIPTURES CONTRADICT THE GOSPEL? PT.2

Romans 2:7-8, is an example some will use to support the idea that God's Wrath will be executed against individuals who reject the Truth in Jesus. How can we explain this verse in light of Trinitarian Theology which supports Everyone being Adopted and Included in the life of God from before the foundation of the world?

Paul is the Apostle to the Gentiles and writes to the Gentile church and those who are being exposed to the truth. In chapter one Paul is dealing with those who because of their wickedness and desire to remain in it refuse to see who they are in Jesus, deny the Creator and worship the creation, and who bring all kinds of suffering on themselves by depraved sexual practices. He calls them 'God haters" in vs.30, and describes their character even when they know what God's decree on these matters is.

Chapter 2 doesn't have any break in the original writing and is just a continuation of chapter 1. Paul says they are without excuse and how can they escape God's judgement. He says they are unrepentant and stubborn storing up FOR YOURSELF wrath when God's righteous judgement will be revealed.

Vs.6, says that God will give to each according to what he has done. Then vs.7-8 show that some will receive eternal life and for others there will be wrath and anger.

Very interesting. Are we to believe that those in vs. 7 who ," ...by persistence in doing good and seek glory, honor , and immortality get Eternal Life" by DOING those things? ( Jesus is not mentioned here in this verse. Will they gain eternal life by these works?)

Or, is Paul showing that these people OBVIOUSLY are only going to receive Eternal Life IN Jesus. By believing who they are in Jesus with their life resulting in this mode of living of vs. 7. Jesus is obviously included in the Eternal Life process here.

Likewise, in vs.8, Paul goes on to describe those who are self-seeking ( They say I'm right and God and Jesus are WRONG), and who REJECT the TRUTH (Jesus) and who follow evil. For them there will be wrath and anger. ( Indignation and anger, Gk.). Is Paul here saying that the anger and wrath will be directed at and taken out on the individuals here who are making the wrong choice of not believing the Truth and Who they are in Jesus?, OR, is he saying that by these individuals making this WRONG CHOICE that the "Indignation" of God and His anger is directed at the CHOICE they made—but not at the individuals personally?

Let me give you an example. There was a little boy who was told not to ride his bicycle out in the busy highway. But, he did ride it there and was hit by an automobile almost killing the child and putting him in the hospital for an extended length of time. He made a wrong choice. Are we to assume that his parents should be Wrathful and angry at him and should go to the hospital and further beat him up in ICU because he made a wrong choice and nearly got killed? Or should we think that the parents are EXTREMELY ANGRY at the wrong Choice the child made. They still love the child very much but by a wrong choice suffering and misery takes place. ( This is a real example by the way.)

Remember, there are only two categories of people who have ever lived, live now, and will live. Those who know who they are in Jesus and those who don't know who they are in Jesus.

It seems there can be no end to the scriptures that people will cite as being contradictory to the Truth that is in Jesus. Whenever these scriptures are brought up there are several things we need to keep in mind.

\*\*\* First and foremost we must always focus on **WHO IS JESUS** and how does this focus fit with whatever scripture we are interpreting.

Then ask these questions:

1. Who wrote the verse?
2. Who is it written to?
3. Why was it written?
4. What is the context the verse(s) is in?
5. What is the Historical setting?
6. How does it 'fit' with the absolutes of the Gospel?
7. How would this verse(s) be applied today by proper Theological Interpretation?
8. Does it uphold the LOVE of God?

Generally with these questions answered one can come to a proper explanation of any verse in scripture. There will be some, however, which are very difficult to explain but with those we just have to do the best we can being led by the Holy Spirit!

# DO SCRIPTURES CONTRADICT THE GOSPEL ?

Just wait a minute!!! What about the scripture that says, .........this, that, or the other thing which 'contradicts' what is being said about Trinitarian Theology and the Adoption, Inclusion, and Salvation of ALL mankind? There are numerous ones which don't seem to reconcile with this understanding of Theology. The question to ask is Who is doing the reconciling and what criteria are they using?

Are different paradigms being used? Are Augustinian, Calvin, or Armenian theologies being used to interpret the Gospel, or do we interpret with certain 'Absolutes' being given and established from the start? All varying interpretations will only serve to confuse a right understanding of the Gospel.

So, when looking at some scriptures which seem to oppose Trinitarian Theology, we must ask ourselves where do we start in our understanding? We must start with the beginning!

We start with God! The Eternal Father, Son, and Holy Spirit. The Triune God. The Trinity. We start with Jesus who is the Word who has always existed and who is God.(Jn.1:1). "In the beginning was the Word and the Word was with God and was God"

Then we go next to Triune God's 'blueprint' plan. Gen.1:26-27. Here God desires to create humankind in order to share His abundant Love which God has existed in as Father, Son, and Holy Spirit Eternally. And, not just creating 'creatures' to have physical life only, but humans to be ADOPTED into the very life of God. We see this purpose in Ephesians 1:3-14. Vs.4-5, tell us that it was God's purpose BEFORE the creation of the world to choose us in Jesus Christ and to ADOPT us AS HIS SONS and DAUGHTERS according to His pleasure and His WILL.

This original plan of God was fully accomplished in Jesus Christ as He came into human existence as Immanuel and created the Union between God and man. As Jesus said describing the Union in John 14:20, " ... you will realize that I am IN my Father, and you are IN me, and I am IN you."—UNION. Jesus repeats this truth in John 17:20-26 in His last prayer on earth!!!

As far as the sin question goes, Jesus took care of that for all of mankind by going to the cross and shedding His blood which provides forgiveness for all of humanity and the sins of the world. (I Jn.2:2).

Paul says it this way, " In Adam all die, but in Jesus ALL are made alive." (I Cor.15:22). And in Romans 5:18-19, Paul emphasizes, " that just as the result of one trespass was CONDEMNATION for All men, so also the result of one act of righteousness was justification that brings LIFE for ALL men."

Since we are IN Jesus by His divine act and appointment whatever happened/happens to Jesus also happened/happens to us as well. Jesus died. We are crucified with Him and we died. ( Ga.2:20) Jesus rose. We rose. Jesus ascended and we ascended to the right hand of the Father. (Eph.2:6).

What we are describing here is what HAS happened in GOD'S Theology. Of course our physical change into spirit is yet to occur. But it is a done deal with God. It is His music the symphony of life is playing.

The kicker, however, is that man with his free will has the option NOT to believe what God has done in Jesus for his benefit. Man can deny and continue to deny his divine relationship with God. And, man CAN continue to do so FOREVER if he chooses.

Now we come to scriptures which seem to contradict Adoption and Inclusion Theology.

They must be viewed in light of THE LIGHT of the world—Jesus. Viewed in light of what has been said above concerning GOD'S WILL and GOD'S PLAN.

Everyone, all humans, all who ever lived are the ADOPTED SONS AND DAUGHTERS OF GOD and have a place reserved in the eternity of heaven for them.(Jn.14) But, here again, all might not experience that heavenly homecoming or party or existence by their own CHOICE by DENYING WHO THEY ARE IN JESUS.

So, we can say that not all will experience eternity in the same way. Most will experience it 'Gloriously' while others will experience it in a MISERABLE, SAD, and ALIENATED condition. The Bible calls this state or condition HELL.

The concept of a torturous, fiery, ever burning damning Hell Fire is an idea which was originated by the Greek philosopher Plato in the 400's BC. The concept came into the Christian church through Augustine in the 5th Century AD in order to keep church members in line through fear. It remains current teaching in the Catholic Church today and many Protestant churches as well. It is not a theologically sound and Biblical teaching. ( You may want to study this understanding in greater detail, i.e. Lazarus and the rich man, etc.).

A word study would be helpful in various passages showing God's 'indignation' towards the CHOICE some make as to their belief in Jesus. God's eternal perspective towards even those who choose not to believe and who experience 'hell' is still one of LOVE. God is love. He was Love. He is love. He will always be love. He doesn't EVER, EVER, EVER, EVER hate His children. His indignation and anger is directed at their WRONG choices, but His love for the individual still remains. Hence, the POSSIBILITY that eventually those making the wrong choice may change their mind, repent and assume their heavenly reward. ( Luke 15 and the Prodigal son parable indicates this concerning the older brother as a possibility). Much more can be said on this topic.

Hopefully this will give perspective on scriptures as you find them, which seem to mitigate against the proper and Godly vision of Trinitarian Theology—simply called THE GOSPEL.

The key for all interpretation of scripture is to answer the question, " WHO IS JESUS?"

When we get this question and answer correct then we can proceed to answer all other questions relating to Theology.

May God richly bless your studies.

Amen

# DO SOME 'NOT' BELONG TO CHRIST ?

( Or do ALL Belong to Christ ? )

In this paper let's look at one of the most used verses in all of the Bible to try and discredit or disprove a position of Trinitarian Theology which says that ALL humanity is IN Jesus Christ and that ALL are Adopted (Ephesians 1:5) and ALL are Included in the life of God by the Spirit.( John 14:20).

This verse is Romans 8:9. Specifically 9b which alludes to someone who "has not the Spirit of Christ is none of His." Some would use this verse to try and undo all the other verses which demonstrate that we all belong to Christ.

It is helpful to read ALL of Romans chapters 1-8 to see what Paul is addressing to the Christians at Rome. Paul declares that ALL have sinned and come short of the Glory of God. (Rom.3:23). And that there is no difference between Jews, Gentiles, Christians, non-Christians. ( Rom.2:11, " God does not show favoritism."). Paul is writing therefore to EVERYONE for ALL have fallen short of the Glory of God.

In Romans 5:18, Paul writes that " the result of one act of righteousness was justification that brings life for ALL men." This act of Jesus 'trumps' the condemnation which was brought upon ALL men by Adam. This life Jesus brought was 'signed, sealed, and delivered' by His LIFE, DEATH,

RESURRECTION, AND ASCENSION. And this LIFE was for All descendents of Adam!! EVERYONE.

Back to Romans 8. Paul is simply comparing two ways of life a person can choose to live. One is out of conforming to the dictates and desires of the FLESH, and the other is to yield to the Spirit of Christ within everyone thereby walking or living and being motivated by the Spirit of Christ within.

Verse 9 begins by pointing out that these Romans are no longer CONTROLLED in life by their sinful nature (flesh) but now knowing WHO THEY ARE IN JESUS are now able to live motivated by the Spirit of Jesus living within them. Paul says that if anyone does not have the Spirit of Christ, he is none of His. Paul is not saying that there are some who don't, he is pointing out that since All things BELONG to Christ obviously they belong and they DO have Christ's Spirit and therefore they ARE Christ's.

Verse 10 makes it more plain. "But SINCE...ei, in the Greek and here in vs.10 is what is referred to in the Greek language as a first class conditional clause which assumes that the statement which follows is TRUE, therefore Since should be used here and not if . Since and if are both translated from "ei" in the Greek. (see Colossians 2:20)...Christ IS IN you, your body is dead because of sin, yet your spirit is alive because of righteousness—Jesus' righteousness declared to us! Paul knows what he is talking about.

There are only two ways to live. One is not to know who we are IN Jesus and walk according to the fallen, sinful, flesh we possess, and the other is to know we belong to Jesus, believe we belong to Jesus, and behave and live our life out of the Spirit of Jesus which lives in us ALL. One is called walking after the flesh, and the other is called walking and living after the Spirit—motivated by grace and the Spirit. The question then is what is MOTIVATING our life?

When one realizes Who he or she is in Jesus and believes it and lives accordingly then Jesus can claim this individual as ONE OF HIS who is a BELIEVER. Those who live in Jesus but who are non-believers still belong to Jesus but they are NONE OF HIS BELIEVERS-----YET! Remember ALL things were and are created IN Jesus, By Jesus, Through Jesus, and FOR Jesus and are upheld and sustained BY Jesus. (Colossians 1:16-17). Obviously All humanity belongs to Jesus and are His.

Paul is not going to claim a spiritual fact in one book of his only to nullify it in another. He does not speak out of 'both sides of his mouth'.

There are other verses such as this we have discussed here that seem to contradict the Gospel. However, when understood in LIGHT of the LIGHT OF THE WORLD--JESUS, they become much more clear.

( For more information on this Gospel message go to www.newlifewcg. org ) and see the links provided there.)


# DOES CREATION PRECEDE COVENANT ?


What came first, the chicken or the egg? All Christian theologians know, of course, the chicken did! Now this may seem like a simple or stupid question, but a similar question also comes to mind, which is, 'When did God decide to make man?' Was this decision BEFORE or AFTER the creation of the cosmos—universe? Another way of asking this is, 'Does Creation precede Covenant, or does Covenant precede Creation?' Did God create a vast Universe and then look around it and ask Himself, 'Now what am I going to do with this?' Maybe I'll just make humans!!!

How we answer tells us VOLUMES about the Plan of God for Humanity and when understood WHY God created man.

Some would answer that Creation was first, then man was created, man sinned, and God then made various covenants with certain individuals and the nation of Israel. With this model God had to 'fix' the sin problem and then get on with the salvation of those who would 'accept' His Son Jesus as their savior. In this model of Covenant after Creation shows God NOT knowing originally all things which would unfold in human history and at some point having to establish a 'Saving Covenant" with humanity. Sort of Creation and Covenant by 'Crisis", if you will.

When all that existed was God, The Triune God-- Father, Son and Holy Spirit, This One True God formulated a plan out of His overflowing love which would allow His love to be shared with His Creation and this love to be shared with humanity by God literally Choosing man and ADOPTING humanity as His children –get this—BEFORE THE CREATION OR FOUNDATION OF THE WORLD. (Ephesians 1:4-6). This declarative covenant of God is based entirely in the WILL of God to share His life with His children and was THE reason for God bringing the Universe into existence. This Universe will Ultimately be under man's feet and in subjection to man. (Hebrews 2:8).

So we see by this that Covenant preceded Creation. From the very 'start' it was God's desire to share His eternal life and existence with His created children. And God has never abandoned that ORIGINAL purpose for creating man. And He NEVER will. !!!

Sometimes Romans 8:23, is referred to as meaning that our Adoption does not take place until the resurrection. But just as a child is adopted from a foreign country by one in another country he just waits coming to his new home since he has ALREADY been adopted. Arriving at his new home does not 'make' his adoption. He can now BEGIN to experience the adoption. The legality of the adoption preceded the experience.

In the same way Romans 8:23 is saying that our Adoption will be experienced fully with the 'REDEMPTION OF OUR BODIES.' The Adoption had already occurred BEFORE the foundation of the world when God chose us IN Jesus. Further God declared that we would be Holy and Blameless in His sight IN Jesus!!!

When sin entered the world death entered the human experience. God in Jesus Christ redeemed, reconciled and saved the world and all humanity which put God's original purpose for the creation of man back to its original state. God created man to be IN Him and WITH Him forever. (John 14:20; Also see John 17:20-26). This INCLUSION was Never meant by Jesus to be temporary, but Everlasting.

Jesus makes it clear that those who BELIEVE who they are in Jesus are the Adopted Sons and Daughters of the Father and will live now in the assurance of salvation and forever in the bliss, peace, pleasure, joy, and happiness at the right hand of the Father—Just as Jesus does. (Ephesians 2:6).


# DOES SCRIPTURE ADDRESS US ALL ?


One comment which comes up often concerning scripture is the concept or idea that the particular verse or verses were written to specific persons in the particular book being addressed and at a particular time.

For example. In Ephesians 1:1, this argument would say that Paul is addressing ONLY the saints in Ephesus, the faithful in Christ Jesus. If this were true, then when these Christians in Ephesus died off or had children who came along much later and were even in areas or cities surrounding Ephesus, then they would not be included in Paul's address here. So, after this group of Christians there in Ephesus died, then the books could be closed since Paul is not referring to anyone else in the future. Stay with me here.

There are similar numerous verses in scripture which are written in this same manner. It is not our purpose here to go through each of these but to show that these really are all inclusive for all individuals, not just the ones being spoken to or written to at the original time.

Ephesians 1:3-6. Are these verses referring ONLY to the persons IN Ephesus at the time of Paul's writing? If that were true, then they would be the ONLY ones who were blessed in the heavenly realms with every spiritual blessing in Christ. The only ones who were chosen in Christ before the creation of the world, the only ones who were predestined to be adopted as His sons through Jesus Christ and the only ones who received redemption the forgiveness of sins through God's Grace. So, if this is true, then the persons at Corinth, Philippi, Rome or any other city, then or now, would not be included! This obviously is not making much sense at all.

Another one is Romans 1:7, where Paul writes, " To all in Rome who are loved by God and called to be saints." With this stated, lets look at Romans 5:1. Paul says here that "We" have been justified through faith, gained access by faith into His Grace in which we now stand." Is this referring ONLY to the saints in Rome? Or, are these versed All-inclusive?

I think this all comes clear when Jesus is talking in John 6:53 and says, " I tell you the truth, unless YOU eat the flesh of the Son of Man and drink His blood, you have no life in you." It would be foolish to the nth degree to argue that Jesus is talking ONLY to the disciples then and there.

Jesus, Paul, and the other writers of scripture are demonstrating various aspects of the RELATIONSHIP we humans have with our Heavenly Father through the Spirit. Scripture is the Revelation of that RELATIONSHIP.

Scripture is not some convoluted maze of smoke and mirrors to see if we can some how navigate through all the machinations, intricacies, secrets, and hoops and ladders in order to understand that God loves us and wants us IN His life and Him IN our life. The MYSTERIOUS HOLY UNION! John 14:20 !!!

Finally, the place to START in answering questions such as these dealing with specific scriptures is to start with John 14:20. That Jesus is in the Father, YOU are in Jesus, and Jesus is in YOU. John 17:20-26 echoes the same concept. RELATIONSHIP,. RELATIONSHIP, RELATIONSHIP. Christ in YOU the hope of Glory. ( Col.1-26-27.)

Understanding Trinitarian Theology is not rocket science. Beginning with the proper foundation and building upon it is essential. There is no other foundation than that of Jesus Christ. And, that He has loved us, predestined us, Adopted us, and included us in his life since Before the foundation of the world!!! ( Eph.1:3-14).

# EVERYONE IS A THEOLOGIAN !!!

Everyone is a Theologian! Everyone has a concept of a higher power, or God. One does not have to be a graduate of some theology school to have an idea of God. The problem is that most people's concept of God is flawed from previous misunderstandings and false interpretations of scripture which make God out to be some kind of 'hanging judge' waiting to fry rotten humans in some eternal punishing fire if they don't snap to it. In effect God created mankind only to put man in eternal torture forever for being lost! God and Satan the Devil are seen as competitors for the souls of men in an eternal battle and struggle to see who wins. Man is seen as 'separated' from God and wandering around trying to get back to a God who is way off 'somewhere' disconnected and watching from afar.

Some have a deist view that God just created the cosmos and man, wound it up real tight and is now watching it unwind to see how it all shakes out—disconnected, dispassionate, uninvolved, not personal, not intimate with His creation, and waiting to see what happens.

God is seen as some kind of titular monarch with not very much ruling power or authority and no real means to bring about His purposes and will. God is relegated to some kind of Cosmic Santa Claus with a big bag of rewards for being good and a big bag of ashes for those being bad. No more or less real than Santa Clause.

God really doesn't enter into most people's thoughts on any kind of a regular basis one way or the other. Only when trouble or disaster presents itself do most people even think of God. Sort of a hip pocket God, like an amulet, to be rubbed or used in these times of distress.

So you see we have all kinds of Theologies in reference to God.

Now let me tell you about the REAL Triune God. The One God who is Father, Son, and Holy Spirit. One single God with three 'persons' comprising His Oneness. This Triune God is LOVE. Pure Love. He has always existed and will always exist. He doesn't just exist, He lives and lives Abundantly and Fully. The Father, Son, and Holy Spirit live in such close communion with one another it is like a Great Dance, as one great Theologian calls it. To use a Greek word, it is Perichoretic. A beautiful dance. Full of joy, peace, respect, honor, appreciation, and love.

This great Love that God has always had was a love God decided to share with a creation. Before God created anything, He decided to create humanity and Adopt humanity INTO His very life and Include man in the very Divine Nature God possesses. (Ephesians 1:3 -14; John 14:20 and John 17:20-26.)

God reveals Himself as a Loving Father. He is close, involved, sharing, giving, loving and liking His children. He shares His Spirit with all of mankind. He made all the arrangements to forgive all the sins of man through the Life, death, and resurrection of His Son, Jesus Christ from before the foundation of the world. ( Rev. 13:8).

He has allowed Jesus to take all of man's sins, man's death, man's resurrection to life, and man's ascension to the right hand of the Father upon Himself. In Jesus Christ all these things are accomplished. By Faith. By the FAITH OF JESUS.

God loved us all so much that He prepared His 'Bullet Proof Plan' before the foundation of the world and sent Jesus Christ to ensure its complete and total success. All things were created by, for and through Jesus Christ and He Upholds or sustains all of Creation by His power. ( Colossians 1:16-17).

The correct Theology is that Triune God Loves us all so much that He does not want to live forever without us!!! And that Great God who has ALL POWER in Heaven and earth will see His eternal plan to its completion.

# EZEKIEL CHAPTER 37
## DRY BONES AND RESURRECTION

Whenever resurrection is being discussed, inevitably Ezekiel chapter 37 comes to "life", pardon the pun. The chapter describes a valley with a vast number of 'dry bones' of the dead in it. Through the prophecy the bones come to life.

However one may interpret this section of scripture there is one thing we need to establish as indisputable fact. There is only ONE source and power for resurrection and that is Jesus Christ. "I AM the resurrection and the life." ( John 11:25 ).

These people pictured here in Ezekiel 37 represent dead people. Dead a long time due to the fact of the dryness of the bones. These bones, representing the people who had died, say metaphorically that their hope is gone. The meaning here is that for many, if not most people, the feeling of lostness or hopelessness is how they approach dying as their last thought. When one dies not knowing the truth of the Resurrection in Jesus it is only natural that one would have this feeling of despair.

Ezekiel 37 is a powerful encouragement showing that all who have died are NOT lost, they are NOT cut off, and that there is Hope in God. For those in this category in Ezekiel 37, God shows through the prophet Ezekiel that God has not abandoned them in the grave but that He is going to bring them up out of their graves and place His Spirit in them in its fullness at that time. Verses 13-15 show that these people will then know WHO they are in God's plan and WHO the LORD is.

It is interesting to note that in this narrative that bones, tendons, flesh, and finally air are brought together to recreate the persons. BUT, blood is NOT. In vs.23 God says they will be His people and He will be their God. Vs. 24 says they all will have ONE shepherd. There is only ONE GOOD Shepherd, and that is Jesus Christ. Vs. 27 says that God will have His dwelling place with them and be their God.

While there are a number of explanations of Ezekiel 37 including these people coming up in a 'physical' resurrection ( no blood, however), and including Israel's coming back from captivity and leaving their idols and now being 'renewed' in the Spirit and living in peace, I feel that a closer look at this being a type of resurrection of ALL humanity to know WHO they are in Jesus and learning about it on the other side of death is also a plausible interpretation as well.

Whatever the correct interpretation is GOD KNOWS. How He brings it about and finally concludes His Magnificent Plan is in the hands of Jesus. As we push the envelope in understanding Prophecy from a SPIRITUAL perspective we ever see Jesus more and more fully in charge of the future which He has ALREADY seen. As in Adam all die, in Christ all will be made alive. Christ the first one. But, all others in the time order God has for them.( I Corinthians 15:22-23). Ezekiel 37 represents those finally being made fully alive in Christ FOREVER.

# FAITH VS. SCIENCE

Faith vs. Science. Consider this before finalizing your opinion. Everything in the entire universe is mathematically connected. Whether macro or micro elements are concerned, they are all mathematically constructed and connected universally. The universe is actually a giant clock from which we get our correct time on earth.

The universe has not **always** existed. Uranium which becomes lead proves that fact since if uranium had always been around it would now be lead. The universe had a start or beginning. It is made up of elements none of which change from one to another by evolving. It is interesting to note that while not all do, most astrophysicists realize the complexity of the cosmos and realize it started from a giant predetermined blue print plan and is perfectly constructed in perfect balance and harmony. Also, that all the physical bodies in the universe have been **perfectly in place** from the beginning therefore not evolving from any previous state or condition. And they all are in place in perfect gravitational balance to keep each in its place.

There may be other solar systems and planets in the cosmos similar to our earth with all the 100 plus elements of the atomic chart on those planets. But to maintain life as we know it they would have to be exactly the same distance from their sun to their "earthlike" planets, **and,** with an atmosphere of oxygen and nitrogen in the right balance, **and,** with water, plants, food sources in a food chain, on a planet spinning at precisely the same speed to create days and nights while tilting on an axis to create seasons in a right balance so as to allow life sustaining conditions to remain constant to support the life on the planet. But note: Astrophysicists have never discovered such a solar system outside of our own which has all of these elements in place.

This just scratches the surface of the complexity of our existence. But one must exercise a great faith in **science** to believe that it all just happened or one can exercise belief in the facts of the cosmos as they are by design. Take you pick.

# GOD HAS FULLY BLESSED US ALL IN JESUS

What do you think of when you hear the words Blessings of God? The health wealth babblers would have us to believe that God will "bless" us with bountiful incalculable riches and abundance in response to our 'giving' to him our offerings and our 'seed' money. But are the blessings of God something that are future for us? And if they are what could they possibly be? What do I mean by all of this?

Let's see. What are the greatest blessings that could possibly be poured out and or given to man by our loving Father in Heaven? James 1:17 gives us insight into God's giving nature and His sharing heart when James says that "every good and perfect gift is from above coming from the Father." But are these gifts God gives something future based on how we perform, or what we do or don't do, or based on some kind of work we may do or even on our faith?

In answering these questions we need to go to Ephesians Chapter 1 and notice carefully what Paul is saying to **all** of us. Eph.1:3, Paul says for Praise to be given to God the Father of our Lord Jesus Christ who HAS BLESSED us in the heavenly realms—or with the 'Treasures of Heaven'—with EVERY spiritual blessing in Christ! What Paul is saying here is that God has ALREADY, PAST ACTION, PAST TENSE, blessed us all with the Treasures of Heaven and with every spiritual blessing that it is possible to give and it is all done in the person of Jesus Christ!

There could be much discussion as to what all these Blessings are, but a better understanding of verse 4 here will shed a little more light on the subject. Vs. 4, " For He chose us in Him before the creation of the world to be holy and blameless in His sight…"

Holy and blameless in His sight here would better be rendered, " to be face to face in intimate relationship with God." This is how the Father, Son, and Holy Spirit are in relationship. They are "face to face". Intimate. Relational. Loving. When John speaks of the Word being 'with' God in the beginning in John 1:1, 'with' doesn't mean side by side like three statues of some sort like relics in a museum, but FACE TO FACE. Divine Loving INTIMACY. And this is how God chose us to be IN Him before the foundation of the world. Triune God wants to SHARE this love relationship With us, in us, and we in Him/Them.

Jesus phrases it this way in John 14:20, the Heart of the Gospel, that the Spirit will reveal to you this, " On that day you will realize that I am

IN my Father , and you are IN me, and I am IN you." It is all a matter of the Intimacy God has desired from the start of this plan of His.

Unfortunately some have looked at verse 4 from a very legalistic, morally straight, squeaky clean understanding of what it means to be 'holy and blameless in His sight' and have missed the beautiful relational aspect of the Triune God and our Inclusion IN that relationship. Triune God does not exist in a structured, law defining, legalistically calculable three in one and one in three sterile grand state. They exist in RELATIONSHIP, IN LOVE, IN HONOR, IN RESPECT, IN INTIMACY Face to Face!

We humans have no need to look for any greater blessing ever in all of eternity than the BLESSINGS God has ALREADY GIVEN to us in Jesus Christ. If we have been given the 'Treasures of Heaven' and every Spiritual blessing in Christ—PAST TENSE—what more could possibly be given to us now or in the future.

What we are looking for in our life now and forever is how to enjoy and experience these FANTASTIC Blessings God has in His loving heart already given to us.

Eph.1:4- 6 , " In God's great Love He predestined us to be ADOPTED as His sons/and daughters through Jesus Christ in accordance with His Pleasure and His Divine Will to the praise of His Glorious Grace which He has FREELY GIVEN US IN THE ONE HE LOVES."

Vs.7, shows how this can happen to all of us fallen, pitiful, sinful, wicked humans. "In Him we have REDEMPTION through His blood the forgiveness of sins in accordance with the RICHES—unbelievable RICHES—of God's GRACE that He LAVISHED on us."

More and more of an understanding of God's Great Love for us should come clearer to all of us when we really realize what God has actually done For all of us and To all of us in Jesus Christ.

The awesome thing to comprehend is that all of this was done BERORE THE FOUNDATION OF THE WORLD, BEFORE CREATION. BEFORE ADAM!

And God planned it all this way so that it had His GUARANTEE of Success on it before it ever started. Done. Done Deal. Victory. Jesus said, "It is Finished", and it was, before it ever got started to begin with!!! The only question remains is , "Will a person accept this and believe it?" I pray all will.

Amen

# GOD LIKES YOU! REALLY !!!

"God loves you." How often have we heard those words? For some of us it is hard to actually believe that God really does love us. We have all kinds of reasons why He shouldn't or can't. Scripture just tells us that He does love us unconditionally. He is our Dad and He simply loves His children. Deal with it.

This paper is not about the fact that God loves all of us, it's about the fact that God **LIKES** us as well. Now I can almost hear the roar of reasons why God doesn't like –choose any person in history, or even yourself—so and so. We humans are a pretty sorry lot in our fallenness inherited from the first Adam. We sin beyond description, our hearts are desperately wicked ( Jeremiah 17:9), we are selfish, judgmental, arrogant, proud, weak, vain, greedy, lustful, envious, jealous, lying and blaspheming. Not a pretty picture. How could God in His pure Holiness actually love us?

But first let me ask a few questions. What would humans be like in their personality and human actions if there were **NO** "god of this world" around? **NO** "prince of the power of the air" around? **NO** influence by the spiritual wickedness in high places to influence any human being? Who is the "father of lies?" Who is the father of accusation? Who is a liar from the beginning? Who is the one who "perfected" pride and wanted to BE "like or BE the Most High?" Where do the spirits of anger, hate, murder, envy, strife, rebellion, adultery, rape and all other fallen attitudes generate from that humans are so strongly influenced by and in some cases almost controlled by? I think this becomes obvious before long. Satan literally HATES the fact that our Heavenly Father likes us.

When God made each of us He formed us in the womb.( Psalm 139:13). He MADE us creating us in His image. He made us for eternal **relationship.** He allows His life to live in each of us. We demonstrate much good that is His good coming through us to others. He loves it when we exercise the life of Jesus in us outward to others. He likes us when we laugh, cry, hurt, sympathize with others, comfort one another, lift up another little one. He likes us when we kiss a puppy or cuddle a kitten. He likes us when we enjoy beautiful music or a pretty sunset He created. He gave us His life and He **LIKES** us!!!

But what about all the negative things mentioned earlier? Dear ones, God is smart! He knows where all of those things come from. He knows all of those negatives ( corrupt rough edges of us all ) have been forgiven in

Jesus.( I John 2:2). He knows Jesus has actually entered into us becoming sin for us. ( II Corinthians 5:21). He knows our old man is dead and that we live in newness of life. He knows we drag around our old man in a body of sin and death. He knows that one day we will put on Incorruption and put on Immortality in a glorified body just like Jesus. ( I John 3:2; Psalm 17:15).

God likes us for who we really are! We are His Adopted children Included in His life. His life lives in us through Jesus Christ by the Spirit and we have been placed **inside** His Triune Life forever by the Spirit.

Our Father does **NOT** like sin and evil but He knows the source of it. He does not like it when we commit terrible offenses and sins. But, He does not count our sins against us. ( II Corinthians 5:19). He does not hold our sins against us in any way that would affect His love for us or His liking us. God **chooses** to LOVE us and LIKE us unconditionally. After all, He has all eternity to continue shaping and molding us into the perfection He gives to us all—the fullness of the measure of the Stature of Jesus Christ. God will always LOVE and LIKE you and me forever. Now deal with it.

Isn't it nice, make that good, make that wonderful to know that Triune God Loves you and Likes you no matter what?

# GOD SEES IN THE PRESENT

We have heard that God sees everything in the present. Of course from our perspective living in linear time—past, present, and future—we only see in the present. God created time and space and everything in it as well.

When we see the light from a distant star, that light left that star in some cases millions of years ago. It left in the past those millions of years ago. But because it is just now reaching our human eyes on this earth, we see it now in the present although that light was emitted from that star in the past.

Since God FILLS all space with his Omnipresent existence, it should be obvious that he sees that light from that star as it left the star and all along its path through space until it reaches this earth and our eyes. It is in the present to Him since He is present IN all of Space. The light can't outrun God as it were.!

When dealing with God seeing the future in the present we have to expand our minds to the concept of God's being the creator of time and space and therefore being above or outside of the "bubble" of time and space. ( Of course God is inside time and space as well as outside of them.)

Outside of the "bubble" of time and space God sees the beginning of creation as well as the end of any and everything. He is the Alpha and the Omega. The beginning and the end. He foretells prophetic events because of being outside of time and space He can see them before they actually happen within time and space. In Psalm 139, He sees the entirety of our lives before we are actually born!!! He knows the page of every day of our book of life and the very instant we are going to die. Hence, He can say that our days are "numbered" and He alone knows the number.

This is an important concept to wrap our minds around because it has bearing on the present reality of us being dead in Christ, alive in Christ, resurrected with Christ, and seated with Christ in the Heavenly realm. All present realities in God's sight.

We wait physically and literally for the completion of these things from our human life perspective. But in God's mind, it is a DONE DEAL.

# GOD'S ORIGINAL PLAN STANDS FIRM FOREVER

Let's make the Plan of God and the Gospel, the GOOD NEWS real simple. After all, it isn't rocket science! We are the ones who have made a man made gospel. Man has made man far too important in the salvation process with far too much dependence on his salvation placed on man.

Originally when Triune God decided to share His love with a creation and with His created children He is the one who devised the plan with all contingencies to make absolutely sure that plan would follow through to completion.

God planned to create man and send His Son, the Word, to become human and bridge the gap between God and man so that man could live in Union with the Father, Son, and Holy Spirit inside of God's life FOREVER. To ADOPT man into the very life of God.

This is what the All Powerful, Almighty God wanted to do. No matter what happened in the new life of His created children, Adam and Eve, God's Plan would stand secure.

So man was chosen in Christ before the foundation of the world to be Holy in Jesus and to live eternally with God in God's life. (Eph.1:3-14). Jesus had to become human in order to create the "bridge" of humanness into the LIFE of GOD and create that Union, that connection.

God knew, however, that if or when Adam sinned that would pose a problem that needed a fix so that God's original plan could continue on and man would still be headed to eternal life and existence in the original plan God had from the beginning.

We read in Rev.13:8, that Jesus was slain before the foundation of the world. So we see that God chose humanity IN Jesus before the foundation of the world and foresaw that Adam (man) would sin and bring the death penalty on all of his descendents thereby necessitating the need for a sacrifice for man's sins and a Savior that only Jesus could provide. That eventuality was planned for and taken care of in Jesus. In other words, Jesus undid what Adam did! Jesus corrected the problem. He CONQUERED the problem.

God wanted man in His Life from the beginning. God being all powerful and all knowing and all loving was not going to let sin and Satan thwart His eternal plan and purpose for man. Jesus would fix or "undo" what Adam did by Adam's sinning.

We read in I Cor. 15:22, that in Adam ALL die, so IN Jesus Christ ALL—the SAME All-Are made ALIVE. We could look at it this way. God's plan from the beginning started. It was proceeding along very well. Adam sinned and took mankind OFF of the track, but Jesus put man BACK on the track, took all responsibility for the sins, life, death, new birth, resurrection and ascension of man by becoming human in the Incarnation, living a perfect life, and QUALIFYING all humanity to live in God's presence forever just as was originally planned by The TRIUNE GOD.

God further states this fact in Romans 8:31-39. What happened with Adam by the influence of Satan is NOT going to happen again! Jesus took care of that possibility. God's plan and purpose stands. It is His Good Pleasure to give us His Kingdom and Life. (Luke 12:32).

"It is Finished", Jesus said. He is the Alpha and Omega. The beginner and finisher of our faith. He is the originator and Perfector of our faith. It is ALL in His hands. All creation was created in and by and for and through Jesus Christ. And, He sustains that creation. It is HIS. Jesus has done EVERYTHING to ASSURE The Great God's Plan is fulfilled and completed.

God's Original plan stands. The Inclusion of man in His life forever. The Glorification of man into the Life of God Forever. And nothing can ever change that REALITY. (Rom.8:31-39). And why? " For God so loved the world…"

# GOD'S PLAN

## PROUNOUNCEMENT OR POSSIBILITY ?

Possibility or Pronouncement? Most people look at the plan of God revealed in scripture as a wonderful concept yet one which may or may not be attained by the individual. For example scripture is read from a viewpoint of this or that concerning salvation as a "can be " experience. We "can" be saved IF… Or, we "can" be forgiven IF… This type of understanding places the finality of Salvation upon us the humans God created to be with Him forever.

What is worse is that the "can" can be just as easily "won't" as in what if the individual "won't" accept Jesus, or chooses NOT to be forgiven by Jesus. With this kind of reasoning the whole plan of God becomes the operation of weak, sinful, fallen and wicked human beings. The ultimate success of the Plan of GOD rests in man's hands not God's.

So the Plan of God becomes one of "possibility" for mankind. The potential is certainly there for man to accept Jesus and His salvation but it all becomes "Iffy" at best.

The Great Triune God is not an "Iffy" God. His Eternal purpose from before the creation of the world stands firm in the Incarnation—the birth, life, death, resurrection and ascension of Jesus Christ. ( Ephesians 1:3-14).

God simply purposed to create a human family and adopt that family into His very life and share eternity with His children He loves. Adam sinned and the original plan had to be "fixed" and was fixed in the redemptive reconciling life of Jesus Christ. God's original purpose still stands.

Humanity BELONGS to God. We are His children. We are bought with the precious blood of Christ. Man's sins are all forgiven in Christ. Man stands clean, forgiven and righteous in Jesus Christ. Sin has been defeated. Death has been defeated. Satan has been defeated. In John 19:30, " It is finished", Jesus said.

The Plan of God revealed in scripture is a PRONOUNCEMENT. It is a DECLARATION of Fact. It is the REALITY OF GOD.    And, it is so for all of Adam's fallen children. It is not possibly true for anyone, it Is TRUE for Everyone. Humanity is the Elect of God. What is true for one is true for ALL.

In Jesus Christ humanity, all humanity, is RECONCILED, REDEEMED, SAVED, CRUCIFIED, AND RAISED AND RESURRECTED TO THE FATHER'S RIGHT HAND. ( Ephesians 2:6).

HOWEVER, for any to experience the Abundant life Jesus Christ brought he or she must BELIEVE. All the blessings and joys and pleasures at the Father's right hand are reserved for those who BELIEVE.

Once an individual realizes that he or she has belonged to God from the very beginning and BELIEVES just WHO he or she is IN Jesus then he or she can now live and behave in a way consistent with who they really are. A son or daughter of The Father.

# GOD'S PLAN ASSURED FROM THE START

In Genesis 1:26-27, we find WHY the Great Triune God wanted to create human kind in the first place. He wanted to create 'man' and place him inside of His great Triune Life to be with man forever. "Let's make man IN our image." God simply wanted to create humanity and place him inside of the life of God and enjoy the eternal relationship with humans forever. Can He do it? Was it possible without fail? Could Triune God lay out this blueprint for all eternity and successfully bring it to fruition? Not only could He, He did !!! He did in Jesus!

We read of the absolute success of the plan in a couple or so scriptures. Let's notice. In II Timothy 1:9, we read, " ...God, who has saved us and called us to a holy life---not because of anything we have done but because of his own PURPOSE and GRACE. This grace was given us in Christ Jesus BEFORE the beginning of time..." This IS the plan of God!

We also see this basic same thing mentioned in the book of Ephesians 1:4, " ... for He chose us in Him ( by Name, personally and individually with ALL other humans who have ever lived or will live) BEFORE the creation of the world to be holy and blameless in His sight; then in verses 5-7 , we read, " In love He predestined us to be Adopted as His sons ( and daughters) through Jesus Christ, in accordance with HIS PLEASURE and WILL—to the praise of His glorious grace , which He has freely given us in the One He loves. In Him we have redemption through His blood, the forgiveness of sins, in accordance with the riches of God's grace that He lavished on us with all wisdom and understanding."

From the very 'beginning' this plan of God was completed in Jesus Christ. Jesus who was 'slain from the foundation of the world." (Rev.13:8). This Jesus who came to earth as Immanuel, God with us, to connect us to the Triune God's eternal existence; this Jesus who finished His work on earth saying so in John 19:30; this Jesus who with the Father and the Holy Spirit planned the whole thing out before time, space, or the cosmos was ever created. So perfectly planned that there would never be any room for mistakes, mishaps, or anything that would or could thwart this perfect plan.

Then finally, in Matthew 25:34, Jesus says, " to come and inherit the Kingdom prepared for you since the creation of the world." The Plan of God has always been on God's heart. His design. His purpose. His desire to live eternally with us humans. And, Jesus life, death, resurrection and ascension made it a REALITY for All.

It just simply is a done deal for humans and has been since God devised the plan originally. Jesus has made it happen for everyone. You included.

Can you turn loose of your Platonic Western Theological Christian thinking and just believe the GOOD NEWS? God has always loved you since He thought of you and your name before time. You are that IMPORTANT to God.

Now: Accept it and believe it.

Amen


# GOD'S PLAN INCLUDES EVERYONE !

A very brief outline


Ephesians 1:3-14 Triune God's original purpose for man

Romans 6:23 Wages of sin is Death But, the GIFT of God is Eternal life IN Jesus Christ our Lord

Romans 5:18-20 Adam's trespass was condemnation For ALL men, Jesus' righteousness Brings LIFE for ALL humanity; All Made righteous in Jesus

I Corinthians 15:22 In Adam all died, but IN Jesus Christ All are made alive

II Corinth. 5:14-15 One ( Jesus) died for all, therefore ALL Died.

Colossians 1:16-17 All things created by, for, in and through Jesus Christ

Colossians 1:19-20 ALL things reconciled in Jesus Christ

I John 2:2 Christ paid for the sins of Everyone

I Timothy 4:10 Christ the Savior of ALL men through Belief

I Peter 1:3-5 Given New Birth in Jesus' Resurrection And kept by God's Power.


# GOD'S PLAN OR YOURS ?


If you were God, just how would YOU have done your perfect plan? How would you have made it "fool proof" ? Since you were the creator with all power in all things, just how would you have devised a plan to adopt and include other beings—humans—into your plan and life forever? Would you have made the plan applicable for everyone or just a few 'good folk' who could somehow measure up to your lofty standards? Would you have been all inclusive of your offspring or somehow selective in your choice of those you save and those you DAMN to be tortured and punished in suffering and 'hell' fire forever? Would you have given specific rules and regulations and qualifications to determine those saved and brought into your eternal life, or would you have done it differently than just about everyone thinks you should have done it? Would you have trusted in the glorious teachings of brother Plato and other 'great' Greek philosophers to determine YOUR plan for all humanity, or would you have come up with your own plan irrespective of Plato's thoughts one way or the other---from before all of creation???

After all it IS your plan.!!!!!!! So, my man, how would you have done it?

Can you improve on what has been articulated in scripture and through the great theologians of the centuries or would you cast aside the truth they have discovered and come up with your own truth? There is only ONE truth. Remember!

So. Where are you in YOUR vision for the plan of God? Coming along O.K are you? Does your plan include God's LOVE for ALL of His offspring. His children? Who you gonna leave out? Why is your sacrifice for them not good enough? Maybe something else can be used!!!

Let's see. You think you can improve on the process. Let me hear it. But I don't think so. Not in a Million years, No, make that a gazillion years. Not ever.!!!!!!!!!!!!!!!!!!!!!!!!!!!!!!!!!!!1

When it comes to Truth, God is the Truth. Let every other man be a liar. Where do you stand with that?

Maybe you get the gist of what is covered here. God's LOVE and Plan are perfect. Jesus is Perfect. The plan for all made applicable for all is a done deal in the ONE and ONLY one it could have been made perfect in. JESUS.

AMEN


# GOD'S REALITY AND OUR EXPERIENCE


Satan is a master of illusion and an inveterate liar deceiving the whole world. One area he deceives Christians is in the area of their being new creations in Jesus.

We as well as many other Christians have thought that when one is saved, born again, converted, walking in a newness of life, eternally existing in Jesus, or whatever other term we may use, that there is this "magical" change that takes place in their thinking and they begin to live out this new life "just the way Jesus would" from then on.

It is true that the reality of our life is now in Jesus and Everything He is we are as well. He is our life. Our life is hidden with Christ in God. (Col.3).

In the Father's reality we have been adopted, included in His life, redeemed, resurrected, ascended, glorified, and seated at the right hand of God WITH Jesus. This is God's vision of REALITY.

It is good that we know all this because this is NOT what humans have been experiencing in the human family for thousands of years. Even in Jesus as Christians we all too often experience the old pulls of our past (and present) sinful inclinations. We are greedy. We lust. We are selfish. Arrogant. Hateful. Judgemental. Vain. Prideful. Jealous. And whatever else you want to add to this list.

Satan has done such a "fine" job of instilling these things in our innermost being as a lie that we live out our human lives BELIEVING these lies. We feel lost. That we don't belong. That we are unworthy. We strive to be accepted and to belong. We feel insecure and we strive for security in physical preparations. Satan has lied to us and we have bought it.

Jesus entered our darkness as the light of the world. He enters into us where Satan has deceived us with his lie and brings the TRUTH. The Truth is that IN HIM we do belong. We are accepted. We are secure—eternally.

Here is the challenge for us and this does not happen overnight. The challenge is to replace the lie of Satan with the Truth of Jesus. Sounds simple huh? It is not. The lie of Satan is DEEP SEATED within all humans. It goes to the very depths of the soul and being. It motivates humans to do all the carnal mind can devise. It produces untold wickedness. It produces human history.

But with the Light of Jesus shining into our minds and hearts and with His Truth replacing the lie we all experience we see in practical fact a LIFE LONG exchange occurring. What we see in the Christian's life is not something that happens like magic overnight or instantaneous, but we see the Christian growing in the mind, heart, attitude, and Spirit of Christ over A LIFETIME.

It helps to know this because if we don't we will be continually beating ourselves up by seeing ourselves as not "measuring" up to the fullness of the stature of Jesus Christ.

The children's tee shirt says it truthfully. " Be patient with me, God is not finished with me yet." And, this is true. Our Christian life is a lifelong walk. Growing. Allowing more and more of Jesus Christ to live His life in us and replace the life of the lie we have been experiencing from THE LIAR.

Jesus has ENTERED our life. He has removed all the spots and blemishes. He has cleaned us up. He has justified us. He has healed us. He has saved us. He has raised us up WITH HIM. He has given us His ETERNITY.

We are just waiting to see the finished "product" revealed IN US. And when we do , we " will see Him as He is!"

# GOOD NEWS FOR......YOU !!!

YOU are the child God always wanted.
God chose you, in Christ, BEFORE the creation of the world.
Christ died for you BEFORE the foundation of the world. Rev 13:8
God loves YOU with no strings attached. Unconditionally.
Jesus SAVED the ENTIRE world. I Jn. 2:2
Jesus came to save what was LOST. Luke 19:10
Your SINS were forgiven BEFORE you were born.
Your Salvation had NOTHING to do with you. Eph. 1:3-14
God has placed you INSIDE His life forever. John 14:20
Salvation is a DECLARATION for ALL, not a challenge for any.
Your salvation and life are SAFE and SECURE in Jesus.
You are SEATED with Christ at the Father's side. Eph. 2:6
You DIED in Adam, but were made ALIVE in Jesus. I Cor. 15:22
You are INCLUDED in the life of God by the Spirit forever.
Sound too good to be true? You are reading the Theological truth of the Christian Church for the first 400 years after its start. The Gospel of Adoption into the life of God.

# GROWING SPIRITUALLY FOREVER

What have you done in your life that you feel further qualifies you to live in the abundance and glory of eternal life in the heavenlys? How far have you come in your growth process as a Christian and what impact will that have in heaven once you arrive?

How much growing into the fullness of the measure of the stature of Jesus Christ can one actually achieve in this short physical life we are assigned?

When we stop to think about how "long" eternity is and how short human physical life is one must ask , " ...is God only using the 70 or so years of physical life to perfect our faith? Is the humanity we carry over into eternity perfected only in the short three score and ten, or maybe a little longer, going to be how we shall be from then on? Or, is there more going on here we need to consider.

We are told that " the Good work God has begun in us He will finish it!" But how much 'finishing' can God do in the short human life as compared to the length of 'time' He has to work with us in eternity? How could we ever be "groomed" enough here and now compared to what God has in mind in our future with Him? How much growing in the grace and knowledge of our Lord and Savior Jesus Christ can we really accomplish in the here and now with all the obstacles thrown at us from all angles in this physical existence?

However long man would have lived physically if Adam had not sinned would only have been a temporary period of time for God to work with each person to get them **ready** to transition over into eternity with Him inside His Triune existence where the REAL learning and growing experience would then take place. The spiritual maturing growth process God has in mind for all of His children continues on after one arrives in Heaven where God will have our FULL ATTENTION with His pure love guiding and leading us on toward the perfection He has in mind for us.

How long will this take? How far will we be able to grow IN Christ then? Can we see that what is transpiring now in this physical life is but a mere seed or beginning of what God wants for us?

God has some fantastic plans for His children and He is going to take however long it takes to share what He has in store for us in His Spiritual Maturity Program In The Life of the Father, Son, and Holy Spirit. After all, He has all the "time" in the world, errrrr, make that all eternity to accomplish His perfection in all of us.

# GROWING UP IN JESUS—FOREVER !

"It is too good to be true!" We often hear this concerning what Jesus has done for us and to us. The Gospel of Jesus Christ declares to us that we are loved, accepted and adopted by God and have been since before creation. (Ephesians 1:3-14). Further, Romans 8, declares to us that we have been predestined, called, justified, and glorified and that absolutely nothing can ever separate us from the amazing love of God.

We have died with and in Jesus Christ, we have been buried with Christ, we have been raised with and in Christ and we have ascended to the right hand of the Father in 'the heavenly realm' and are seated there WITH Jesus at the Father's right hand. ( Ephesians 2:6). But you and I don't see all of this subjectively speaking. Yet, God sees it objectively from His eternal vantage point.

The question in my mind, at least, is at present with all of our weaknesses, deceitfulness, sinfulness, vanity, lust, greed, jealousy, animosity, and all other human foibles you can throw into the mix—how are the above two paragraphs to be understood?

God loves His creation! He has an eternal plan for it—you included. It is while we were and are all yet sinners that Christ died for us. And rose for us. And ascended for us. And seated Himself at the Father's right hand for us and with us.

But. And here I think is the big But. We are going to be changed from what we are now into something too wonderful to even explain. Mortals are going to put on incorruption. We are going to be raised in glory. We are going to see Jesus AS He is. We are going to grow spiritually into the fullness of the stature and likeness of Jesus Christ. Growing in the grace and knowledge of our Lord and Savior Jesus Christ does NOT end when we are given our redeemed body and move into our Heavenly mansion with the Father in Heaven. Eyes have not seen and ears have not heard what God has in store for those who love Him. Eternal life is not a reward for getting it all right in the here and now. It is a gift and God is in the growing and perfecting business and that does not stop at our death. Heaven is not the reward of the saved. Life with and in God IS. Relationship! The reward occurs IN the Heavenly realm. If heaven is the reward of the saved, then we could just get a box in heaven and sit in it forever and never "see the light of day"! Our Father desires to share with us real life and relationship in love with us forever. Not just give us an "atta-boy" and leave us alone forever.

Revelation 21 tells us that the old is going to pass away. That tears are going to cease. That death and mourning and crying and pain are to be no more. The old order of things will have passed away. God is making all things NEW—including our new heavenly life. He will give us the fresh water of the spring of the water of life. And all of this is done in Jesus.

Yes, God loves us now. He even likes us now. But He does not like all the sins and weaknesses we have now even though they all are forgiven in Jesus. In other words, as it has been said, "God loves us just as we are, but He loves us too much to leave us just the way we are." There are wonderful and glorious changes in store for us as we move from the earthly realm into the Heavenly one growing and forevermore becoming more and more like Jesus Christ. Growing up into the fullness and stature of Jesus Christ may just take forever. And that is going to be a wonderful experience!

# THE HEALING OF THE PRODIGAL SON

Brace yourself. You are about to read a comment on the 'Parable of the Prodigal Son' ( Luke 15: 11-31) you most likely have never heard before. Yet, human history bears out that this is the way the story relates to all of us.

Most of us are familiar with the story Jesus told of a father who had two sons and he divides his estate between them. The older son remains with the father and the younger son takes his part of the estate—money— and leaves home and spends his life in riotous living on wine, women, and song. So much so that he probably became an alcoholic, sex addict, drug addict, diseased, most likely maimed and partially blinded by his excesses. Not a pretty picture. But, human suffering and failure never are pretty.

Because of his now 'ruined' condition the only employment he could find was slopping the hogs in an unfamiliar environment. Apparently he was neither educated enough nor physically able to command greater and more respectful employment. He was hanging on to life by a thread.

After most of a lifetime he realizes that there is security, protection, sustenance, and acceptance at his father's house. Most people require a lifetime to learn life's lessons and this man was no exception. He is probably in middle age—maybe 40 to 60—when he 'comes to himself and his senses' and heads home.

I want you to note that when his father saw him far off he had compassion on his son. Let me describe this scene as it encompasses all of us. His father SAW him and had compassion on him. No spoken word yet, just years of being away from his son and now what he SEES evokes COMPASSION on his son. (Or daughter as applicable). What did he see?

He saw a son in the distance barely able to walk. Tired. Dirty. Sore infested. Unkempt. Disheveled. Lame in one leg. Dragging a foot. An arm in a sling hanging limply at the man's side. One eye bandaged. A body racked in pain. A body emaciated from the lack of dietary necessities. And later to find out realizing his son's mind was confused and wandering from all the abuses he had subjected his body to. But he was HOME.

No matter what the father saw he saw it through the eyes of LOVE and COMPASSION. This was his son who was lost, gone, alienated, away, and now he is home. The father weeps in drenching tears of joy.

Why did the father run to the son? I submit to you that the son was not able to run to the father in his condition. A myriad of emotions, questions, doubts, weaknesses, and physical circumstances prevented his running to his father. He did not wait until he was WHOLE to come home, he came home TO GET WHOLE. TO BECOME WHOLE. TO BE HEALED.

The father realizes all these things and can't wait for the slowly moving son to painfully make his way to the father's house. The father is overjoyed at the sight of his son returning regardless of his condition. His son was JUST AS HE WAS. HE CAME. (Just like Charlotte Elliot's hymn, JUST AS I AM). And his dad was unconditionally accepting of his lost son. So he RAN to embrace his dear son who was back. Never mind the condition. The father's love and forgiveness already covered EVERYTHING.

Nothing mattered in this son's past. No addictions mattered. No indiscretions mattered. No shortcomings or failures mattered. No weaknesses mattered. No sins mattered. No physical impairments mattered. The son was home and there was healing and health to be received at his father's house. His dad runs to embrace his son and the healing began.

The father threw a celebration not for what the son had done in his life, but for what was now going to take place in the NEW LIFE he would have by in fact starting over in his father's house. Unconditionally loved.

Unconditionally accepted. Embraced as the son the father had always dreamed of having back.. And now he was!

Do you see yourself in this story? We All are the child who went our way in life. And our Father waits for us to come home. When He sees us coming He will RUN TO US. UNCONDITIONALLY LOVING US. FOREVER.

# HEAVEN-- MORE THAN GOLD AND PEARLS !

Heaven. Oh, the bliss of Heaven. Gold streets. Pearl gates. Beauty everywhere. The full wealth of the Eternal God. Let's stop for a moment and think about Heaven as the reward of the saved human race. We know Jesus made this all not only a possibility but a reality. So what is so good about Heaven? True enough, Revelation pictures the glory of Heaven as beauty beyond compare. Wealth beyond our wildest dreams. Pearls so large that they are doors. Man! It's going to be great living eternally in all of that beauty and splendor and perfection. Right? Well, let's see.

For starters what good is all the wealth, gold, pearls, precious stones, and other eternal accoutrements going to do for glorified sons and daughters of God? We can't 'spend' the wealth, or purchase anything with it. We can't use it for any personal use or personal gain. We can only look at how beautiful it is. And, that is great and will be great for a while. But if looking at all this beauty, having a room in a mansion—a little cubicle to sit around in-- having a crown with jewels in it, and having everlasting life surrounded by great wealth, beauty, and splendor is ALL there is to it, I don't think I want to go!

So what makes Heaven such a fantastic place for humans to live in forever? It is NOT the 'things' that are there. The Triune God lived forever in past eternity in a joyous, harmonious, peaceful, loving, accepting, appreciative, caring, dynamic, sharing, and WONDERFUL ...... RELATIONSHIP. It never got old. It never will. Things can get old. But a dynamic LOVING RELATIONSHIP in and with God never will. It is the face to face relationship inside the eternal God's Divine existence that will NEVER get old or boring. Our Father will NEVER run out of things to teach us and share with us.

We are talking about relationship with the one who created this vast universe and everything in it. This Finite universe. We are going to live in FRIENDSHIP with this creating Genius. We will talk with, learn from, admire, walk with, grow evermore, and live in this eternal RELATIONSHIP with the Triune God who loves us personally and individually as He loves Jesus Christ.

The Triune God, Father, Son, and Spirit, has so much to share with us. Look at just how vast the Cosmos is. God made it. He is so much bigger than the creation He designed and spoke into being by Spirit Power!!!

Heaven is going to be what eyes have not seen. Nor ears heard. But it is going to be more than gold streets and pearls. It is going to be a joyous eternity of building relationships with other of God's sons and daughters and Jesus Christ and the Father. It will never get boring. Never grow old. Never be exhausted in what is available. But it will always be relational. It will be the greatest RELATIONSHIP God has to offer. John even refers to it as a Marriage with the one Who created it all to begin with. Forever. Now that's reason to want to be there.


# HEBREWS 6:4-6—FALLING AWAY FOREVER?


Hebrews 6:4-6, presents somewhat of a challenge to the Trinitarian Theologians who claim redemption for all and Adoption and Inclusion for all in Jesus Christ.

Again, whenever we endeavor to explain scripture we should always approach the scripture from the standpoint of " WHO IS JESUS". What has He done TO all of creation and Why. Isolated scriptures such as these two verses in Hebrews 6 then offer a different understanding than what at first seems to be the ONLY way they may be understood.

**One** of the ways Heb.6:4-6 is understood is that Jews who professed to be believers progressed to the point of full belief and acceptance of Jesus but at the last moment backed down in denial and therefore fell away from the truth and the life they could have had in Jesus.

**Another** way of looking at these verses is in the "hypothetical" sense. This says that if one **could** fall away from their salvation, or deny their salvation in Jesus , or nullify their salvation in Jesus, then it would be impossible to reposition them in the state of salvation since Jesus would have to be crucified again. This would make the individual more powerful than Jesus who has redeemed the entire world and reconciled it in Himself.

So, this hypothetical approach is only that, hypothetical. Remember this is Jesus' doing , not ours. So we can not undo what Jesus came to do and did.

One way of looking at this is what did Jesus do and did He have the authority and the Power to do it and was He successful in doing what He came to do? If these presuppositions are true and correct, then it is infinitely presumptuous on anyone's part to assume that we humans can UNDO what Jesus did.

Greek philosophy, of which I have written extensively in the past, has had such a bearing on our understanding of scripture that it sometimes is difficult to dissociate that thinking from the Absolute Truth that is in Jesus. Our brains are SEARED with false premises and paradigms.

Paul is simply saying here in Heb. 6 that **IF** it were **Possible** for one to fall away then this is what the picture would look like for them. But, since it is **impossible** for one to fall away from Jesus ( we are in His hands, we do not have Him in our hands), Jesus is the **Guarantee** of the better covenant which is a Declaration, a Gift, based on God's Unconditional love of His creation. ( Hebrews 7:22).

We have been so influenced by Plato, Platinus , Aristotle, Socrates, Augustine, and Jonathan Edwards, it is difficult for us to see the real Love of God for all of His creation and the purpose He has for all of us-----if only we will **BELIEVE.**

We need to always ask the question, Whose idea is this anyway? Whose plan is this anyway? How did He plan it out originally anyway? Can we undo His sovereign plan by our puny human efforts—either good or bad?

Final disclaimer: Some of us are of the mind set that what we have learned in the past is somehow superior to the Truth that is in Jesus.. That it **WAS** the Truth that was in and is in Jesus. If that is so, then there is obviously NO room for future or further growth in the Spirit of God. We shut ourselves off. Completely. Why would we want to stand in the gap and defend **ELLEN G. WHITE? OR, JOSEPH SMITH, OR JIM JONES, OR ELMER FUDD, OR MICKEY MOUSE.?**

The truth is only to be found in Jesus Christ. Can we just look to the Love of God and purpose He created all of humanity for in the first place for our truth? Jesus made it so. Jesus made it happen. You are Adopted, and Included in the life of God forever. Why argue with this?

Now I know some of us reading this will still argue for the principles we **"PROVED"** 40 years ago in "college". We are stuck in the paradigms of the 50's and 60's. Well, stuck is stuck. What can I say? What can anyone say? Some will go to their grave defending lies and heretics and wrong ideologies for their personal defense. For these people to admit their error is somehow demeaning or belittling to their self worth. How foolish. Hell, I have been wrong before and I readily admit it. I was wrong when I slugged my mother in the stomach and knocked her out. I am not proud of that. I am fully and humiliatingly ashamed of that. But it is true. I am sorry. I repent of that. Now let's move on. Let's quit defending something that is wrong. False. Heresy.

May God bless all of you,

Thank you Jesus for your Grace,

# HELL IS GOING TO BE " HELL"

In Trinitarian Theology of Adoption and Inclusion the whole world has been saved in Jesus Christ since before the foundation of the world. (Eph.1). Jesus said in Luke 19:10 that He came to save what was LOST. We know He did what He came to do.

Some see this from a perspective that EVERYONE will be included in the "Party of heaven" experiencing joy and pleasure at the Father's right hand forever. While it is true that any who repent/believe Jesus will share this glorious eternal existence. What we want to discuss here concerns those who REFUSE to believe what Jesus has done TO and FOR them.

Scripture makes adequate provision for a state called "perishing", or, "weeping and gnashing of teeth", or, "utter darkness", or, "hell". Here we want to talk about this concept because it is wrong to think that everyone who does any and all evils in this human life will get away Scot Free and live along side everyone else in Joy in Heaven. Again, I emphasize all sins are forgiven but individuals must accept/believe Jesus in order to experience the Abundant Life Jesus gives now and Forever.

No one is going to get away Scot Free who will not accept/believe Jesus. And, scripture makes this clear. We need to understand. It is God's will for all to come to repentance/belief and not continue in this state of "perishing" or "Hell". (II Pt.3:9).

Yet scripture shows that apparently there will be some who will refuse to believe who they are in Jesus. Remember all are IN Jesus and at the Father's right hand. Let's talk about those who refuse to believe this.

It would be foolish to think that those who refuse Jesus would just be having their own party away from the Father, away from the Ball Room of Heaven, or the Royal Supper of the Lamb.

They are going to experience eternal life quite differently than those who believe. In the common terminology of the day scripture and Jesus show that Hell or the state of perishing will be anything but a party.!!! Those in this state will continue experiencing continued suffering by their CHOICE of NOT ACCEPTING/BELIEVING JESUS!!!

It is not the Father who punishes them because they would not believe Jesus, but they choose this continued suffering by THEIR CHOICE of refusing to BELIEVE just WHO they are in Jesus.

Make no mistake, this suffering is going to be SUFFEERING in the Extreme. Misery unimaginable on the human scale. Anxiety, angst, depression, confusion, doubt, fear, uncertainty, worry, insecurity, mental chaos, and unhappiness all experienced to the degree unparalleled in the human experience. A "party", hardly!!! This is what scripture tries to show. This is a vast difference in those who believe and those who don't!!!

Can you imagine people living FOREVER in this "state" knowing that they DON'T HAVE TO, but have chosen this PERISHING and MENTAL torment for themselves?

The GOOD NEWS is that they don't have to continue in this state forever IF they will see the Light of Jesus and come to acceptance and belief. Who knows, maybe a few thousand years—or longer—will bring them to their senses!!! Remember they will always be God's children. They are included and adopted in Jesus. They are, however, experiencing eternal life vastly differently than those who believe what Jesus has done to and for them. They will always be the ones Jesus came to save who were LOST. And it just may be that through the Father's continued encouragement for them to believe and their continued SUFFERING that they will change their minds and come to believe and live FOREVER with the Father. This we can not answer here. We just know that God will ALWAYS love them and their future decisions are between them and God. Finally, God is big enough to help anyone overcome unbelief with BELIEF! The question remains though, will they?

# HELL. NOT WHAT YOU MAY HAVE THOUGHT

People are 'hell bent' on hanging on to their ever-loving Hell Fire of Punishment and Torment for sinners who they think are not saved. We all grew up with the concept of Hell and Heaven with Hell being the place people were consigned to for living less than moral and perfect lives or who did not measure up spiritually. Hell was a bad, bad place to be sent upon death. An Eternity of 'hot flames' licking our bodies with unimaginable pain, anguish and suffering...forever. FOREVER. How could we believe anything else in our Christian walk? Our parents held Hell over our heads. Preachers held Hell over our heads. Even our own mind held Hell over our own heads!

The question to ask, is where is the loving God the Father of the Bible when all this Hell is going on for all eternity? For most of us this is all too easy to see and understand and believe. We hang on to this 'theology' because it speaks to bad people—really bad people. Humans like Hitler, and Mussolini, and others of the same persuasion. We certainly don't want people like that in heaven with us so the only alternative is HELL.

We require "JUDGEMENT" for these people and other bad people as well. Judgement is right. Fair. Equitable. Suffering for suffering. Punishment for sins and evil. Well, you get the picture.

Could it be that this whole picture is not scriptural? Could it be that this whole picture has its origins, not in the Bible, but in the pagan mind of Plato of ancient Greece? For four hundred years before Christ Plato's concept of an ever burning and torturing hell endured. Could this be true?

Then in the 5th Century A.D. a church leader by the name of Augustine of Hippo, St. Augustine, perpetuated Plato's hell doctrine in the Christian church because he saw that this 'fear tactic' helped keep Christians in line and away from sin. Some sins were classified as 'venial'—which weren't all that bad, but others were classified as 'mortal sins' and they were very bad, so bad in fact that the person committing them had to GO STRAIGHT TO HELL upon death. And SUFFER. FOREVER.

When we understand that the Great Triune God planned our Adoption through Jesus Christ BEFORE THE CREATION OF THE WORLD ( Ephesians 1:3-14), and that Jesus Died for ALL mankind from the foundation of the world ( Revelation 13:8), and that Jesus' sacrifice was the payment for ALL mankind's sins ( I John 2:2), and that Jesus Christ has reconciled the whole of creation and ALL of mankind to Himself ( Colossians 1:20), then maybe we need to rethink what hell really is.

We are created in Jesus to live with Him forever in RELATIONSHIP. We belong to Him. He has prepared a joyful and beautiful eternal existence and relationship for us and with us that can not be described in earthbound terms. When we see this and realize who we are IN Jesus we can act like who we really are.

HELL: When we deny who we are in Jesus or continue living not knowing who we are in Jesus we can live out of our fallenness in Adam and continue suffering, or as scripture says, PERISHING, until such time as we believe who we really are in Jesus.

The sad thing is that we being free moral agents can choose to NEVER accept and believe who we are in Jesus and continue suffering and perishing from now on, even forever. And that is HELL.

# HOLINESS AND HOW WE GET IT

Holiness. What is it? How do humans achieve or gain or get holiness? Is there Anything we can humanly do to be holy?

We know that God, Father, Son, and Holy Spirit are Holy. They exist eternally in a Holy loving relationship. But what makes them Holy? Do they have some heavenly set of laws to obey that when and if followed produces holiness in them? The answer is that the holiness Triune God experiences is the loving, face to face relationship the three have with each other. There is mutual love, respect, honor, agreement, and joy the three share with each other face to face. It is not "based" on anything since this relationship has always existed and there was nothing before God to base it on!

But what about us? Are there laws we can obey, ways we can dress, actions we can effect, thoughts we can have, or anything else we can do which will produce holiness in us? The answer to this question is NO. Paul expresses this in Romans 3:10, "..as it is written, there is NONE righteous." Nothing anyone can DO produces righteousness, otherwise it would have been produced by some at some point.

Note here that the words holiness and righteousness can be used interchangeably since they have essentially the same meaning. Our holiness does not and CAN NOT have ANYTHING to do with ANYTHING we can DO or NOT DO. There are no works we can do to help our righteousness along. In fact Isaiah 64:6, tells us that, " all our righteousness is as filthy rags" to God.

Matthew 19:17, tells us, " there is none good (righteous) but ONE." This should tell us that our obedience, our morality, our law keeping, our 'goodness', our dress, our hair styles, our cosmetics or lack of cosmetics, do NOT make us Holy!

The mystery of our holiness is simply, " Christ IN us the hope of glory." (Colossians 1:27). Christ is our life. (Colossians 3:4). God has GIVEN us a righteousness (holiness) apart from the dictates of any law through faith.

(Romans 3:21). Jesus Christ who is the only one who is good, righteous, and holy declares His Holiness to us. He imparts His Holiness to us. It is an act of God's love.

What makes us Holy in this declaration of Christ is that the Father, Son and Holy Spirit live in us and we in them. (John 17:20-26). We are now face to face with God in this eternal relationship with Triune God. As God is Holy in His relationship—Father, Son, and Holy Spirit—we are INCLUDED in this same relationship and this is what makes us HOLY.

But you say what about the sins we all have and still commit? Doesn't that nullify any holiness we now have? Paul says it this way in Romans 5:20, "where sin increased grace increased all the more." Jesus took care of the sin problem ONCE and for ALL. For ALL people and ALL sin. We stay clean (Holy) through the word Jesus spoke to us. (John 15:3).

Let's be clear. Our life, our righteousness, our goodness, our holiness, our EVERYTHING which is Godly is a gift of Christ's life bequeathed to us. Christ IS our LIFE ! James says it this way in James 1:17, " EVERY good gift comes down from the Father in heaven."

The gifts of Salvation, Redemption, Adoption, Reconciliation, and Holiness all come from our Father given to us IN Jesus. This is GOOD NEWS. But it is only going to get better as eternity unfolds.

# HOW GOD SEES

Jesus is the Eternal Contemporary of all time. He is present in all time in creation history and in the future as well. He is simply the " I AM". Eternal.

When we read in Rev.13:8 that Jesus was slain from the foundation of the world, or we read in Eph.1:3-14 that we were chosen in Christ before the foundation of the world, an interesting question is brought up. How could this have happened before the birth of Jesus recorded in the book of Luke?

We are reminded here that God not only exists IN time and space which He created, but He also lives outside of time and space where He has always existed as Father, Son, and Holy Spirit—Triune God. And as is the case, He sees everything in the PRESENT from that vantage point. He sees the whole panorama of the human experience "from the foundation of the world". Of course we don't because we are finite beings who only live and exist in time and space. We see from a perspective of past, present and future.

God clearly says in Isaiah 55:8-9, that His thinking, thoughts, ways, perspectives, etc. are Higher, more advanced, Supremely advanced compared to the thoughts and reasonings of man. Man really can not comprehend the magnitude of the complexity of God's thought processes.

God knows everything in advance. He sees everything in advance from His perspective ORIGINALLY. Even before creation He sees everything clearly played out on the human stage. (See Psalm 139 and Romans 4:17)

When we see in Isaiah 7 and Isaiah 9 the account of " a virgin shall conceive", and the announced birth of Jesus as well as the account of the birth of Jesus in Luke 2, these in God's reality are "reenactments" of what already occurred "before the foundation of the world".

If Rev.13:8 is true and Jesus was slain before the foundation of the world, then in God's eyes, objectively speaking, He was born before the foundation of the world as well.

Understanding Theology a little better allows us to process biblical concepts with greater care than would otherwise be possible.

# HOW LONG UNTILL CHRIST RETURNS ?

How long will it be until the 2nd Coming of Christ? How long until Christ returns? How long is the end of the age and when did it start? Many interpretations and speculations about these things have infatuated Bible students and Prophetic Prognosticators for centuries. Many have figured times and years and dates from decrees in the Book of Daniel and other places. Then by adding up 'years' and half-years and seasons based on certain events during THEIR time they came up with any number of dates for the return of Jesus. Needless to say all have been wrong. And, those who are doing the same thing now suffering from "Prediction Addiction" will find themselves to be wrong as well.

All of these predictions are based upon the assumption that now—whatever time in which one lives—is THE END TIME. Furthermore, that these are the LAST DAYS as indicated by numerous events and happenings which 'fulfill prophecy and complete scripture.

There are several references to 'last days' and 'last times'. But when is this time? Hebrews 1:2, says that God has "in these LAST DAYS" spoken to us by His Son. In I John 2:18, John says, "Little children it is the LAST TIME....whereby we know it is the LAST TIME". (KJV). The NIV says, " it is the LAST HOUR...this is how we know it is the LAST HOUR.". Jude 18 says, " in the last times (plural) there will be scoffers who will follow their own ungodly desires." I Peter 1:20, says that, " Jesus was revealed in these LAST TIMES for your sake." (NIV). II Timothy 3:1, says , "that in the LAST DAYS perilous times would come."

When we stop to look at these various scriptures we can readily conclude that these very things have been happening in the world for the last 2000 years. Scoffers, perilous times, famines, pestilence, disease, and horrific wars have been commonplace for all of these last days. And that is just the point.

The former days, scripturally speaking, ALL occurred before Jesus Christ came on the scene. Hebrews 1:2 makes this plain. That from now on in these LAST TIMES beginning with Jesus Christ and His Ministry God speaks to us by His Son. In other words, the end time, the end times, the last days, and the last times all began with Jesus Christ and His ministry. They did not start in 999 A.D. at the end of the first millennium. They did not start with the Reformation in the 1600's. They did not start with WWI, or WWII, or the invention of any weapon of destruction. They did not start with the coming to rule or power of any one particular man whose "number" is thought to be linked to any one specific individual in prophetic verses. Men have tried over the centuries to do this very thing. But "that dog won't hunt !" Time marches on. The end time marches on.

How much longer before the return of Jesus Christ to this earth? Scripture is pretty plain about this. We may not like to hear it speak. But the truth is that only The Father in heaven knows. It has been 2000 years since Jesus was here the first time. Paul and others originally thought that Jesus was going to return in their day. All who have prophesied Jesus Return have been woefully wrong. And they are all still wrong. Could it be another 50 years? Or, 100 years? Or 1000 years? Or 3000 years? The answer whether we wish to hear it or not is a resounding –YES. God is revealing His true nature and life as the Great Triune God, Father, Son, and Holy Spirit, and the reality that He created mankind to share in His life and His sharing in man's life. And this is going to take time before it covers the world as the oceans cover the earth.

Jesus gave the sure sign of when He would return. It is found in Matthew 24:30, and He says that when He returns, "all the nations of the earth will SEE Him coming with POWER and GREAT GLORY." Believe it or not that is the ONLY sign Jesus gave of His return. WHEN YOU SEE HIM COMING. That is the SIGN. When is it? Only the Father knows!

You mean to tell me that all the figuring, calculating, searching, postulating, interpreting, cross referencing, and looking for certain alignment of the stars is not going to somehow tell us when Jesus is going to return? Correct. They aren't.

The day is coming when the modern soothsayers and Prophets who speak, but not because God spoke to them, are all going to be out of a job. No more T.V. hype. No more emotionalism. No more fear tactics.

We all collectively have a job to do. Let's be about our Father's business of sharing His Son with the world and the GOOD NEWS that is Good News for them all.

Jesus is coming when He comes, and not before!


# " I HAVE OVERCOME THE WORLD ! "


"Be of good cheer; I have overcome the world." Jesus said in John 16:33. What does this mean for you and me? Are we just to stand back in awe at Jesus' accomplishment of the feat and congratulate Him with 1000 "at-a-boys"? Just what is the significance of Jesus' overcoming the world?

Jesus came as the Incarnate Son of God to create the union between God and humanity so that man could enter into the very life and existence of the Triune God. Whether or not Adam sinned was not the determining factor as to the success of this foreordained plan of God. But, when Adam did sin, bringing untold misery and death upon his descendants, it became necessary for what Adam did to humanity to be undone by Jesus.

For 33 years Jesus' life was a living sacrifice. Every day of His sinless life was racked with suffering and pain finally ending with His supreme sacrifice—Death. At the end of his earthly life and ministry Jesus utters two dynamic statements in the Book of John. One is, "It is finished" in John 19:30. What Jesus came to do, He did! He finished the work the Father gave Him to do. (John 17:4). The other statement is in John 16:33, "...but be of good cheer; I have overcome the world." He overcame the world of the first Adam and the authority and power of the evil one, Satan the Devil." So here again, do we just give Jesus 1000, or more, "at-a-boys" and marvel at His accomplishment?

Jesus is saying He overcame the world not to brag or lift up Himself in any way, but to inform John and every other human who ever lived that this MEANS something for all people.

Since there is NO WAY we humans can possibly overcome the world the only way we can be considered as having overcome the world is in Jesus' overcoming it! As the 'Vicarious' human Jesus' single life becomes the propitiation / payment for everything we need for Life. He is our **overcoming.** He is our **sin.** He is our **faith.** He is our **life.** He is our **death.** He is our **new birth.** He is our **resurrection.** He **qualifies** us for life. He has **OVERCOME** the world. He has defeated sin and death and **crucified** all of Adams descendants and **ADAM'S WORLD** making it **Null and Void** as having any implications for our future life with Triune God. Jesus **DID IT ALL.**

So where does this leave all of us? There is nothing left for us to overcome **Spiritually.** We simply **Rest** in what Jesus has already done for us all. In this human existence in the age of man under the influence of Satan the Devil we have all kinds of trials and tribulations ( John 16:33) which are a product of living in the fallenness of Adam and the fiery darts of Satan. We are promised a certain degree of suffering in this physical life. But the **GOOD NEWS** is that all of this is going to pass away and we are left only with what Jesus did, does, and is doing in the life all people.

Jesus is saying, since He has overcome the world and everything in it and the god of it, to **Look Up. Be of good cheer. Be positive. Be thankful. Rejoice. Celebrate. Know who you are in Jesus. Know where you are going. Know your future is secure. Know God loves you and has done all these things in Jesus because He loves you THAT much. Believe. Trust. Be free.**

**Lord, I believe, help my unbelief!**
**AMEN**

## "I NEVER KNEW YOU!" MATTHEW 7:21-24

God loves us all unconditionally. No stipulations. No requirements. Not anything. He loves us from before the foundation of the world and wants to be with us forever. His total and complete Grace was extended to us individually in Jesus Christ before we were even born! Our sins were forgiven, we were redeemed, we were reconciled, and we were saved in Jesus before we started our human walk through life. We did not get a say so or a vote. We have ascended with Jesus to the Father's right hand in the heavenly realm and have been seated there with Jesus. ( Ephesians 2:6).

With this being said, how would verses such as Matthew 7:21-24 be explained? (see text). The kingdom of Heaven is first and foremost a relationship with God through acceptance and belief in Jesus Christ. Jesus said that the kingdom was here and among us presently. Jesus wants a relationship with all of us and to give us all the abundant life he offers. Acceptance and belief of WHO we are IN Jesus is critical for this to be experienced.

Of course Jesus knows our name. He knows the name of ALL people. When Matthew 7 speaks of Jesus not knowing these people it means He has not known them in the right relationship based on their belief and trust in Him for the things they were doing in their life. People have "prophesied" or preached in His name, people have driven demons out of others, and miracles have been performed. But, these people doing these things have done them out of personal talent and ability and in some cases with the aid of Satan and even with the help of the Holy Spirit. However, most importantly, they have done so for wrong personal motives and personal exaltation, which did not glorify Jesus, nor did they accept and believe WHO they were in Jesus. They trusted in themselves and not Jesus. It is they who never 'knew' Jesus.

These people were adopted and included in the life of God from before the foundation of the world like everyone else. ( Ephesians 1). Yet, for whatever reason they did not have the relationship of belief and trust in Jesus they needed.

With this kind of self-centered approach to ministering and self-aggrandizement, Jesus is left with no other choice than to say to " get away from me." Jesus calls this kind of action "evil doing". The question is, do they have to stay away from Jesus forever?

God is not willing for any to continue suffering in their own personal mental captivity. He wants all to come to a change of mind about Jesus— what we call repentance. God is very patient and will allow someone all the time necessary to come to this repentance. When they do and accept who they are in Jesus and believe it they will be blessed by experiencing the abundant life eternally God grants in and through Jesus Christ.

May we All come to see WHO we are in Jesus Christ and Praise His Name Forever.

AMEN

# "I WILL MAKE YOU FISHERS OF MEN !"

Let's go fishing! I remember learning how to fish from my dad years ago in the lakes in central Mississippi. How vivid some of those fond memories are. Jesus Christ calls all of us to go fishing with Him. But not the kind of fishing that brings in swimmy creatures.

Jesus said, " ...come and follow me and I will make you fishers of men." (Matthew 4:19).

Most people do not take this very seriously. Most Christians in their Christian walk for however many years just "sit in the boat" and float around. They never wet a hook! There are so many ways to fish that it would be difficult to define all of them. As we become fishers of men we need to examine just how it is that we can go about Christian fishing. It requires a paradigm change from just boating to fishing. Literally there are thousands of ways we can follow Christ's commission to fish.

I think first off we must realize that it is Christ Who MAKES us fishers of men. It is by His power, inspiration, guidance, direction, encouragement, and strength that empowers any of us to "fish".

We live in the most information available age ever. We have access to all types of printed material. Radio. Television. Internet. News Papers. Books. Booklets. Fliers. Tri-folds. The only thing left out of the equation is our personal and collective inspiration as to how all or some of these may be used.

There must be a paradigm shift from boat floating to FISHING. Energy, effort, and determination need to be utilized if our efforts are going to prove successful.

Some of the ideas we come up with are not going to work very well. Some not at all. But, some WILL. And, those are the ones we can rejoice in. We need to fully understand that people—all people—need what we have to offer. They all need to know the Father in Heaven loves them. Jesus loves them. That there is peace and assurance in knowing WHO they are in Jesus Christ. We have EVERYTHING to give that they all really need to know about. The question is how do we go about getting this truth to them and into them?

Jesus said I will make you fishers of men. He did not say HOW He would require us to fish! He gave us intellect to figure that out with the help of the Holy Spirit and the tools available to us at any particular time in history.

Let me suggest getting an interested group together to have a BRAIN STORMING session to come up with viable ideas of just how to do all of this. That way this core group can all be on the same page and supportive of the ideas.

Well, you get the point. Now let's do what Jesus said. " Let's go FISHING!"

# IMMANUEL IS NOT JUST FOR CHRISTIANS

Today is the second Sunday of Advent. Advent pictures the coming of Jesus Christ. Jesus fulfills the meaning of the name IMMANUEL given in Isa.7:14. God with us. And us with God. Moreover, as Jesus said in John 14:20, God not just with us but God IN us and we IN Him.

Being the elitist creatures that we are, we would look at this truth and apply it conditionally to those who consider themselves Christian. We would say that this is a possibility for any to accept and therefore experience and dwell in once they "came to Christ".

But the truth of IMMANUEL is more profound than this. The truth of IMMANUEL is that God has come into human existence to be IN man and for man to be IN God. This was made possible only by Jesus coming and fulfilling the IMMANUEL reality. Jesus bridges the gap, the gulf between God and humanity. He is the connection. The unifying factor. He is the WAY that this happens.

The truth of Immanuel does not only apply to those considering themselves Christian, but this truth applies to ALL humans on earth. Let's notice a few scriptures which illustrate this.

The Apostle Paul, in talking to the pagan religious leaders in Athens, says in Acts 17:28 that they, the pagans live and move and have being IN God. So Paul is obviously NOT talking to Christians here, but to ALL men. Creation exists IN Jesus Christ. He created it for Himself, and in Him all things hold together—are sustained by Him. ( Colossians 1:15-17). Colossians 3:4 tells us that Jesus IS our LIFE. ALL peoples' life.

Without getting too deeply into Theological arguments at this point, let me just say that in truth Immanuel has existed since the creation of Adam! God has always been IN man and man has always been IN God through the connection of the Holy Spirit. The Fact of it is revealed to man through the INCARNATION of Jesus.

IMMANUEL then becomes the Truth of Truths. Immanuel is Jesus. Immanuel is the secret, the Mystery of the Ages as Paul says in Colossians 1:26-27.

Now a few more scriptures which demonstrate this inclusion of all mankind are:

I Cor. 15:22 …in Adam all die, but in Jesus ALL are made alive.

Rom. 5:18 …..ALL men

I Tim.4:10……Salvation for ALL men

II Cor.5:14…..One died for ALL

I Pt.3:18……..Christ died once for sins for ALL

Heb.9:12……..Christ died once for ALL

I Jn.2:2……….Jesus is the atoning sacrifice for the WHOLE WORLD

John 3:16…….for God so loved the world

Heb.10:10……ALL made Holy through the sacrifice of Jesus

Rom.8:15-16…We are adopted by God, we are the children of God

Ephesians 1:3-14, is especially revealing since mans Adoption into the life of God took place BEFORE the creation of the world. It has been fact and reality all along the human path of existence. This is understood, however, from a proleptic understanding in Theology. God is EVER PRESENT in the life and existence of His creation. He is the was, is , and will be. He is the I AM. The Eternal.

Immanuel is the truth for all men. God has come to be IN man and takes man INTO Himself. Not just Christians, but all men. He is the Father of ALL. Jesus is the Savior of ALL.

It is nice to reflect on Advent four weeks before Christmas every year and the birth of Immanuel. But the truth of Immanuel is 24/7/365. God is indeed with us and in us perpetually and we are in Him as Jesus proclaimed

in John 14:20, " I am in the Father, you are in me, and I am in you."

Immanuel is Revealed. Immanuel is the Secret for ALL. Will you believe it?

# IMMANUEL—MORE THAN GOD "WITH" US !

We are in the first week of Advent today. I want to share a concept with all of us that if we are not careful we will overlook it in its importance and view Advent like most all other churches do.

Most would look at Jesus' coming as is related in Isa.7:14, that the son born to the virgin would be named Immanuel, or as we all are familiar with, "God with us." But as we will see here, it is more than that.

Jesus did not come "to visit" earth 2000 years ago! He was not a spectator on the human scene. He did not show us how to imitate him and thereby earn the right to be called Christians. Immanuel means so much more.

History is replete with those claiming to know the "secret" of life. The Gnostics had their hidden secrets. The Rosicrucians had theirs. The Zoroastrians had their mysteries of life. All relating to self helps, pull one's self up through mindsets and man made philosophies. Today we have New Age, and even a book out and a movie by the name, "THE SECRET". Robert Collier wrote a book in 1926 entitled, THE SECRET OF THE AGES.

Understanding IMMANUEL unlocks the greatest secret or mystery man has ever been blessed with. Immanuel does mean God is with us. But, it also means that man is WITH God—and this 24/7/365,

Jesus says it this way in John 14:20. "On that day,( or we would say, one day, or sooner or later, ) you WILL realize that I am IN my Father, and you are IN me, and I am IN you." Immanuel. God LIVES in us and we live in Him. We live, move and have our being in HIM. Acts 17:28. And when you realize this truth of all truths, you will know the greatest secret that has not been understood by the natural mind of man since Adam. No philosophy will know it, or come to see it, or hypothesize it, or stumble across it. It is a spiritual realization.

The apostle Paul says it this way. Colossians chapter one. Immanuel reconciles us to God. He places His life in us and takes our life INTO Himself. Connection. Unification. Uniting of man and God. Jesus is the bridge between earth and heaven. Paul then says in Col.1:26-27, 'The MYSTERY that has been kept hidden for ages and generations, but is now disclosed to the saints, to them God has chosen to make known among the Gentiles the glorious riches of this MYSTERY ( secret), which is Christ IN you the hope of glory." Vs. 29, shows Paul's Passion to proclaim this Mystery to ALL PEOPLE and to present EVERYONE Perfect in Christ.

Immanuel , the Secret and all that it entails is by God's doing. It is an ACT OF GOD! It does not need or require our vote or approval. It is God's declaration that He has come to be IN man and man IN Him. Immanuel therefore takes all of humanity into Himself and then what happens to Jesus also happens to all of humanity. Jesus dies, humanity dies. Jesus is resurrected, humanity is resurrected. Jesus ascends to the right hand of the Father, humanity ascends to the right hand of the Father as well. "I am in the Father, you are in Me and I am in you." See that?

As powerful acts of God, God has the power to Reconcile, to forgive, to place all sin ON and IN Jesus thereby NOT counting man's sins against man. ( II Cor.5:17-21).

There have been MANY imposter saviors in world history. There have been those who claimed that their saviors were born of virgins, died after three days and were resurrected. But, there has been only ONE IMMANUEL who is the one in whom we live, move, and have our being AND who lives IN us.


# IN THE IMAGE OF GOD

### ( MORE THAN A REFLECTION IN A MIRROR )

Genesis 1:26-27 says that God created man in God's image, both male and female. There has been much speculation on this statement over the ages with books being written on the subject.

It has been postulated that what it means to be created in God's image is to have the ability to think, possess creativity, be human in appearance as Christ was human. Further, to be able to love and be loved. To give and to receive. Also, to have a mind capable of great thinking and concepts of physical, metaphysical, philosophical, and theological understandings.

While all of these are God given capabilities which no animals possess they all miss the point of what it means to be created in God's image.

God speaking in Genesis 1 is not some unknowable, untouchable, cosmic Giant possessing "all everything" only to be revered, bowed down to, exalted, worshipped, and who is unapproachable as if He were some cosmic Budda, or Zeus, or similar to these but only infinitely greater.

John 1:1 shows God to be Father, Son, and Holy Spirit, a Triune God of ONE essence but three personas or persons. The word "with" here relates to relationship as the Triune God is "face to face" one with the other. Not just "existing" but living in RELATIONSHIP with one another in an entwined 'perichoretic' relationship of love, acceptance, appreciation, honor, fun, and the mutually sharing of life together.

This love relationship overflowed to the point that this Great Triune God decided to make children to share this abundance of love with and to share LIFE with in this perichoretic relationship which would take humanity INSIDE God's life and include man in God's life through man being 'Adopted' as God's very own children and placed inside this Divine relationship FOREVER. (See Ephesians 1:3-14 and John 14:20 ; John 17:20-26 ).

And all of this to be done IN, BY, FOR, and THROUGH Jesus Christ. The Divine UNION was to be and WAS completed in Jesus. God in effect established man's destiny before ANYTHING was ever created.

Triune God is Spirit. Father, Son and Holy Spirit are Spirit. For man AND woman to be created in God's image, created for this divine relationship demonstrates God's esteem for both sexes equally and His love for all of His children without partiality.

There simply is no other being in God's creation that in any way fits the description of one(s) being created IN God's image. Man and woman and only humanity can and does fit this profile.

The rest of the creation including all animals and all of nature and all of the cosmos was created FOR humans to be in charge of. Hebrews

2:5-8 shows that EVERYTHING created is to be under the "feet"—under subjection to man. That day is coming, but it is not here yet. The future world to come is not even going to be put under the authority of angels, but MAN.

This relates to man and woman being created in God's image. The fact that God is sharing His Divine Nature, His Divine LIFE with humanity demonstrates God's confidence in placing ALL things ultimately under man's "feet". In subjection to man.

In the image of God is to be IN eternal RELATIONSHIP with Father, Son and Holy Spirit. It is to share mutual Trust, love, confidence, and nature. God will have billions of sons and daughters IN his image sharing in the maintenance and care of the cosmos with all things being under their feet.

Great theologians such as Karl Barth, the great Athanasius, T.F. Torrance and others knew this truth and taught it.

Maybe now we can understand a little better another dimension of God's great love for all of us – love that will allow Him to share His very Divine life and eternity with us.

In the Image of God. More than a reflection in a mirror!


# IN WHAT "TENSE" DO WE READ SCRIPTURE?


What tense do we read scripture in? Past, Present, or future? This is vital to understanding what the great Triune God has done to us and for us and with us in Jesus.

For example, in Colossians 1:27, …"the Hope of glory" is stated. Hope here is not some wished for happening in the future like, " I hope I get married", or " I hope I get a new car", or " I hope I win the lottery". Rather, Hope IS the end result or product of what God has destined for us. Hope is a reality. Hope is a present reality as well as a future reality which never fades away.

Another. Hebrews 12:2, " Jesus is the author and finisher of our faith." Here again do we look at this as a future "possibility" but not a now present reality? Since it is Jesus' FAITH which makes all things possible and He shares His faith with us to accomplish what His purpose has always been and He has ALL power to do His will, He has authored our faith and He has finished our faith --NOW. This is a done deal and the author of Hebrews wants us to know it. This is not something that is going to be finished" in the future. It is finished NOW. We are GLORIFIED AND SEATED AT RIGHT HAND OF THE FATHER WITH JESUS NOW. ( Romans 8:30; Ephesians 2:6 ).

One more. I Peter 1:9. ..."you are receiving the goal of your faith, the salvation of your souls." Vs. 3 points out that He " has given us NEW BIRTH through the Resurrection of Jesus Christ from the dead INTO an inheritance which can never spoil." This is not something that might happen in the future but a present reality. NOW.

Scripture is not 'conditional'. We do not make it happen by believing or not believing. God does not need us to help Him make His Word work. Scripture is a DECLARATION of the Plan and Purpose and Will of the Triune God. When the Holy Spirit reveals the true meaning of scripture to us He allows us in our free will to accept its Truth and believe His Word or to reject it and not believe it. He allows us to choose to experience it or to not experience it now and/or forever. He will not force us to choose or believe. But, He wants us to choose to experience the life He offers in Jesus.

As far as tenses go, we have been saved, redeemed, reconciled, justified, adopted, glorified, resurrected and seated with Jesus at the Father's right hand in Jesus. PAST TENSE. Present Reality in God's Objective View. We just wait to see it all in its fullness when we are changed to immortal beings (I Corinthians 15) and " see Him as He is." ( I John 3:2). When He appears a lot of things are going to become CLEAR. We see through the 'eyes of faith' and through a glass 'darkly' or dimly now.

We need to understand that the Triune God is IN CHARGE. He knows what He is doing. His Plan is PERFECT. Can't be improved upon. He Loves us, likes us, and wants us to be with Him and each other forever. He makes it happen and He has made it Happen in Jesus Christ.

And He is so Good that He allows us to BELIEVE IT !!!

Lord I believe, help my unbelief.

AMEN

# INCARNATIONAL THEOLOGY- GOD ACCEPTS US!

## ( Who is in charge here anyway?)

For those who oppose the Theology of Adoption and Inclusion ( Incarnational or Trinitarian Theology) of all of mankind into the life of God since before the foundation of the world (Eph.1:3-14), and who deny that Christ's sacrifice was once and for ALL for all time (Heb.10: 12), stating UNTIL the individual accepts Jesus these facts are NOT applied to the individual, my question respectfully is this: For the billions of humans who have lived before Christ and after Christ who did not ever hear of Him so that it was impossible for them to "accept" Him so that these various scriptures could apply, are they just lost forever? How do they get to accept Jesus? Did Jesus die and save that segment of the LOST as well as all other segments of the lost? What question would be asked of those who have not heard the Gospel when they face the Father in Heaven? Was Christ's sacrifice from before the foundation of the world applicable to these who never heard the Gospel witness? Could it be possible that Christ chose them and adopted them from before the foundation of the world like He did believers? According to Christ's adopting humans before the foundation of the world, what is the difference between those who never heard the Gospel and believers since at one time believers had never heard it as well? Lots of questions but I think you can follow!

I think the MAIN MOST question, the NUMBER ONE question to ask is - Whose idea is it to grant Salvation to humans in the first place? Next, with that answered ( God of course ) was it God's purpose originally to save what was LOST (what became lost in Adam), and did Christ come to save that which was lost and did He actually SAVE WHAT WAS LOST—ADAM AND HIS DESCENDANTS.? (Luke 19:10). Was Christ's life, death, resurrection and ascension ENOUGH for the salvation of the human race?

Calvinism says that it was God's purpose originally to SAVE SOME and to have SOME LOST. Did God love the ones they say were chosen to be lost? And, would He not be showing favoritism and respecting persons to choose for some to be lost and some to be saved? John 3:16 says that God loved the WORLD. God is LOVE.

Really, the only thing left was for God to decide to Adopt and Save EVERYBODY and then go from there in how He would bring the knowledge of that adoption and salvation to ALL and allow everyone the free will to choose to believe it or not.

Here is where many Christians and the Christian Theology of Adoption and Inclusion actually have some agreement. The common Christian thought is that individuals must hear the Gospel and decide whether or not to "accept" Christ as their personal savior. If they don't , then they are consigned to Hell and suffer the consequences.

Trinitarian or Incarnational Theology says believe what Jesus did FOR them and TO them by His divine acts and His gift of life in and with God. One has the dynamic of believing and accepting so that the process of salvation will NOW take place, the other says the dynamic of salvation and adoption has ALREADY taken place in Jesus' life, death, resurrection, and ascension and that the individual must believe it in order to **experience** living in God's abundant life now and forever. By not believing it, the individual would just continue in misery and suffering and perishing ( Hell ) indefinitely, or until such a time they did come to believe it.

The general concept is that we Christians must get to people now and get them to accept Jesus and 'get' saved so they can go to Heaven, otherwise they will GO TO HELL!!! Can you see that this places the 'success' of salvation for humans in the hands of humans? Do you think the Father in Heaven would leave the FINISHING of our Faith and Salvation in man's hands when He is the Author of our salvation----and He is the FINISHER as well? ( Heb.12:2; Phil.1:6). Remember this is the Triune God's Master Plan.

For those who think that there is a free ticket and free ride for EVERYONE straight into the Glory of Heaven the caveat is such that it is NOT a free ride and a free ticket where man has no involvement since man himself has to CHOOSE this LIFE that is in Jesus by BELIEVING WHO HE OR SHE IS IN JESUS! ( This choosing is what separates this theology from Universalism or Universal Salvation.)

The really Good News is that God Loves us all and He has made all the arrangements necessary for man's complete and eternal salvation and inclusion in His life forever!!!

We can argue 'till the cows come home' and it is not going to change what our loving Heavenly Father has done for us IN Jesus Christ. Thank you Jesus !!!

Amen.

# INSTINCT ? OR GOD ?

Why do Swallows fly to Capistrano every year—and at the same time, on the same day every year? Why do Salmon swim up stream to the place where they were born (hatched) to spawn? Why do Monarch Butterflies migrate to Mexico every year by the millions? Why do birds build nests in every conceivable design and from all substances available to them at the time? When we take time to examine some to the peculiarities of the animal kingdom we are faced with amazing activity which we all normally ascribe to "instinct".

We say that various species just do this or that by instinct. That this instinct is just in them from birth and passed on generation to generation from whatever beginning or origin they had. Some may call it evolution while others see it as creation by a creator.

The animal world is truly amazing to say the least. The methods of procreation, of protection, and of mothers caring for their offspring is beautiful when carefully observed.

We are witnessing something so marvelous and inspiring, yet often we relegate what is going on to 'nature', Mother Nature, instinct, evolution, or some other reason other than what is truly going on.

Could it be that the great Tripersonal—Triune God is actually involved with His creation? That this creation is actually filled with the Spirit of God and that He has an active hand in loving what He has created and involves Himself personally with His creation?

Colossians tells us that All things were created In, By, and Through Jesus Christ. ( Colossians 1:16-17). And that He UPHOLDS or SUSTAINS ALL of His creation. What does that mean to you?

The Spirit of God is at work in this present world. And always has been. Ecclesiastes 3:19-21, speaks of the breath and 'Spirit' of animals—beasts. What spirit is this? Whose spirit is it? Where does it come from? God is personally and actively IN His creation caring for the 'lesser' creatures as well as those created in His image! God loves His creation. It is beautiful to Him. And interesting. And fascinating. And complex. And FUN. FUN!!! God laughs at monkeys doing their monkey business. ( And at us doing ours at times!). God swims with the whales and soars with the Eagles. God enjoys His creation. He is in it and He sustains it by His Spirit.!!!!!!!!!!!!!

There are over 12,000 different types of ants in the world. Thousands of insects. Butterflies, Birds, fish, vertebrates and invertebrates. Amazing creation. And this, not to mention what is going on throughout the universe, is all upheld and sustained by our Savior Jesus Christ.

Luke 12:6, reminds us that even when five sparrows are sold for a few cents—not worth very much to us—that not one of them is forgotten by God! Ecclesiastes Ch.3, reminds us again that there is a 'spirit' in these created creatures of God. They are not created IN God's Image, but they are CREATED and cared for and sustained and upheld by the loving God who made them!

The next time we see puppies playing, or kittens rolling around on the floor, or calves frolicking in a pasture let's be sure to see the hand of God IN them. Let's see the beautiful expression of the Father's love to create something so sweet for us to enjoy along with His enjoyment of it. Let's not relegate what is happening in this life we share with the creation to be ascribed to Nature or Instinct. Let's praise God for all that he has wonderfully made.

The "heavens declare the Glory of God", but so do the things on this earth that God Upholds. Thank you Father. It is so Beautiful.

# IS GOD BIG ENOUGH ?

What are our choices when it comes to the various Theologies and church doctrines which pervade the religious landscape of Christianity?

Much on the smorgasbord of religious feasting is available. We can choose from Old Covenant practices which are obsolete to New Covenant grace oriented worship of Jesus Christ which stand forever.

One question that needs to be addressed is What God are we going to worship? The God who is a Father, is Love, who forgives all, who is patient, and whose mercy extends forever, or, The God who is austere, cold, callused, vengeful, cruel, judgmental, overbearing, unmerciful, unforgiving, and a God who would punish and torture His children forever separated from Him in the flames of Hell forever if they don't love Him back and/or obey Him?

Or, are we going to worship the God who was big enough, powerful enough, all wise, and all knowing –including knowing the entire future as it would unfold in the creation—that He would orchestrate a plan out of His Love that would insure His entire creation would always belong to Him and share in His love for it. Did He make all the preparations in advance to insure the ultimate outcome of His plan in accordance with His purpose, will, and desire?

Is our God big enough to stand against any attack of evil forces or human rejections and still emerge as the Only Triune God, the Loving Father, the Alpha and Omega, the Beginning and the End, the first and last cause, THE God of Forgiveness, and the one whose plan is assured of success because He is big enough to MAKE it happen?

Is God's Love, Grace, Mercy, and forgiveness big enough to deal with man's hate for God and man's disobedience to everything God is? Will God still love unconditionally all His children and extend His adoption, inclusion, and salvation to them when they are so determined in their heart to resist and rebel against Him?

Was the Incarnation of God's very being in Jesus and His sacrifice ENOUGH to cause THE PLAN to succeed? Was or is there ANYTHING that can make void or nullify what God has purposed in His heart to do? Is there ANY POSSIBILITY that it can fail now?

These are all insipid and banal questions. They spring from a human mind which is so limited it can not understand the magnitude of God's Great Love or the Greatness of God's ways and thinking. These are questions asked only from the human limited level of understanding. Man can not comprehend the ABSOLUTE SOVEREIGNTY with which Almighty God designs His plan and completes His plan.

Man raises puny questions and postulates puny scenarios of philosophical "what ifs" as if these are going to negate or change the outcome of God's Great plan and purpose for His creation.

To make a long story short (er) let's say it this way.

God is LOVE.

ALL things were/are created BY and FOR Jesus Christ and He sustains All things by His POWER. ( Colosians 1:15-20.)

ALL things were Reconciled to God by Jesus Christ.

Creation, the Cosmos, the Universe, All mankind—everyone who has ever lived or who will ever live—everything on earth or in heaven has been reconciled to God and Belongs to God. This is His deal. And, it is the real Deal.!!

Any efforts to contravene this Deal will fail.

Jesus Christ is VICTORIOUS. All battles have been won in Jesus. What God says will stand. Therefore, a GLORIOUS FUTURE is in the offing for everything and everyone in God's home. Behold He makes ALL things new. He destroys Death. He replaces tears and death with JOY and LIFE.

And He does so for EVERYONE who Believes His WORD.

# IS GOD DISTANT AND UNINVOLVED

You are aware of most people's view of God. Distant. Disconnected. Non-involved with His creation. Jesus talked about His Loving Father and the Triune existence of God that is in human beings. ( John 14:20; John 17:20-26). The early church leaders talked about Adoption and Inclusion in the life of God. Men like Paul, John, Polycarp, Irenaeus, Athanasius, and others wrote of this truth. So how did we come to view God in the 21st Century the way most Christians do as distant and uninvolved?

Just prior to the Reformation in the 1600's great church leaders such as John Calvin, Martin Luther, and others were seeing the great truth of the Triune existence of God in humanity and His connection to His creation. But something monumental was happening in the world of thought that eclipsed the theological thinking of the Reformation.

The European world had been dominated by the Church during the lower and Middle Ages. The time was ripe for a change in thinking and attitudes. Partly as a backlash against the tyranny of the Church and the domination of politics extant in the world, great thinkers emerged with what came to be known as the "Enlightenment". Or, the Enlightenment of Reason, or the Age of Reason. This dramatic change in thinking occurred from the 17th Century on through the 18th. The faith in the church was hijacked by this revolution in thinking. Where God had been central in theological thinking, now reason, intelligence, philosophy, invention, mechanics, politics and science would replace God in man's view of 'authority'. The saviour of man would now be man and his intellect with no real need for God.

Famous men of the Enlightenment, just to name a few, included Rene Decartes, Edmund Burke, Edward Gibbon, David Hume, Immanuel Kant, Thomas Jefferson, John Locke, Montesquieu, Thomas Paine, Voltaire, Rousseau, and Isaac Newton.

The Enlightenment religion of the day became what is known as DEISM, from the Latin word deus meaning god. Deism emphasized reason. It believed in one God as creator of the cosmos, but was opposed to revelation and the thought that God dwelt in man or was continuously active in the affairs of the world. Or to put it another way, God created the cosmos and the world and wound it up like a giant clock, turned it on, and let it go on its own. So after creating the cosmos God just walked away.

This "religion" essentially did away with God as Frederic Neitzhy would say, " God is dead." Man could now do as he pleased with no restraints from a God who was distant and uninvolved. Romans 1:20-25 describes what reasonings are behind this kind of thinking!

But the Enlightenment and the Deism which pervaded the period were not the finishing blow to the faith of the church. That esteemed honor came to a refined, educated Englishman and graduate of Cambridge University, Charles Robert Darwin.

Darwin published his Origin of the Species in 1859 which formed the basis for the evolutionary thought which would push the creator completely out of the cosmic picture. Although Darwin did not specifically write defining the evolution of humans, only plants and animals, his assumptions and theories were expanded by others to mean the evolution of man from lower forms in the anthropological assent to humans.

The world today continues to suffer under these false concepts and God remains distant and uninvolved.

But what is the Truth? We read in Colossians 1:16-17; Ephesians 1:22; Hebrews 1:3, that Jesus Christ is the Creator and that All things were created BY and THROUGH, and IN, and FOR Jesus AND that He SUSTAINS or UPHOLDS ALL THINGS.

Jesus said that the Kingdom is among us. Jesus said that He and Father and the Holy Spirit would make their home IN us. And for Jesus to uphold all things and sustain all things, He must be in all things. Paul said in Acts 17:28 when debating with the pagans at Athens that, " we live, and move, and have our being in the Creator God."

Jesus is the 'Light of the world'. That light has not gone out and did not go out with the Enlightenment and the philosophy of Deism. Not only is Jesus the light of the world, John says in John 1:4 that in Him was/is LIFE. There is no life apart from the source of life which is the indwelling life of Jesus in all living things. After all, He did breathe the breath of life into all living-breathing creatures! Ecclesiastes 3:19-21 speaks of this breath and spirit of life in animals and beasts.

God knows when a sparrow falls to the ground. He is in it and there. (Luke 12:6). We are told in Psalm 148 and in Psalm 8 for all the creation to praise God. God is very much in His creation. His life permeates all living things. His Spirit permeates all of the cosmos. All of the Universe. David said this in Psalm 139:7-12. God swims in and with the whales by His Spirit. He soars with the eagles by His Spirit. His Spirit is alive and in and upholding and sustaining ALL of the Creation.

Our loving Triune God, Father, Son, and Holy Spirit has desired to share His life and eternity with us His children—FOREVER. He is not far off. He is here and now. He is personal and relational. He LOVES you, always has, always will. And He has made all the provisions for you to be with Him for all eternity in Glory. Can you believe this?

Lord I believe, help my unbelief.

AMEN

# IS GOD FAIR ?

II Peter 3:9…"God is not willing for any to perish, but for all to come to repentance / belief.." He is not necessarily overly concerned as to when or how one comes to belief / repentance, but that a person does. And He is VERY patient.

God's heart desire is to have life and relationship with His children in joy and happiness forever. It PLEASES God to share His love and life with man. (II Peter 1:4).

Often times it does not seem fair to us the way salvation applies to some people. They are too bad, having too much fun, too evil, etc. But, what is fair to God is NOT always what seems fair to us. Take for example the parable of the Laborers in the Vineyard in Matt.20:1-16. Here those hired in the early morning were paid one penny for the days work as well as those hired throughout the day and at the last hour of the day. All received one penny. We say this is not fair. Not equitable.

This parable is a pure example of GRACE. God giving as He pleases. Gifts not based on what one as earned or on what one deserves or on what one has done, but gifts based on God's love and what Jesus has done.

In Luke 13:4, is an example of people looking at the sins of others in a disproportionate manner compared to one's own sins. The Tower of Siloam killing 18 people. But Jesus says that it is an individual matter of one's personal repentance / belief in order not to perish.

In Luke 10:12-14, Jesus is not condemning of Sodom, Tyre and Sidon, but says it will be more tolerable for them in judgement than for Korazin and Bethsaida because when miracles were performed in Korazin and Bethsaida they still did not repent. They refused to believe Jesus.

Why doesn't Jesus condemn sinners, publicans, tax collectors, prostitutes, malefactors and any other sinner? Jesus is not interested in condemning, but in hoping for individuals to come to belief in Him. (John 3:16-17; II Peter 3:9).

God does NOT keep records of the sins of man. Psalm 130:3, tells us that, " If you should mark or record iniquities/sins , who would be able to stand.?" God is in the forgiving, saving, adopting, including, and indwelling business, not the condemning and destroying business.

God's plan and purpose is for all to come to see and believe who they are in Jesus and who they have ALWAYS BEEN in Jesus. If you were to ask God, He would tell you that yes, " HE IS FAIR.!"


# IS IT FINISHED OR IS IT DONE ???


Jesus said, " It is finished". (John 19:30). But we see evil, sin, corruption and every kind of abomination in the world today. Jesus said this in reference to the job He came to do in connecting mankind to God to complete Holy Communion, or Divine and Holy Community in Union with the Triune God. He did His Job. He made all the arrangements, provisions, payments, and fulfillments necessary for man to be united forever with the Triune God. In His own words from the cross at Calvary, He said, " It is finished." And it was.

Now we read in Revelation 21:6, Jesus says here that, " it is done.". So is it finished, or is it done? This is an honest question not sharp shooting anything at all.

We need to consider that what the Triune God originally purposed was to have a human family, Adopted and included into His life forever had to be completed in the life of Himself becoming human and thereby uniting humanity to Himself. ( Ephesians 1:3-14). Then we can understand that the WORD had to become flesh and live as a human and die to connect man to God in this intimate relationship. Jesus is the connection. Without Jesus and the Incarnation there is no connection.

Jesus did everything the Father and He decided and purposed before the foundation of the world. The Plan was the original blueprint. There were explicit elements in the blueprint that had to be exercised. Jesus did it all and said so in John 19:30 when He exclaimed from the cross, " It is finished!"

Now the price was paid. The debt was satisfied. The connection was made. So Jesus in his own words says, " It is finished!" There is nothing more that "I " can do. He says.

The plan from before the beginning of the Cosmos is now ASSURED. IT IS FINISHED. BUT, BUT, BUT, Now there is a history of man to be lived out before all is **DONE.**

Man lives in the fallenness of Adam. Evil and sin permeate the world. Satan is still the "prince of the power of the air…" Eph.2:2. And he is the god of this world. II Cor.4:4.

God has given man and the age of man just so long to endure and suffer in the sin filled existence of Satan's influence. But, N F L. ( That's not National Football League ). It is Not For Long. !!!

Satan has been defeated. Jesus Won the Victory for all of the Cosmos.

Now we come to Revelation 21:6. Here Jesus is just proclaiming that after all is said and done that what He came to do is climaxing in the final analysis and that now what He finished is DONE. IT IS DONE. IT IS OVER. GOD WINS . WE WIN. **IT IS DONE.**

# IS JEREMIAH 10 ABOUT CHRISTMAS TREES ?

At the expense of kicking a dead horse to death again, I want to share some OBVIOUS truths concerning Jeremiah 10 which you may have overlooked. Coming from a history which said that Jer.10 was describing a 'Christmas' tree and therefore we should not have Christmas trees because they were Pagan and of Pagan origin we are not to worship God like the Pagans did. Do you really want to be honest with what Jer.10 is REALLY describing? Good. Let us just go there and read what it PLAINLY says.

Jeremiah 10 is a discussion describing FALSE gods and their LACK of influence in mankind's and the True God who does have impact in mankind's. With that in mind let's look at the verses as they proceed through Ch.10:1-16.

Vs.2, warns against the practice of ASTROLOGY with the pagans being horrified by what they thought those signs portrayed.

VS.3, says that a tree is cut out of the forest and a CRAFTSMAN then with a chisel shapes the tree, ( block of wood),

Vs.4 says it is ADORNED with silver and gold ( inlaid with gold and silver) and it is nailed down so it doesn't move.

Vs.5, Now begins a more clear picture of what is going on. It is LIKE a scarecrow , as an IDOL, it can not speak, nor can it walk, don't fear this idol because it can not do harm or good.

Vs.6, This verse now compares the Eternal, LORD, saying None is like you, YOU are great, and YOUR NAME is mighty in Power. ( now look at this puny idol !!!)

Vs.7, says Who is it that should not REVERE you (LORD)? There is NONE like you.

Vs.8, GOES BACK TO TALKING ABOUT THE "TREE" or IDOL. They are senseless, and foolish; they are taught by worthless WOODEN IDOLS.!!!!!

Vs.9, Hammered silver and gold are then OVERLAID on the wooden idol, and the idol is then DRESSED IN BLUE AND PURPLE ALL MADE BY SKILLED WORKERS!!!

( Did you ever see a tree dressed in blue and purple? Why no.

Vs.10, Now swings back to the true God. But the LORD is the true God., He is the living God, the Eternal King..

Vs.11, says, " Tell them this : These gods who did not make the heavens and the earth will perish.

Vs.12, says, God made the earth by His power.

Vs.14, ….."Every Goldsmith is shamed by his IDOLS. His images are a fraud. They have no breath in them.

Vs.15, says, "They are worthless, the objects of mockery; when their judgement comes, they will perish."

Vs.16, The final blow is the statement in vs.16 which says that , "He who made Jacob is not like these idols. The ALMIGHTY IS HIS NAME.

# IS JESUS' RESURRECTION ALL INCLUSIVE?

Jesus makes a profound statement to Martha, Lazarus'sister, in John 11:25. Lazarus has died and four days have passed. Lazarus had been a "good" man and therefore in Jewish Pharisee philosophy would be resurrected at the last day in the resurrection. Martha states this to Jesus in verse 24.

But Jesus makes a POWERFUL statement to Martha when He says, " I AM the resurrection and the life." Let's carry this statement a little further to understand its impact. Jesus is saying, " Here is a situation with Lazarus which will allow me to state just WHO I AM and demonstrate why I have come and that I have the Power to resurrect the dead. So, let me tell you who I am. I am the Incarnate Son of God and I came to rectify the fallenness in Adam of ALL Humanity who are DEAD in Adam—Past, Present, and Future—and to be THE RESURRECTION and THE LIFE for ALL Humanity and raise ALL people up in my Resurrection thus bridging the gap between God and man thereby creating UNION between God and man. I am the source and the ONLY source for ALL of humanity to be resurrected. Let me begin to show this power to resurrect now by raising Lazarus."

Matthew continues this theme in Matthew 27:50-53. This is the account After the Resurrection of Jesus when the graves in and around Jerusalem were opened and the DEAD came up in resurrection. This demonstrated again God's power to raise the dead. But it was also a FORESHADOWING of the Resurrection of ALL of humanity in Jesus in God's time order—Jesus, of course, being the First ( I Corinthians 15:23).

In I Corinthians Paul further shows that the resurrection of Jesus Christ and ALL of Humanity's resurrection stand or fall together. If one is not true, then NEITHER is true.

( I Corinthians 15:16 ). Paul then goes one step further when in verse 22 he says, " For AS in Adam ALL die, SO in Christ ALL WILL be made alive." No one is excluded. Just as no one has ever been excluded or will ever be excluded in dying as a result of Adam. No one is excluded from being made alive IN Jesus Christ. Paul says it this way in Colossians 3:1-4. "...you have been RAISED with Christ "Christ IS your LIFE."

John tells us in Revelation 13:8 that the Lamb of God was slain from the foundation of the world. When Christ was crucified and died in the early 30's A.D. His blood reached all the way back to Adam and ALL of Adam's descendents and forward to every human being who would ever live in the human family line of Adam. Therefore, ALL are redeemed in the blood of Jesus no matter when they live! There can be NO ONE excluded. And NO ONE is!

Jesus came to seek and to save what was lost, Humanity, and He did. ( Luke 19:10). Jesus came to REVEAL Himself as the Resurrection and the Life. ( John 11:25). Jesus came to live, die, be resurrected and to ascend to the Father's right hand AND to carry Humanity to the Father's right hand WITH Him by being humanity's life, death, resurrection and ascension. (Ephesians 2:6).

God had a 'lock tight' plan from the very beginning to Adopt and Include humanity into the life of the Triune God—Father, Son, and Holy Spirit. ( Ephesians 1:3-14). Throughout the history of man God has NEVER wavered in His Plan for humanity. In Jesus the Plan is complete. " It is finished," Jesus said in John 19:30.

In Jesus the FULLNESS of the Plan will ultimately be REALITY. God WILL wipe away all tears. Joy and happiness and peace and righteousness will reign in the FULL KINGDOM OF GOD FOREVER.

All of this will be completed because of one man. The man who was fully human and fully God, Jesus Christ.

The question is, can we believe this magnificent truth? Can we believe the WORD? Can we believe the Son of God, Jesus Christ?

"Lord I believe, help my unbelief."

# IS THE GOOD NEWS FOR "EVERYONE" ?

One of the basic arguments against Trinitarian Theology of Adoption and Inclusion and salvation for everyone is that scriptures concerning these elements only apply to Christians or those who Believe or those who accept Jesus.

There are numerous verses which state the full inclusion of EVERYONE in the Salvanic Plan and process God originated. I will list just a few here:

Romans 5:18 ..."for ALL men" (and women ☺)

John 3:16........."the World"

I Timothy 4:10 "salvation for ALL men ( and women ☺)

II Cor. 5:14......"one died for ALL

I Peter 3:18......"Christ died once for sins for ALL"

Heb.9:12........."once for ALL"

I John 2:2........"Atoning sacrifice for the WHOLE WORLD"

What God says through Paul in Ephesians 1:3-14 is that man was blessed by being chosen in Christ before the creation of the world...and Adopted and redeemed through the blood of Christ (Who was also slain from the foundation of the world, Rev.13:8).

The Good News is really Good News. It is not the "Good Idea" that God is trying to make happen. Any "news" is the reporting of something that has ALREADY happened! And the Good News of God is Good News for ALL of His children. EVERYONE.

We read in Colossians 1:16-17, that ALL things were created by Him—Jesus—and for Him and that in Him All things are held together—sustained.

With this in mind, let's look at Acts 17 in answering the question does all of this apply to everyone. Beginning in vs.16, Paul is in Athens speaking to Jews, Greeks, Epicurean and Stoic philosophers and various other foreigners and men of Athens. He says in vs.25 that..."God gives ALL men life and breath and Everything else." Then in vs.28, Paul tells all these Pagans with whom he is disputing, that " In Him we –including them—live and move and have our being....We are his offspring." EVERYONE, including You.!!!

Verses such as these mentioned here should make us realize that God loves His creation. That the Creation was created by Jesus and for Jesus. That He created man, loves man, lives in man, adopted man, saved man, and wants man –all men—to know it so that they can begin to Live like it.

Again the Gospel is News. It is an announcement of what HAS ALDREADY HAPPENED IN JESUS—FOR EVERYONE.

When God poured out His spirit on the Day of Pentecost in Acts 2 and fulfilled what Joel had prophesied in Joel 2, that pouring out of the Spirit was available for All people to be connected to and enjoy living in the ABUNDANT LIFE which Jesus brought.

The connection, the circuit of the active relationship activating the Union between Jesus and His children is BELIEF. Knowing and believing the Gospel activates the New Life and Abundant Life Jesus gives.

This is what Paul is doing in Acts 17. He is ANNOUNCING the Good News to those gathered in Athens. Once they knew it as Paul declared, some "few" became followers of Paul and BELIEVED.

The Good News is for Everyone. But like as Paul did in Athens that same Good News must be announced today by those who Know it.

We can't put it under a bushel basket, we can't turn out the lights on the Hillside. We can't get on a ship and avoid "Nineveh". We can't go around Samaria. We can't omit the "ends of the earth". We are called to tell the story. Tell it on the mountain. Tell it when we rise up. Tell it when we lie down. Tell it to our children. Tell it to anyone who will listen. But tell it.

After all, it really is GOOD NEWS—FOR EVERYONE.


# IS THE HOLY SPIRIT GOD OR A POWER?

The question we ask here is, Is the Holy Spirit God? "The Holy Spirit is a **POWER!**" Some say this at the expense of saying the Holy Spirit is not God, or it is not part of the Triune God. Scriptures used are ones such as Acts 10:45 to say that the Holy Spirit is only a Power, or the Power of God, which can be poured out thus demonstrating that the Holy Spirit is not a person or a part of the Trinity and therefore not God, only His Power.

While it is true that the Holy Spirit has been 'poured' out on all humanity there is as Paul Harvey says, " The rest of the story." Let's examine some to the attributes here of the Holy Spirit and then determine its God Traits in complete honesty.

There are no less than seven (7) qualities of Godly existence we shall look at now. None of which are properties of a power such as electricity or magnetism or any 'power'.

1. Acts 5:3-4. Here Peter confronts Ananias and his wife over their lies to the Holy Spirit which lie Peter tells them they have not lied to men but to **God.** So the Holy Spirit can be lied to. Not denied only , but lied to.

2. Psalm 139:7-8. The **presence** of God is everywhere through the Spirit. God is omnipresent in His existence as the Holy Spirit.

3. I Corinthians 2:10-11. The Holy Spirit **reveals** things, He **searches** things, He **knows** the deep things of God. Electricity does not. ( Of course, Electricity is only a power.)

4. I Corinthians 2:10-11. The Holy Spirit **thinks,** And knows.

5. Ephesians 4:30. The Holy Spirit can be **Grieved.** Powers can not.

6. Romans 8:26-27 The Holy Spirit **Intercedes** for us. Goes to bat for us. Defends us.

7. I Corinthians 12:7-11. The Holy Spirit makes **decisions** according to **His** will.

8. John 14:16,26; 15:26. The Holy Spirit is a **Comforter** and a **Counselor** which Jesus said He would send.

Electricity is a power. Nuclear energy is a power. Magnetism is a power. An internal combustion engine produces power. But, do any of these function remotely as the above 8 characteristics demonstrate. The conclusion is, The Holy Spirit is the third Person of the Trinity.

The Great Triune God is that ..Three in One and One in Three. One God. Three distinctions all equal. The Father is God. The Son is God. The Holy Spirit is God. And we are included in that God relationship.

God has power. The Holy Spirit is All powerful to be sure. But God is Father, Son and Holy Spirit. And you are included in that life of God forever. Now you know the

"Rest of the Story."

# IS THE HOLY SPIRIT IN ALL HUMANS ?

Does Jesus live in all people? Is the Holy Spirit "in" all people? If so, why are humans in so many instances vile, filled with hate, and all the other works and fruits of the flesh?

Our immediate response to the above questions is to say NO. Jesus is not in them at all.

Jesus is the source of life. ( John 1:4) Paul tells us that Jesus upholds or sustains the whole creation ( Colossians 1:17) and Luke recorded in Acts 17:28, quoting Paul, " that all people live and move and have their being in Jesus." Jesus is the source of life. He is our life. ( Colossians 3:4). Acts 2:17 ( Quoted from Joel 2:28-32) shows the Holy Spirit being poured out on all flesh. All flesh, all humans, have had the Holy Spirit "poured" out on them. It is not that the Spirit of God was not there before, but now since Acts 2 it has been given to all mankind in "greater" or more fuller measure to REVEAL to man who he is in Jesus. The Spirit had always been in man giving him life but now, as God desires in His time, is there to reveal to man his true identity.

With this being said, here is the problem. Most of mankind does NOT know this truth! The Spirit has not revealed this to most of mankind. We may say it this way, Jesus lives IN all humans but by their not knowing this they do not allow Jesus to live "out" of them with His mind guiding and leading them. Hence, we see all the fallenness of man expressed in the life of these who are not aware yet of who they are in Jesus.

This is what sharing the Gospel is all about. It is letting people know that God loves them, has adopted them, included them in His life, and has saved them in Jesus. Also, that they have always BELONGED to God and now coming to know this truth they may live and behave consistent with who they are in Jesus.

Jesus sustains all of creation, humanity included. Jesus is in all life in one way or another. Just because we may not understand this does not make it not so! Scripture is plain about this. If the Spirit of life of Jesus were not in a living thing or person, that thing or person would not be living!! If the Spirit of Jesus were not in and upholding or sustaining ANYTHING or any molecule in the entire cosmos, that thing or molecule would NOT exist. Jesus is the source of all existence!!! After all, ALL THINGS were created IN and BY and FOR and THROUGH Jesus and in Him all things consist or are upheld. ( Colossians 1:16-17).

The day is coming when ALL will know the truth of who they are in Jesus. They will know God loves them. They will know that they were taken INTO to very life of the Triune God by the Spirit through Jesus Christ and may live forever in the family of God.

No one is excluded from finding this out. No one is left out. God loves the world and all of humanity. All die in Adam, but all live in Jesus! ( I Corinthians 15:22). Then the question will be, " Will you believe it? " Yes, Lord, I believe, help my unbelief."

# IS THIS YOUR VIEW OF HELL—REALLY?

The view of God and the reward of the wicked by some people goes like this:

" I am God and everyone had better accept the sacrifice of my Son Jesus Christ and live in obedience to my Laws from then on or I can't begin to tell you how horrible it is going to be for you for all eternity." And by the way, for any of you who do not hear about my LOVE and my Son, you are going to Hell and suffer.

If you don't make it to heaven, then a Hell you can not imagine awaits all of you heathen ungodly reprobates. And it is going to be gruesome. Flames much hotter than the sun in its full brightness and heat. Scorching flesh day and night with no relief ever in all of eternity. No rest. Just extreme torture and punishment for you who are wicked.

My Son only died and rose again for those who are going to heaven. He did NOT die and pay any sacrifice and payment for the rest of you who are so ungodly and sinful that evil is all you can think of and do. So you are going to burn. I am a just God and I say you must be punished for all of your evil deeds FOREVER. In your seventy or so years on the earth you earned the horrors of Hell and Hell's fury and wrath FOREVER because you were thoroughly bad and evil. I have reserved a place for all of you who are ungodly at the table of justice and you will eat of perishing fruit day and night with no respite or relief as you agonize and suffer eternally out of my sight FOREVER. I don't want to have anything to do with you. You are like illegitimate sons and daughters to me. I can't stand the thought of you. I just want justice for all of you incorrigibles in torturous flames FOREVER.

I remind you, however, that I am LOVE. Love is my chief characteristic and I am fair. But because you will not love me back and you have rejected my dear son then you will not see my love, only my WRATH, but I will administer it in LOVE.

Weep and gnash your teeth. Suffer. No punishment but eternal suffering is good enough for any of you since you rejected my son and you would not invite Him or Me into your life. I can not stand rejection and I have prepared a place for all of you who have not accepted my LOVE. That place is Hell. Burning, scorching, agonizing, suffering Hell fire FOREVER.

Now who do you want to love and serve, Me the loving creator God and My son Jesus, or do you want to serve yourself and the Devil--- FOREVER?"

Sincerely,

Your LOVING HEAVENLY FATHER.

## JESUS ACCEPTED US INTO HIS LIFE ORIGINALLY

A common concept in Western Christian doctrine is that humanity is SEPARATED from God and that man must accept Jesus into his life after repenting and that this moves the believer from the state of 'lost' to saved and 'unseparates' him from God.

Often a verse such as Colossians 1:21 is used to show this separation. But is this actually the case? Is man lost until he 'accepts' Jesus into his life? Is man 'made right' with God when he—man—believes that Jesus died for his sins by shedding His blood? In other words, is the salvation of humans left up to their 'making' it happen by what they do or don't do, believe or don't believe? Who is the author and finisher or perfector of man's faith anyway?

Before we go further in this, let's look at Colossians 1:21 and see what it really says. " Once you were "ApallotrioO" in the Greek.. It means 'estranged' or 'alienated' in our language. It does not mean separated and can not mean separated here. Acts 17:28 says that mankind lives, moves, and has his being in Jesus Christ. If one were to be separated from Jesus totally, he or she would cease to exist at all !!!

This kind of thinking is really backwards. The truth is that Jesus from before the creation of the world ADOPTED humans into the life and family of God, INCLUDED man into the life of God, REDEEMED, RECONCILED, SAVED HUMANITY and ACCEPTED man INTO His life originally. This is the starting point. See: Ephesians 1:3-14.

Adam side tracked the plan of God by sinning and introducing sin into man's world. That sin brought death on all humans. ( I Cor.15:22 ). With Jesus' perfect ATONING Sacrifice man was forgiven all of his sins and made alive with Christ and declared to be RIGHTEOUS through Jesus Christ. ( Romans 5:18-20 ).

In reality Adam LOST the human race by sinning. But the Good News is that Jesus Christ came to 'seek and to save WHAT WAS LOST.!!!' (Luke 19:10). Jesus came and accomplished what He set out to do by becoming the 'Propitiation' for the sins of ALL THE WORLD. ( I Jn.2:2). No one escapes the 'Propitiatory' act of Jesus' saving work. Absolutely NO ONE!

When we use terminology such as 'one must accept Jesus into our life', what we really should be saying is acknowledging that Jesus has already accepted us into His life from the beginning and that we NOW have come to believe this FACT of ADOPTION AND INCLUSION AND SALVATION. We need to keep the "horse before the cart'—so to speak.

Sin has done a serious detrimental number on mankind.      Sin  has brought untold suffering, misery and pain on humanity. Through sin we have alienated and estranged ourselves from God—but we have NOT SEPARATED ourselves from Him. We have broken fellowship with Him. But we have never broken our RELATIONSHIP with Him. We are His Children—FOREVER. He is our FATHER forever.

Our Triune God has always purposed to have us in His life forever and He in our life forever as well. ( Jn.14:20 ; Jn.17:20-26). All the plans and preparations were designed by our God ORIGINALLY since before anything was ever created in the first place.

God's FINISHED PLAN does not depend on the puny efforts of weak, sinful, puny, mortal, human beings. It all depended on and depends on JESUS CHRIST. And He finished it. ( John 19:30). " IT IS FINISHED!"

The problem most of us have in explaining all of this comes from past misunderstandings stemming from wrong Western Christian Theological errors which have focused on the cross only and Atonement.

God is not mad at ANYBODY. God LOVES everyone. YOU too. God is not OUT TO GET anyone. God is not out to condemn anyone. God's plan has been perfect from the beginning in ETERNALLY SHARING HIS LIFE WITH HUMANITY. He wanted it to work. Imagine that!!! And the GOOD NEWS is that He HAS MADE IT WORK in, by, and through JESUS CHRIST's life, death, resurrection and ascension.

AMEN

# JESUS AND NICODEMUS-WHAT'S GOING ON?

( Why is John 3:16-17 in scripture in the first place ?)

John 3 and the account of Jesus and Nicodemus is well known to most Bible students. Maybe there is more in this chapter of John 3 than what at first appears. John 3 is actually FULL of the Gospel.

Nicodemus was a member of the Sanhedren , a Pharisee, a teacher of the Law and one of the rulers of the Jews. The Jews position was that the Jews were born into the kingdom of God which they attributed to the Jewish people, calling themselves the children of God. To the Jews the Jews were the Kingdom of God and that SALVATION only applied to the Jews! Jesus' reference to being born of water and Spirit in vs.5 is a direct reference to HIMSELF. Not water baptism which the Jews practiced . Jesus is telling Nicodemus that no one can enter the Kingdom of God through physical means.

Jesus then says in vs.14, that as Moses lifted up the snake in the desert, so the Son of Man must be lifted up that EVERYONE, not just the Jews, who believes in Him may have eternal life. Or, experience it in a God Plane relationship—fully.

John 3:16-17, is probably the most famous and oft quoted verse(s) in the entire Bible. Jesus is saying here that unlike what the Jews thought about Gentiles who they considered to be less than dogs and unworthy of life after death and only good for perishing, Jesus is telling Nicodemus that God so loved the ENTIRE creation/world and ALL people and that any who would believe in Him would not perish but have eternal life –like Nicodemus thought only the Jews would have.

In effect, Jesus is shattering the Jews Religious philosophy concerning what they thought was the Kingdom of God and that they thought they were physically born into it, thus being the children of God. Further that He was the living water and Spirit needed to be born into the Kingdom of God, and that ANYONE, not just Jews could be in it through Jesus.

Jesus then gives a little discourse on how light (Himself) exposes the evil works of men INCLUDING the Jews and their leaders all the while they were claiming to be the kingdom of God on the earth through their physical birth into it.

Lastly, it is interesting what Jesus says in vs.3 concerning being born again and seeing the Kingdom of God when NOTHING is mentioned by Nicodemus about it in the first two verses of chapter 3. Nococemus is just verifying the fact that the leaders KNEW who Jesus was and that He had been sent from God. But Jesus wants to teach Nicodemus THE TRUTH ( vs.3). Jesus then launches into this beautiful discourse which Nicodemus does not understand at this time. It seems that later at the time of Jesus' death that Nicodemus did understand much more of it than at the first here in John 3.

# JESUS CAME TO SAVE WHAT WAS LOST

Jesus came to seek and to save what was **Lost.** (Luke 19:10). When you look at the people Jesus associated with you see the 'lostness' of persons in the fallenness of Adam. Jesus did not normally seek to spend a lot of time with the elite, educated, successful, and influential members of society. Jesus wanted to demonstrate His love and care for the lost and the ones He mostly associated represented that group very well.

The lostness Jesus came to seek and to save was not some game of hide or seek. The lost Jesus came to save was lost to the nth degree. Those sinners Jesus spent time with were types of the lostness of all humanity. The fact Jesus was with prostitutes, publicans, and sinners of all types demostrates His reaching down to **ALL lostness** of all people of all time. Humanity was not just a little displaced or temporarily misplaced or kinda-sorta misdirected. **NO!** The cosmos and humanity were LOST. So lost in fact that there was NO possible way for the cosmos and humanity to become "Un-Lost". Extreme **ALIENATION** from God was what Jesus came to seek and to Save humanity out of.

In the fallenness of Adam under Satan's influence the sins of humanity have been evil and hurtful practically beyond human comprehension. The list is practically endless. Murder, Adultery, Child Abuse, kidnapping, war, psychopathic torturings, child prostitution, extortion, false religions, and an endless list of other crimes of evil. All defining **LOSTNESS** springing from Adam's wrong choice of eating of the Tree of the Knowledge of Good and Evil. Adam not only brought the death penalty on all humans ( I Corinthians 15:22) he also brought on extreme misery and suffering leading up to that certain death. The ramifications of **Lost** become exceedingly hurtful and ungodly.

Jesus was not playing some children's game. He wasn't seeking 'some' who were lost so they could come on over to the other side like a game of "Red-Rover". Jesus was playing for keeps. This was a matter of life and death for all of humanity.

The Father had sent His Son to be the Saviour of the WORLD. ( I John 4:14). Jesus came to seek and to save what was lost. He did. Jesus said from the cross in John 19:30, " It is Finished." What He and the Father and the Spirit had planned from since before the foundation of the world would be completed in Jesus.

Everyone and Everything became lost as a result of sin. Jesus came to seek and to save what had become lost. All humans . All of the cosmos. Everything. The **GOOD NEWS** is that the Father, Son, and Holy Spirit were big enough with all power to accomplish what they started out to do.

Thank God that there are none lost through Jesus actions of redeeming and reconciling all humanity to Himself. The Holy Spirit is beginning to show this truth to the whole world. It is just a matter of time until He finishes that job.

# JESUS IS THE RESURRECTION FOR ALL-- NOW

We are all familiar with the story of Jesus' raising Lazarus from the dead in John chapter 11. So what's new? Well maybe there is more going on there than we had previously thought. Briefly, Lazarus of Bethany, the brother of Mary and Martha, became sick and died. Jesus comes to Bethany from Jerusalem and by the time He arrives Lazarus had been dead four days. Martha tells Jesus that if He had been there then Lazarus would not have died. ( vs.21). In vs.23, Jesus tells Martha that Lazarus 'will rise again.'

Vs.24, Martha answers, "I know he will rise again in the resurrection at the last day." Now the question is, What resurrection is she talking about? She doesn't have I Corinthians 15, nor I Thessalonians 4, nor Revelation 20. She is obviously conversant with Pharisee Jewish theology which said that resurrection would occur when MESSIAH CAME. And, that those who had done "good" would be resurrected. Those who were evil would not be resurrected at all. And the resurrection would not be just for Jews or Israelites who had died, but for ANYONE. Messiah would come and establish what they called , "The World to Come. "

Vs.25, Jesus says, " I am the resurrection and the life. He who believes in me will live, even though he dies; :26, and whoever lives and believes in me shall never die. Do you believe this?" In effect, Jesus is saying to her that He is the resurrection NOW. And He is saying that He is the Messiah. And He is saying that He HAS COME. He is also saying that no one has to wait until the 'last day' or at His Second Coming to be resurrected. He is the Resurrection NOW. For all people. AND, THE LIFE for all as well.

Martha responds in vs.27, "Yes, Lord, I believe that you are the MESSIAH, THE SON OF GOD, WHO WAS TO COME INTO THE WORLD." Notice, Jesus does not correct her and say, " Oh no I'm not either!" And notice she says this BEFORE Lazarus is raised by Jesus.

We presently participate in Jesus Who is the Resurrection and the Life. Jesus physical resurrection in 31 A.D (?) only reaffirmed the fact that He had the power of resurrection and WAS the resurrection. We participate in the Power of Jesus Who IS The Resurrection.

Maybe the terminology we need to use for our Physical change when Jesus returns in Glory, is not Resurrection—since we already are—and seated with Jesus at the right hand of the Father in the Heavenly realms ( Ephesians 2:6), but use instead the term our change from corruption to incorruption, or mortal to immortal, or simply " our change " or the redemption of our bodies. (Ephesians 4:30.) Job even used this type terminology in Job 14:14, " If a man dies, will he live again? All the days of my appointed time I will wait 'till my **change** comes ( the NIV says , 'renewal'). Objectively speaking, humanity IS resurrected in Jesus Now. If we are all seated at the right hand of the Father it is obvious that we are resurrected as well. And all of this in Jesus Christ who is our life. (Colossians 3:4).

We need to understand that we are IN Jesus Christ now. We were crucified with Him. (Galatians 2:20). We died with Him. We were buried with Him. We rose with Him. (Romans 6:1-4). We ascended with Him. And we share in His life (Eternal Life) NOW with Him.

Can we understand? Can we live our lives commensurate with WHO we are? We are the children of the Father, Adopted from before the creation of the world in Jesus (Ephesians 1:3-14), Saved by the life, death, and

Resurrection of Jesus Christ and we live perpetually in that Resurrection and LIFE who is JESUS.

Whatever lies you have been told in the past about who you are and where you are spiritually—Forget them. The Truth is you are the son or daughter the Father has ALWAYS LOVED and wanted to live with Him Forever. He loves you so much that He refuses to be God without you. He has made all the arrangements. And as Jesus asked Martha, " Do you believe?" Lord, I believe.....Help my unbelief!!!!!

# JESUS REVEALS OUR INCLUSION

With the coming of Jesus through the Incarnation God accomplished something that was never done before. No pagan god, no mythological god of any description had ever appeared to man and established a RELATIONSHIP with humans. Obviously so because pagan gods and mythological gods do NOT exist! Those gods always remained distant, disconnected and while they were worshipped they were never nor ever became relational and in relationship with man.

But Jesus was different. John says it this way in John 1:14, " the word was made Flesh and DWELT among us!"

I Peter 1:20 says that .."This Jesus was chosen before the creation of the world, but was REVEALED in these last times for your sake".

When God chose this Jesus before the creation of the world, He also chose US IN Him before the creation of the world and ADOPTED us into His very life blameless and Holy. ( Eph.1:4-6).

Paul says it this way in Colossians 1:26-27, that the MYSTERY OF THE AGES is revealed to the saints, " Christ IN you the hope of Glory."

Some have thought that this 'Adoption' and 'Inclusion' theology originated with Paul since he states it in a number of places. Some have even thought that it was invented by modern day Theologians. But the purpose here is to go back to the source of this theology and show that it did NOT originate with Paul, but with Jesus Christ.

Many churches have used John 14 through John 17 in conducting Passover services, or Lord's Supper services and used these verses to echo the very LAST prayer of Jesus Christ before he was taken and killed the next day. And this is not a wrong use of these scriptures. But if we are not careful we will look at them with the wrong glasses on or from old paradigms and miss the concept of INCLUSION which Jesus states clearly in these chapters.

Let's focus on a verse in the middle of John 14, verse 20. Jesus here makes a statement for all people. He says , "...On that day( or we would say in time, or sooner or later) you WILL realize that I am IN my Father, and you are IN me and I am IN you." He introduces the concept of INCLUSION here but this is not all in this passage.

At the very end of this prayer in John 17:20 – 26, Jesus states this concept of INCLUSION in the life of God and it is nearly impossible to overlook it, although many people have over the ages. Jesus prays here for those who carry the message of this truth to ensuing generations for all time. :20..."My prayer is not for them alone. I pray also for those who will believe in me through their message, :21...that ALL of them may be ONE, Father, JUST AS you are IN me and I am IN you. May they also be IN US...notice that again, IN US, that the world may believe that you have sent me.

:22..." I have given them the glory that you gave me, that they may be one AS we are one: 23...I IN them and you IN me. May they be brought to COMPLETE UNITY to let the world know that you sent me and have loved them EVEN AS YOU HAVE LOVED ME. -----( Just the same !!!)

:26..."...I have made you known to them, and will continue to make you known in order that the love you have for me may be IN them and that I MYSELF may be IN them.

The word inclusion means ' to be made part of the whole'. What we see God the Father doing from before the creation of the world is working out His eternal plan in its complete fullness with Jesus being chosen ( I Peter 1:20) and slain ( Rev.13:8) and our being chosen in Jesus, adopted and included in the life of the Great Triune God before the creation of the world ( Eph.1:4-6).

All of this is by God's purpose, plan, declaration, act of God, will and for His pleasure. He is the potter. He is the Master Builder. He is the author and finisher of our faith. He is the perfector of our faith. His Wrath is opposed to anything that would attempt to thwart the purpose of His plan. He has the power to see His plan accomplished in Jesus. And it is!!! Jesus said, " It is finished!" (John 19:30).

Let's never forget that we serve, worship and Love an awesome God. An all-powerful God. An all loving Father. Our God thought this plan out before time and named Jesus as the Captain of the salvation of humanity, and named us PERSONALLY AND INDIVIDUALLY in His great purpose and INCLUDED us IN His life.

# JESUS THE SAVIOUR OF THE WHOLE WORLD

There is a little verse somewhat hidden in I John 4:14 which has the backing of **ALL** the power in the entire Universe behind it. ( Of course most scripture does and some would say all ). In this verse God the Father gives an Unconditional order to the Son to come to the world and be the Saviour of the world. " The Father has sent His Son to be the Saviour of the world." (I John 4:14).

Note here that the Father did not send His Son to see **IF** He could manage to save the entire world and all of humanity, or possibly save some, or a few, or the chosen, or the elect... but **The World!**

In John 3:16, the most quoted verse in all of the Bible, John says, "For God so loved the world..." Not some of it. Not most of it. Not just a few. But the **World.** I John 2:2, says that the sacrifice of Jesus was propitiation—payment—for the sins of the **whole** world. No human being can escape being under the saving directive of the Father accomplished in Jesus Christ.

When Jesus was on the Cross at Calvary, He said that what He came to do He did. That it was finished. What the Father commissioned Him to do He **FINISHED** it.(John 19:30).

When we stop to think that the Greatest Power of Love in all of the Universe ( and outside of it as well) determined for His Son to be the Saviour of the World—all of it—do we not think that He, the Son, and the Spirit could accomplish what they started out to do?

God's purpose from the beginning was to place mankind **IN** His Triune existence forever and have relationship with man throughout eternity. God's purpose was to adopt and include man in His life from before the foundation of the world. ( Ephesians 1:3-14).

There has **never** been a question as to whether or not God had the capability and power to accomplish His plan. Who or what could ever stand in the way of a Triune God who has **ALL POWER IN HEAVEN AND EARTH?**

The evil we see in the world from the sinfulness in the fallenness of Adam is precisely what Jesus came to save mankind and the cosmos out of! No one is **TOO** sinful or evil for the love of God not to touch them and save them. The Father commissioned the Son to save the world and the Son " Made it so". No **ifs, ands, or buts about it!!!**

Scripture clearly shows that the whole world has been reconciled in Christ. (Colossians 1:20). It is when humans are the **enemies** of God that they are reconciled to God with salvation following. ( Romans 5:10-11).

There simply is NO escaping the salvation which the Father has extended to **ALL** humanity in Jesus Christ. He loves us all that much. When a person comes to accept and believe what God has done to and for them in Jesus Christ, they can then begin to live in the abundant life which Jesus provides. Just when will ALL people come to know and understand this and believe ? I don't know, but the Holy Spirit is working on it!!!

AMEN


# JESUS...THE ULTIMATE SURROGATE !


In Hollywood movies often times a stand in or fall guy will come into the action of a picture when real danger would put the star actor in peril. This surrogate stands in and takes the hits, the abuse, the falls from buildings, jumps from speeding cars, and runs through fires and explosions in the picture. The real danger, hurts, and suffering occur to this substitute. The star actor is always safe and in no harm at all due to the actions of the fall guy.

When we refer to Jesus Christ as the "vicarious" human being for all humanity what we are saying is that in all situations and experiences in our life He steps in and takes any and all "hits" for us good or bad. He is our surrogate. He is our substitute. As such He is our faith, our belief, our repentance, our life, death, resurrection, and ascension. He is everything we are not and everything we could never be.

When we question our personal belief in His substitutionary work for us, He becomes our "personal" belief for us. When we sin He steps inside of us and becomes our sin for us. ( II Corinthians 5:21). When we attempt to pray to the Father, Jesus is there as the advocate and intercessor to take our prayers and 'translate' them into just the right prayer to present to the Father. When we focus on daily, mundane, earthly, common, and routine physical things to the exclusion of focusing on our Father in Heaven and all He means to us, Jesus steps in and focuses on the spiritual things FOR us in our stead.

In any and all situations where we fall short in our Christian walk, Jesus lifts us up in Himself and becomes our fullness, our fullness of the measure of the stature of Christ. He is our ALL. He is our All in All. He is our everything. Some will say that Jesus is just doing it all for us and we aren't doing anything. The answer to this is, " What **CAN** we do that would be acceptable to the perfect standards of Almighty Triune God?" We really can do nothing of ourselves of any Godly value and therefore Jesus **MUST** step in and do for us what we could never do for ourselves. Period.

Jesus then becomes our Life. ( Colossians 3:4; John 14:6). Our old man is dead. He is crucified with Christ. ( Galatians 2:20). We now walk in a newness of life which is Christ's life for us. ( Romans 6:1-11.) There is just no way of getting around the fact of Who and What Jesus Christ is to all of us weak human beings. We can take no credit at all for any part of our salvanic experience. It is humbling to admit that we are not capable of doing anything "good" when it comes to attaining life with The Triune God. It ALL has been done and is being done in Jesus Christ.

It is like the old hymn, "I NEED THEE EVERY HOUR." Not only do we need Jesus every hour, we need Him every nanosecond of our life which now really is His life shared with each of us. Thank you Jesus for doing everything for me and all of us that none of us could ever do for ourselves. When it is all said and done, like the praise song goes, " Just give me Jesus."

AMEN

# JESUS, THE VICARIOUS HUMAN

By now we have all heard of Jesus being the "vicarious" human. In this brief paper we want to make this as simple and as understandable as possible. In its simplest meaning vicarious means 'in the place of', or 'substituted for' or 'to stand in for'.

By being the vicarious savior of all mankind Jesus experienced everything in place of humans. We are all probably familiar with the scriptures which speak of Jesus dying for man; tasting death for everyone; being made sin for us, etc. ( Heb.10:10, Heb. 2:9, II Cor. 5:21).

We also know that we are crucified with Him. ( Galatians 2:20). That we are buried with Him. ( Romans 6:1-4). That we are resurrected in Him in a New Birth. ( I Peter 1:3). And we are ascended with Him to the Father's right hand. ( Ephesians 2:6).

We can also say it this way. What ever happens to Jesus happens to us as well. This is not "hocus-pocus" type magic, nor is it just Jesus saying that this is the way it is and is going to be because He said so.

Jesus is our life. ( Colosians 3:4). He is His own life as well. But the miracle of all miracles is that He has opened up His Triune existence, opened up His being and INCLUDED us all IN His being. He has taken us INTO the Trinity. Into the Father, Son, and Holy Spirit by the Spirit. ( John 14:20; John 17:20-26). Through ADOPTION God hasn't just given us a name, but He has given us His Life. Jesus is the only source of Life! It is His to give and He has given it to us humans. "In Him was LIFE." ( John 1:4). This life is the light of men, but many humans have never understood it and John wanted all men to know it and believe it. (John 1:6-7).

The famous verse, John 14:6 says, " I am the way, the truth, and the LIFE. No one comes to the Father except through me." There is ONLY one way into the Triune God's life and existence now and forever. That way is in and through Jesus.

This is what the Gospel is all about. God loves us and purposed from before the foundation of the world to Adopt us into His very life and existence through Jesus Christ. ( Ephesians 1:3-14). Through the INCARNATION Jesus provided the WAY. The ONLY way. Jesus came to do His job. He said, " When I am lifted up from the earth, I will draw ALL men to myself." I am not excluding anyone. And, He did.

"I will BE sin for everyone. I will suffer for everyone. I will taste death for everyone. I will be resurrected for everyone. I will ascend for and WITH everyone. I WILL DO MY JOB." And it "is finished." ( John 19:30).

When we consider that ALL Israel will be saved we must conclude just how big the love of God is and merciful, gracious, kind, patient, and forgiving God our Father is. ( Romans 11:26-27). The story of Hosea and Gomer is a loving illustration of God's UNCONDITIONAL love and complete forgiveness for ALL sin.

I John 2:2 tells us that Jesus is the propitiation ( payment) for the sins of those John is writing to as well and for the sins of the WHOLE WORLD. Now we are back to the "Vicarious" human, Jesus.

Jesus is not only the vicarious human for all of our sins but he gets all the credit for any good in any of us and for any good any of us has ever done or will do. There is only one who is good and the source of good and that is God. Through Jesus God shares that goodness with us. ( Matt. 19:17).

We are saved by Grace through Faith.( The Faith of Jesus ). Not of or by works. Not any kind of works. Not even good works. The Good works aren't even ours, but Christ's living His life in us. So how could we boast? We can't. ( Ephesians 2:8-10).

Jesus is EVERYTHING to us and for us and instead of us. He is the Vicarious human. There is nothing left undone which He is yet to do. It is finished!

Can we believe in the Vicarious human , Jesus? Can we believe He has accomplished EVERYTHING FOR US? Can we REST in what Jesus has done? Can we joy in the blessed ASSURANCE of LIFE FOREVER IN HIM and WITH HIM? ( And with each other, I might add.)

Can we put aside once and for all our works oriented approach to our calling? Can we get rid of our 'legalistic' ball and chain? Can we just trust and rest in Jesus?

Lord I believe that Jesus is the Vicarious human for me. Help my unbelief.

AMEN


# THE RESURRECTED BODY

In Christ's resurrection there are a couple of dynamics which are often over-looked. These have major implications for our own resurrection. There has been much speculation over the ages as to what kind of 'body' Jesus had when He was resurrected. Let's notice a few scriptures which have impact on us.

In John 20:26-27, Jesus appears to the disciples in **bodily** form in the same body He had had but now of flesh and bone. He invites Thomas to handle Him by touching Him and putting his fingers in the holes from the crucifixion. Jesus is making a demonstration for a reason to display His human flesh and bone **body** to all of the disciples.

In Luke 24:33-42, Jesus appears to the disciples and invites them to touch Him and to look at His hands and feet and tells them He has **flesh and bones,** not ghostlike. Then He purposefully asks them for something to eat, NOT because He was hungry, but to demonstrate the fact that one resurrected with a body of flesh and bones can eat!!! Jesus wants all to understand His continuing humanity in a **body** capable of doing physical things.

In Matthew 26:29, Jesus had told the disciples that He would drink of the fruit of the vine with them in His Father's Kingdom.

When Stephen was being stoned ( Acts 7:55-56) he looks up into the heavens and sees the **bodily human form** of Jesus STANDING at the Father's right hand. I would say, "Cheering him on !!!"

Paul further states that Christ is "seated at the right hand of God" in Colossians 3:1 and in Ephesians 1:20.

We can see in these passages clearly that Jesus has a **body.** That He sits, stands, eats, and will drink of the fruit of the vine in His Father's Kingdom. In other words, HE CAN AND WILL **PARTY!** This all has implications for all of us as we shall see.

David had said in Psalm 17:15 that we would arise with His **likeness.** Later in I John 3:1-2, John writes that " when He appears we shall see Him as He is and we will be **like** Him."

**VIP:** Now when we read I Corinthians 15:35-57, we should be more keenly aware of just what kind of body we will have in the Father's Kingdom. This whole section deals with the kind of **body** we shall have in resurrection. ( Just read this passage for yourself.) Lastly, in Romans 8:11, Paul speaks of our mortal bodies being quickened or given life through His spirit who lives in you.

Things to note:

It is OUR **body** now raised incorruptible and imperishable, a spiritual body.

It is raised immortal in honor, power and glory.

We shall bear the **likeness** of the man from heaven--Jesus. I Co.15:49;

I Tim.2:5—" The MAN Jesus Christ.

It is a human body that **looks** like us. Yet spiritual ( I Cor. 15:44)

It has **flesh** and **bones.**

It can **eat** and **drink.**

It can **sit** or **stand** or **walk** or **run.**

NOTE: Jesus still has His human body which is now spiritual. The fullness of God STILL dwells bodily in Jesus. Jesus STILL remains the SON of the Holy Trinity but now and forever retains His humanity with His spiritual body which **LOOKS** physical and NOT limited physically. ( This could get confusing ☺ )

It will be ready for any kind of **PARTY** the Father wants to throw! And never get tired! ☺

My Personal speculation.

Since the resurrected human body can do these things listed above, it makes sense to me that it possibly could play golf, fish, swim, run, dance, and any number of other things humans do. What think ye? Wild Huh? ☺

God is Good. So let's wait and see just HOW GOOD !!!

Can I get an **AMEN ?**


# JESUS—THE EVER PRESENT GOD !


This paper will present some Theological perspectives for your consideration, which are quite different from our past concepts as you will see. We want to deal here with the ever-present contemporary existence of Jesus Christ in human history.

When the Eternal speaks to Moses in the Ex.3:14, He identifies Himself as "I AM". The one who was, is, and will be. This Eternal one spoke to Moses in the burning bush. He parted the Red Sea. He provided manna in the wilderness. He did all the things we read about in Old Testament scriptures. He was, as Paul said in I Corinthians 10:4, The Rock who followed Israel. Paul says that Rock was CHRIST.

When we read in Colossians 1:15-17, that all things were created by and for Jesus Christ and that He upholds all things, i.e., SUSTAINS all things by His power, we see then that Jesus has been IN the creation and with man since the garden of Eden.

When Jesus tells Martha in John 11:25, that He is the resurrection and the life He is stating a reality, a truth, that has been Fact since before the creation and including the occurrences in the garden of Eden with Adam and Eve. He was/is the resurrection and the life now—presently--at the time when He tells Martha this, He was the resurrection and the life when various ones were resurrected in Old Testament times, and He will ALWAYS be the resurrection and the life.

We read of a virgin giving birth prophetically in Isa.7:14, and calling His name Immanuel. But Immanuel is God with us, and as Jesus says in John 14:20, not only with us but IN us as well.

Question. Since Jesus is the "I AM", the 'ever present contemporary of time', when was there ever a time when He was NOT Immanuel? When was He NOT God with us?

In other words, did Jesus become something new He never was before when He was born of Mary in Bethlehem?-

If He has always been the Rock, always been the Resurrection and the Life, always been the Savior and always been the Son in the Great Triune God's existence, then when was he NEVER Immanuel?

Remember He has upheld and/or sustained ALL of creation since He originally created the cosmos—all things. (Col.1:15-17).

What we read in the birth account of Jesus in Luke 2 in reality from an eternal perspective, from a spiritual perspective, from God's perspective is a physical reenactment of what occurred BEFORE THE FOUNDATION OF THE WORLD. The same thing is true of what we read in Revelation 13:8, which says that Jesus, was slain BEFORE the foundation of the world. Therefore, if He was slain before the foundation of the world, He had to be BORN before the foundation of the world as well.

When we read in I Peter 1:20, that He was chosen before the foundation of the world but that the REVEALING of that fact would be IN the Last Times, we then can realize the impact of our being ADOPTED by Jesus Christ Before the foundation of the world as well. ( Eph.1:4).

Many people have looked at scripture from a past, present, future perspective. Or, from a 'dispensational perspective. Man has tried

to fit scripture into various time frames and timetables of his devising. But God is not confined to time. He just reveals the way

things are by virtue of what Jesus Christ has done for His creation and to His creation by being connected to it in person ALWAYS as Immanuel.

Jesus has always been EVERYTHING man needs. He has always been since Adam-- and Paul reveals this to the Pagan religious leaders in Athens in Acts 17—the one in whom humans Live, Move, and have Being—life and existence.

Jesus did not just become all of a sudden the Savior of the world 2000 years ago! He did not just start sustaining His creation 2000 years ago.

He did not just become anything 2000 years ago that He was not already! He is the "I AM".

What He did 2000 years ago in His physical existence in Israel may be applied to all humans since Adam. He is their life too. He is their resurrection too. He is their Savior too. He is their Father too.

We need to reflect on the I AM aspect of God. We need to reflect on the fact of Immanuel, not just for 'Christians', but for all people for all time. We need to stop painting God into the corners we create for Him thereby LIMITING Him in His involvement in the lives of His children.

God Is. He was, is, and always will be. His Name is Jesus. He is Immanuel—God with us and in us ALL. All mankind--

--All humans since Adam and including Adam. He grants Life to all who were 'granted' death in Adam. (I Cor.15:22).

He is ALMIGHTY GOD. ALL POWERFUL. ALL LOVING. ETERNAL. WONDERFUL COUNSELLOR. FRIEND. SAVIOR. And one title we can all especially claim as his children, FATHER—FOREVER.


# JUST HOW BIG IS OUR CREATOR ?


Genesis 1:1, " In the beginning, God created the heavens and the earth." Apart from being the most read and most quoted sentence in the entire world, let's take a look at this amazing statement in light of science.

Note, the verse does not say, "In the beginning God created stuff." We now know, thanks to Albert Einstein, that all of the Cosmos is related to all that exists in the Cosmos. And that the entire cosmos is orderly and perfect in its design and operational physics. (Gravity, Thermodynamics, Inertia, motion, etc.)

Note, further, Genesis does not describe what existed before God created the heavens and the earth. Nor does it say where God came from. Nor does it say how God created it all. It just says He DID!

Modern physicists, and some not so modern, have discovered amazing facts concerning the Cosmos. The study can be divided into the Macrocosmic study and the Microcosmic study. Facts and some speculation in both areas involve extreme mathematical calculations and formulas. Mathematics which go far beyond the analysis of a simple hydrogen atom (one proton and one electron) into Quantum Physics dealing with subatomic particles, their makeup, actions, and impact on existence—to macrocalculations of the size of our Universe, its age, and its relative time of origin.

To further complicate matters, not only are the four dimensions we humans live in are studied and evaluated, science now deals with the 5th, 6th, 7th, 8th, 9th, 10th and what some are calling the 11th dimension, or the, string vibration dimension which gave rise to everything in this universe and the parallel universes which are said to exist by an infinite number!!!

The amazing truth to all of this is that it is ALL MATHMATICALLY CALCULABLE. All is related to everything else in the universe. Time and 2 space are defined by math. Energy is defined by math. Light is defined by math. Power is. Gravity is. Heat is. Everything that is made up of molecules, atoms, subatomic particles, quanta, etc. is mathematically related to everything else in the cosmos and defined by math. One writer once said that mathematics was the alphabet God used to write the universe with.

The order and design in the Creation is amazing. David said it best, " The heavens declare the glory of God." ( Psalm 19:1). All of creation declares the same thing and the handy work of God.

All astrophysicists, who subscribe to the Big Bang theory of the start of the cosmos, have agreed to agree that this is the point where they will start their study. They do not attempt to explain where the matter came from, or the energy that produced the Big Bang in the first place. They just agree to start there.

Scientists have discovered most all they need to know concerning the cosmos and all of its numerous universes. Billions of galaxies. Subatomic particles down to the size of 10 to minus 44. ( The smallest particle matter can be divided into). What they are seeing in all of this is the reality of the hand of God in the next step they will discover. They will discover if they keep looking into the subject long enough the one they have been seeing all along in His creation—The Great Creator God who in the beginning created the heavens and the earth and everything in all of the cosmos! It is just becoming more and more complicated to explain creation without a creator!

One last comment. Scientists are now saying that the universe is only a shadow of 'something' much larger. They just don't know what that something is!

# "LET GO AND LET GOD"

"Let go and let God." Often times we create unnecessary anxiety over certain Bible verses when we try and figure out the exact time frame, order, or possible fulfillment of those verses. Generally we look at those verses through the old lens of old paradigms from old theologies and doctrinal understandings or 'mis'-understandings whichever the case may be. Change is difficult in any area of biblical thought.

When coming to understand scripture there are some basic fundamental givens we must establish in the beginning since everything theologically correct will spring from those basic premises.

First and foremost is to understand that Jesus Christ is the one who was in the beginning with the Father and the Holy Spirit. That these three comprise the ONE Triune God.

Next, That Jesus' original purpose in creating the human family was to Adopt and Include the human family in the Triune God's life for all eternity.

Next, When Adam sinned and brought the death penalty on all humans who followed because of his sin, Jesus had to by His life, death, resurrection and ascension "undo" what Adam did and Redeem, Reconcile, and Save humanity and the creation which had become lost through sin. This Jesus did.

So effectively speaking, God's original plan to have all of humanity live with Him forever was accomplished through the Incarnation of the Son of God.

What we see playing out in human history and in the present day in human affairs has been and is a result of the fallen nature all humanity has received from our human father, Adam. That nature manifests itself in all manner of evil, hate, murder, war, envy, strife, anxiety, and suffering of all sorts. Humanity still operates under the evil influence of Satan the Devil who continues on as the god of this world. BUT, he has been overcome by Jesus Christ and will ultimately be deposed by the King of Kings and 2 Righteousness will dwell in creation in the New Heavens and New Earth forever. Until then, we see all the misery and suffering.

Remember that ALL things have been redeemed and reconciled to God by Jesus Christ. The fullness of His Kingdom is coming one day.

We don't have to debate scripture as to when or how certain things play out. We don't have to determine which scriptures apply from any linear interpretation. We don't need to try and mix the ultimate reality of the salvation of all humanity with dispensational time frameworks.

We don't need to try and figure out exactly who are firstfruits or lastfruits, or first, second, or third resurrections or any other scriptural specific which all must be explained in light of the givens listed above.

Remember, Jesus IS the Resurrection and the Life. All of humanity's eternal life and existence is lived out in Jesus Christ. He has made all the preparations and arrangements for this and He said, " It is finished."

Jesus has it ALL under control. He came to seek and to save the lost. And, He did. He came to create the Union between God and humanity and to take humanity to the Father's right hand and seat humanity there. And, He did.

We must remember when approaching scripture that it is all done, all accomplished, all secured, all assured, and all completed in Jesus Christ for all of us. We don't need to argue over most things we really don't know fully about and just let God do His work. Let's live our lives knowing WHO WE ARE IN JESUS. Jesus is the ONLY BEGOTTEN Son of the Father. We are the Adopted and Included sons and daughters of the Father. Let's live like it. As I said at the start let's live in our Freedom in Christ. Let's...

"Let go and let God."

# LIVING INSIDE THE KINGDOM OF GOD— NOW!

In Luke 17:20-21, Jesus makes a remarkable statement. He says, " The Kingdom of God is WITHIN you." Earlier He had said in John 14:20, that " ...He was in the Father, you are in me and He was in Us! The relationship that the Father, Son, and Holy Spirit had had for all eternity NOW includes man!!! It is a matter of man realizing it. This is WHY Jesus came to this earth in the first place. He came to create this union between and with the Triune God and mankind—humanity.

With this in mind, Jesus did NOT say that the Kingdom of God was 'Available' to humans. He did not say that the Kingdom was a possibility. Quoting Mk.1:14-15, Jesus said the Kingdom of God is 'at hand', Repent and believe the Gospel." Repent, "Metanoia" in the Greek, meaning change your mind as to Who you are inside of the life of Jesus. The Kingdom is Now and here. You can experience it. Then He says, "Believe the Gospel." It is all about changing our mind and believing!!!

The Kingdom of God has always been prepared for humans since before the foundation of the World. Originally. ( Mt. 25:31-34). Triune God has always wanted mankind with Him and Inside of His "Perechoretic" life. He wants to share His divine nature eternally with all of us. See ( II Peter 1:4). And make no mistake, Jesus made it happen for everyone.

Now a few really difficult theological concepts to wrap our minds around. " Beginners, you may leave the room now."

When God proclaims that He is IN us through Jesus and by the Spirit, He is not just saying He is near. Not saying that He is in us to just to ensure our eventual resurrection. Not saying that He is in us IF we want Him there and to do our bidding like some "voodoo amulet". No. Triune God offers and proclaims nothing less than our complete "enmeshing" inside of His life. God offers the same "Perechoretic" dance He shares mutually as Father, Son, and Holy Spirit, with all of humanity. We are IN the dance. We are inside of the life of God. We are inside of His Divine Nature. Can you see that? Is it too good to be true? Have you EVER heard that before? You should have. God is a Dad and He wants us in and inside and with and dancing with Him FOREVR. The really Good News is that He has some really "cool" stuff to share with us in PLEASURE forevermore inside of His life. ( Ps.16:11). Thank you Jesus.

We say God is Good. Brothers and Sisters, we can not even begin to imagine what it will be like to live inside of the life of God forever. But, it will be GOOD. REALLY GOOD!

AMEN


# LOOKING DOWN ON THE ENEMIES OF GOD

Paul Kurts


When taking another look at God's Great LOVE for His creation and His children, we need to focus on a fact of scripture which demonstrated this Great LOVE of God and the enormity and magnitude of God's GRACE.

Christians sometimes can be the most smug people thinking that now that they are accepting of Christ that they are the "we" and connected to God and that everyone else are the "they" that are disconnected or separated from God—the ones who the Bible speaks of as enemies of God. With the attitude that God somehow doesn't love these people as He does "us"!!!

Well, let me blow your theological mind for a minute. In Romans 5:6 we read that Christ died for the ungodly. And, in vs.8, that Christ died for us while we were STILL sinners. And, in vs.10, it is while we were ENEMIES of God that God Reconciled us to Jesus through His death. And, in

Romans 8:7, we read that the human mind is ENMITY against God. And, in Jeremiah 17:9, we read that the carnal, human mind is desperately wicked and only God can know it.

With these scriptures in mind allow me to ask the question, " Who did Christ die for?" Who is the enemy of God? Who is the Ungodly? Answer: ALL of the descendants of Adam. ALL humans who ever have lived. All humans died in Adam. But, the same ALL humans have been made alive in Jesus Christ.( I Cor.15:22).

The ASTOUNDING Good News is that all the while God has loved unconditionally His children in spite of their HATRED of Him! We read in Romans 8 again that NOTHING can separate us from the Love of God.

Now for some mind blowing Truth for all of self righteous individuals. YOU and I are STILL the Enemies of God. And thank God, Jesus took care of our enmity against God and our being enemies of God. Do we NEVER do Ungodly acts? Do we NEVER sin? Do we NEVER exercise the wickedness in our minds? Are we not guilty sometimes of even a "little" bit of hatred toward God?

God just simply LOVES His kids even when His kids don't like Him and even Hate Him. God extends His loving GRACE continually and His love continually to ALL of His children—the ones who are Ungodly and the ones who are enemies of Him and the ones who hate Him. Talk about love. That is love in all caps—LOVE.

When Jesus tells us to "love our enemies" He knows what He is talking about. This extension of God's Grace OVER POWERS any hatred our enemies have for us. God knows what He is talking about. From experience, He knows.

Romans 2:1, tells us to be careful NOT to judge anyone else concerning ungodly deeds mentioned previously in ch.1:29-32, because Paul says that when we pass judgement on others—ie, the "world" and other sinners—we pass judgement on ourselves because we are guilty of the SAME things.

The point of all of this is this. No matter how low God has to stoop into the sinful life of us humans and into our Ungodliness Jesus "absorbs" that sinfulness and enmity and Ungodliness and takes it to the Cross.

Now in Jesus we who were dead are now ALIVE and Jesus makes EVERYTHING RIGHT and NEW.

Praise God.

Amen

# MALACHI 4:3 AND TREADING THE WICKED

Coming from old Calvinistic views of the fate of the wicked, or unsaved, Malachi 4:3 could be interpreted by some and has been by some that the 'Righteous would 'tread' upon the wicked or stomp the life out of them until they were in a state of ruin or 'ashes' under 'your' feet. Somehow verse 3 is seen as some kind of Godly approval of the righteous taking the vengeance of God out on sinful humans. Maybe we need to look at this from a different angle.

We might note here that the Hebrew word used for "tread" does not mean destruction to ruin, or punishment, or stomping the 'hell' out of someone to render them to ashes. It is the same word used for crushing grapes to make wine. It is a type of destruction to transformation.

We tread upon the wicked, all of humanity who are non-believers, whenever we share the Good News that they are Adopted, saved, redeemed, and included in Trinitarian salvation. For the wicked this Good News destroys their belief in THE LIE, but that destroying leads to the beautiful truth of all our inclusion and adoption IN Jesus. Furthermore, speaking of ashes here could be speaking of the wicked's REPENTANCE as it is referenced in other places in the Old Testament.

I am not saying that this is the ONLY interpretation of this verse. However, it would seem consistent with Jesus' Salvation for all of humanity.

Note again Malachi 4 could be describing the 'zealous' evangelizing efforts of believers who know His name—Who they are IN Jesus—and that the message is for Healing—spiritual healing—with individuals carrying the Gospel message out with the enthusiasm of a 'young calf leaping when let out of its stall!' (vs 2).

Then God closes verse 3 with the statement that "I do these things !" Of course it is by God's spirit and power that the Gospel message is shared with anyone and He grants the repentance which is coming to believe that message.

So once again in this short chapter in the last book of the Old Testament God is continuing to pour out His love on all humanity as He shares the Good News with everyone eventually.

August 24/25, 2002

# MORE GOOD NEWS ABOUT SALVATION

By Paul Kurts

What you are about to hear is the Greatest news anyone could possibly hear!

GOD IS LOVE AND GOD LOVES YOU!!!

Jn.3:16-17 God's original purpose for man was to save him, not condemn!

Rev.13:8 Jesus was slain from the foundation of the world. Heb.2:9 Jesus Tasted death for everyone.

Mt.25:34 Kingdom prepared for you from the foundation of the world.

Eph.1:3-14 CHOSEN IN CHRIST before the foundation of the world.

II Thes.2:13 CHOSEN from the beginning to salvation

II Tim.1:8-9 Grace given us B/4 the beginning of time!

Jn.5:24 and Rom.8:1 No condemnation for those in Christ Jesus.

Eph.2:4-10 SAVED by God's Grace.

Heb.12:2 God is the AUTHOR AND FINISHER of our faith.

Phil.1:6 HE who began a good work in you WILL FINISH IT!

Rom.8:28-39 NOTHING CAN OR WILL separate us from God.

I Pt.1:3-5 We are guarded, shielded, protected by God's POWER

Jude 24 We are kept by Jesus and presented WITHOUT fault
Heb.7:22-25 Jesus is able to SAVE us COMPLETELY
I Jn.5:11-13 We have ETERNAL LIFE now in Christ.
THANKS BE TO GOD…..WE WIN. GOD WINS!!!
I Cor. 15:57 God GIVES us the VICTORY through JESUS
II Tim.4:8 , 18 CROWN stored for you. RESERVED IN THE K.O.G.

# NO MORE PRICE TO PAY….EVER !

Retributive justice was supported under the Old Covenant as is seen in Deuteronomy 19:17-21. The "eye for an eye" principle. Or, as one might say today, " let the punishment fit the crime." Under this concept, justice is not served unless payment or retribution for the infraction is imposed. This is at the heart of a legalistic penal system.

Humans are continually committing crimes (sins) which hurt themselves and/or others. Depending on the degree of the seriousness of the sin or crime, when caught, a trial is held and sentencing is levied and justice is served. This is basically how all justice systems operate in the world. It makes sense and sounds fair.

The Grace of God does not operate under a retributive format. There is, however, payment for sin and crimes. This propitiation ( payment) was made and paid in full by Jesus Christ for the sins of the whole world. No one escapes this "paid in full" Grace of God. All are forgiven in Jesus Christ. The sacrifice of Jesus makes the retributive payment for all. All are reconciled to God through the blood of Jesus. All stand in total innocence justified in the Grace of God fully pardoned by God.

There is nothing left to pay. All of humanity's debt has already been paid by Jesus. No one can make it better or more efficacious as it can not be improved upon. It is complete in Jesus.

Now this is a pretty good deal for all of us sinful humans who live out our lives in the fallenness of the first Adam. There is therefore no condemnation for us any longer. Jesus has been made sin for us and has taken the condemnation on Himself and tasted our death for us. The penalty payment has been paid. We are freed convicts. We are no longer held captive by Satan and this world. We are not on parole. We are not on probation. We are set free and made free in Jesus. We are fully PARDONED. We are no longer condemned but we have passed from death into life through Jesus Christ. Can we just live in this total freedom and enjoy the blessing of Abundant Life?

Does this sound fair to you? It doesn't to me either. But, Triune God did not ask for our vote or approval of how He conducts His business. Grace extends from God's love and it passes over our heads. We don't think like God. He does not have to operate on what we consider fair. God operates out of His Love. His Grace. His Mercy. His Forgiveness.

He does what He does because based on His Love it is the only way He can do things.

Since all sins have been forgiven in Jesus Christ, there is nothing left for humans to be held accountable for which would cause retributive condemnation in any kind of Hell. No justifiable punishment required. God is not a retributive God. He is a loving, merciful, forgiving, gracious, kind, patient, generous, compassionate and gentle FATHER. He is a daddy to all of the human family and He wants all of us to know just how GOOD He really is. No one lives outside of the loving embrace of the Father.

He loved us so much that he was willing to become incarnate and do whatever it took to take us into His Triune life forever. Even including dying a horrific death in our place. There just is not a retributive "bone" in His body.

What is left for us is to Believe God. Believe the Gospel. Believe Jesus and Who He has made us to be IN Him. The Abundant life Jesus gives is available to everyone who believes.

Lord, I believe. Help my unbelief.
AMEN

# OLD COVENANT FEAST DAYS

FOUND IN LEVITICUS CHAPTER 23
FEASTS OF THE LORD
GIVEN BY COMMAND TO MOSES
FOR: ALL ISRAEL
COMMANDED ASSEMBLIES

1. WEEKLY SABBATH, THE 7$^{TH}$ DAY OF THE WEEK
2. PASSOVER, THE 14$^{TH}$ DAY OF NISSAN
3. FEAST OF UNLEAVENED BREAD FIRST DAY ON THE 15$^{TH}$ OF NISSAN
4. FEAST OF UNLEAVENED BREAD SEVENTH DAY ON THE 22$^{ND}$ OF NISSAN
5. FEAST OF PENTECOST "COUNT FIFTY" FROM SABBATH DURING U.B.
6. FEAST OF TRUMPETS 1$^{ST}$ DAY OF THE 7$^{TH}$ MONTH
7. FEAST OF ATONEMENT 10$^{TH}$ DAY OF THE 7$^{TH}$ MONTH
8. FEAST OF TABERNACLES 15$^{TH}$ DAY OF THE 7$^{TH}$ MONTH THRU THE 22$^{ND}$ OF THE 7$^{TH}$ MONTH
9. LAST GREAT DAY OF THE FEAST OF TABERNACLES ON THE 23$^{RD}$ DAY OF THE 7$^{TH}$ MONTH CALLED THE 8$^{TH}$ DAY OF THE FEAST

THESE WERE OBSERVANCES GIVEN BY GOD FOR ISRAEL IN THEIR GENERATIONS TO REHEARSE AND REMEMBER GOD AND HIS DELIVERANCE OF HIS PEOPLE FROM BONDAGE IN EGYPT AND THEIR DELIVERANCE FROM EGYPT AND HIS CONTINUAL WORKING IN THEIR LIVES. AS ALL LAW WAS, THEY WERE GIVEN "TILL THE SEED SHOULD COME" –GALATIANS 3:19 , AND THEN THEY WOULD BE REPLACED BY A NEW AND BETTER OBSERVANCE—THE OBSERVANCE OF AND WORSHIP OF JESUS CHRIST WITH THE GIFT OF THE HOLY SPIRIT.

# OUR VIEW AND GOD'S VIEW OF SCRIPTURE

When trying to make sense out of the Bible there are a few concepts that are helpful for us to understand.

When God inspired the Bible to be written, He inspired it to be written from a perspective of time. A perspective of being within time and space. A perspective of linear time. Past, present, future. Etc.

So we see in scripture the Old Covenant and the New Covenant. The age of the history of Israel.. The church age. Prophecy. Apocalyptic writings. References to past events as well as future events and happenings. All related to linear time.

When you think about it, this is really the only way God could have inspired the Bible to be written so that man could read it with any understanding. Man is in linear time and understands from that perspective.

If God had inspired the Bible to be written from a Theological perspective of His existence outside of time and space, from an eternal perspective of a present reality of any and all things, then how confused would man have been in trying to understand ANYTHING concerning scripture.

So it appears that what is written in the Bible has a past, present, and future fulfillment. And as such, man has devised a plethora of interpretations of what the Bible says about any and all things. We see, for example, Pre-millennialism, Post-millennialism, A-millennialism, Dispensationalism, and other ism's that man has created.

An example of what I am saying is in John 11, when Jesus is told by Martha that Lazarus will rise " at the judgement at the last day". A time reference. But Jesus makes a profound statement to her when He says, " I am the resurrection and the life"---NOW. Jesus had always been the resurrection and the life. And he exercised that position in resurrecting various individuals in the Old Testament scriptures. Jesus is the ever Present reality of all that He is. He is the ETERNAL CONTEMPORY PRESENCE OF ALL TIME, to use a quote and expression of Theologian Robert F. Capon.

What we see from God's Eternal perspective from being also outside of linear time and space is that everything in God's view is in the PRESENT. He sees the beginning from the end and He sees it in the present. Therefore

He just makes declarations in scripture that in His view are "current" and have current application in His view, even though they are not literal for us in this physical life right now.

God says that we are buried with Christ in baptism. That we are raised with Christ. We are dead in Christ. We are justified and glorified in Christ. That we are born again in Christ. We are seated with Christ in Heavenly places. That our Citizenship is IN heaven. That we are new creations in Christ. So from God's perspective all things are a done deal, a present reality. Do we understand this? Some of it. Probably not all of it because God's thoughts and ways are so much higher than ours. ( Isa.55:8-9 ).

God is the one who is the author and finisher and perfector of our faith. He is the one who has decreed to share His Devine Nature with us. He has as an act of God declared us Holy, blameless and righteous in Jesus. He has the POWER to do this because He is God and He can do and does what pleases Him. He does not ask for our vote or our approval. He does what He does because He is God. And, He is love. What He does is Good and it is Always Good and always out of love.

If we are not careful, we will try to put everything in a TIME frame of reference and miss out on what God has already accomplished in Jesus. Remember what Jesus said in John 19:30, " It is Finished !"

Can we just believe that everything is a done deal in Jesus? Can we celebrate that God has given us every blessing in Jesus? Can we really believe that, " IT IS FINISHED!"

# OUTLINE OF THE GOSPEL OF JESUS CHRIST

Here in outline form, is scriptural validation for the Gospel of Jesus Christ and the Plan of God. This outline supplements other articles on the Gospel Plan of God. Scriptures are not quoted word for word, but the scriptural essence and meaning is listed.

Jn.8:12 Jesus is the LIGHT OF THE WORLD

Col.1:15-20 All things created IN,BY,THROUGH and FOR Christ and SUSTAINED by Christ.

Acts17:28 In Him, Jesus, we live and have our being. ALL people included.

John 14:20 I am in the Father, you are in me, and I am IN you.

Jn.1:14-18 Jesus is the only Begotten Son of the Father

Mat.11:27 No one knows the Father except the Son, and those the Son chooses to reveal Him in His time. We can only know the Father through the Son.

## ALL CHOSEN AND ADOPTED BEFORE THE CREATION OF THE WORLD

Eph.1:3-14 We were chosen and adopted before the foundation of the world.

Rom.8:15-16 We are the adopted Sons/Daughters of God

## DEATH CAME ON ALL HUMANS BY ONE MAN--ADAM

I Cor.15:21 Death came through one man, the resurrection of the dead comes also Through a man.

I Cor.15:22 For as in Adam , ALL die....

## ALL HUMANS ARE MADE ALIVE IN JESUS CHRIST

I Cor.15:22 ...so in Christ all will be made alive

## ALL THE FALLEN COSMOS AND MANKIND RECONCILED IN JESUS

Col. 1:19-20 The fullness of God dwelt bodily in Jesus and ALL THINGS are Reconciled to God through Jesus

Rev.13:8 Jesus was slain from the creation of the world

## ALL ARE INCLUDED

Jn.12:32 When I am lifted up I will draw ALL men to myself

I Jn.2:2 Jesus is the atoning sacrifice for the sins of the WHOLE WORLD

Rom.5:18 As the result of one trespass was condemnation for all men, so also The result of one act of righteousness was justification that brings Life for ALL MEN..: 19—ALL made righteous by Jesus.

IICor.5:14-15 One died for ALL. And, ALL DIED. Vs. 15, repeats, He died for ALL

I Tim.4:10 God who is the Savior of ALL men, especially to those who believe

I Tim.2:6 Who gave Himself a ransom for ALL men.

Heb.2:9 Jesus tasted death for EVERYONE

Heb.9:12 Jesus entered the Most Holy Place, Once, for ALL and obtained eternal Redemption for all.

Heb.10:10 We have been made Holy through the sacrifice of the body of Jesus Christ Once for ALL.

I Pt.3:18 Christ died for sins once for ALL, the righteous for the unrighteous to Bring you to God.

## ALL RAISED AND SEATED WITH CHRIST ( OBJECTIVELY TRUE )

Rom.6:4-5 ...new life, we were united with Christ in death, we will certainly also be United with Him in His resurrection.

Eph.2:6 God has raised us up with Christ and SEATED us with Him in the Heavenly realms in Christ Jesus.

## PREDESTINED, CALLED, JUSTIFIED AND GLORIFIED

Rom.8:29-38 Predestined to be conformed to the likeness of His Son. He Predestined Called, Justified, and Glorified us .

## ALL DONE BY THE POWER OF GOD

I Pet.1:3-5 God has given us New Birth through the resurrection of Jesus Christ, Kept and shielded by the Power of God

## BELIEVE THE WONDERFUL TRUTH OF GOD—YOU BELONG !!!

Jn.5:24 He who hears my word and believes Him who sent me Has everlasting Life.

Jn.6:40 Everyone who looks to the Son and believes in Him shall have eternal Life

Jn.6:47 He who believes has everlasting life.

Jn.20:31 ...And by believing you may have Eternal Life.

Rom.1:16 Salvation for everyone who believes

Rom.3:22 Righteousness through faith to All who believe.

I Tim.4:10 Savior of all men, especially those who believe.

I Jn.5:1 Everyone who believes Jesus is the Christ, is born of God.

I Jn.5:13 You who believe in the name of the Son of God that you may KNOW That you have eternal life.

# FOR GOD SO LOVED THE WORLD !!!

## PARADIGM SHIFTING ON GOD'S LOVE

Paradigm shifting is one of the most difficult mental activities one can experience in this life. Concepts become so embedded in our minds, whether right or wrong, that changing them is nearly impossible. Growing in the knowledge of and understanding of God requires changing our paradigms of thinking as we come to understand correctly what we did not understand correctly before. What makes it difficult is that it all must be taken on FAITH. Understanding we can not see.

When Jesus told the disciples that they must eat His body and drink His blood some paradigm shifting was certainly required by those men. When Jesus told Nicodemus that you must be "born again" to see the Kingdom of God, same thing. When God told Hosea to marry the prostitute Gomer, same thing. The birth of Isaac, same thing. Abraham and the sacrifice of Isaac, same thing. Of course we could go on and on.

Jesus said in John 16:12 that He had MUCH more to say to you/us than we could now bear. In vs.13, He said the spirit of Truth would tell us what is yet to come. We historically have thought by an old paradigm position that He meant what would come "prophetically". I think what Jesus is saying here is in the area of what is to come in understanding more about God the Father, The Son, and the Holy Spirit. Not prophecy.

By old paradigms we have thought that since we could quote the verse, "God is Love," that we knew God is Love and that we "understood" what that meant. But, God has been continually showing us what the Love of God entails. We have a kindergarten, elementary, and infantile understanding of what God is Love means. Not to offend any one. It is just the truth!

We think we see God's Love in sending Jesus to be The Sacrifice for us all. But, we don't fully understand the depths of what that means. Hebrews tells us He TASTED death for us all and we don't fully understand what that means. Corinthians tells us that He BECAME SIN----SIN FOR US ALL, and we don't understand what that means.

And it all means so much more than what we have thought in the past. The personal being of Jesus entering into our very life, experiencing our brokenness, our sin, our humanness, His seeing and experiencing our "good" and our wickedness, yet loving us and LIKING us as well as His very own. He is Emmanuel, God with us. He is Emmanuel, God IN us. He is Emmanuel, God WITHIN us. He is changing us, growing us and perfecting us one day at a time.

The question is, " How far does and will God go to demonstrate His love for us?" How far does his Mercy extend? How far does His Forgiveness go?" How deep and wide is His Love REALLY?"

When Adam sinned, God could have QUIT! When Israel CONTINUALLY refused God, He could have QUIT. When we continually sin even after Jesus comes into our lives, God says, " while we are yet/still sinners, Christ died for us." Why, to DEMONSTRATE His LOVE for us. (Rom.5:8). Do we understand the magnitude of what this means? My answer is, WE DO NOT!

We have limited the degree into which Jesus has entered into our humanness. We have limited the degree into which Jesus has entered into our SINFULNESS. We have looked at Jesus as the sacrificial Lamb of God to just pay for our sins. We have Not looked at Jesus indwelling in us IN OUR SINFULNESS and thereby His experiencing our sin and becoming SIN FOR US. ( II Cor. 5:21).

Misunderstanding Psalm 22, we have thought that God does not look on sin. This misunderstanding has kept us from realizing not only does God "look" on sin, Jesus enters our life, our being, our SINFULNESS, and experiences that sinfulness with us and continually delivers us from it, forgives us for it, and daily changes us to become more like Him from THE INSIDE OUT. Even in this continuing process as dirty as it gets, Jesus Loves us and Likes us and declares, " You are mine, you are in My hands and nothing can take you out, nothing can separate you from me, no power in all of universe can undo what I have done for you and what I continue to do for you every day of your life. I LOVE YOU. I LOVE YOU. I LOVE YOU. " You just can not comprehend, HOW MUCH I LOVE YOU !"

AMEN


# PAUL INTERPRETS THE GOSPELS !!!

Whoaaaa! Wait a minute. How are we to interpret scripture? Does the Old testament interpret the New? Does the New interpret the Old? Do the writings of Jesus interpret Paul's writings or do Paul's writings interpret Jesus' writings???? Wow!! A Mouth full!

These are essential questions which must be answered if one is to interpret scripture accurately. Most never give a thought to these questions. Do You?

While it would take a volume to explain all of the ramifications of these questions, we would like to look at one of these posed.

Most people do not realize that Paul's writings PRECEDE the writings of the first four Gospel writers. So What? Why would that make any difference in scriptural understanding?

OK. Let's see. Jesus writes and speaks from an Old Covenant understanding and interpretation of the Law. He lived under it. He grew up under it. He taught it.

When Paul writes in the 50's A.D. , he is the first writer of many of the New Testament scriptures. Christ taught him personally concerning Grace and the understanding of the New Covenant in the Blood of Christ. Paul explains everything in the light of WHO is Jesus and in the light of the Plan of God being completed in Jesus. He comes at it from the eyes of faith and Grace. From the eyes of Love and Proclamation. He writes from experience of 25 to 30 years of Christian life AFTER the life and death of Jesus.

Since Paul writes first, compared to the writers of the Gospels, he has no previous writings to confuse him with concerning theology, cosmology, soteriology, epistemology, ecclesiology, paleontology, pigmy marriages or anything else to cloud his understanding of our relationship in Jesus.!!!

Why is this important? OK. When we read the sayings of Jesus in the Gospels we are reading words which came AFTER Paul writes his books of the Bible. There is NO WAY that these sayings can interpret what Paul writes since his writings came first. They do not establish doctrine nor do they undo doctrine which has been established in the inspired writings of Paul. SO, when we read the words of Christ in the Gospels, we MUST see those words in light of what Paul reveals in Grace in his writings. Otherwise, we miss the boat to understand their full meaning as it is intended.

When there is a conflict in our minds concerning the writings of Paul and Jesus, let's remember these principles and continue to grow in the grace and knowledge of our Lord and Saviour Jesus Christ revealed in the writings of the Apostle Paul.


# PHILOSOPHY OR THEOLOGY—WHICH?


St. Augustine's philosophical, doctrinal, and theological interpretations in the 5th Century left their imprint on Western Christian Theological thinking to such degree that the Church in the West focuses its teaching on the Cross and Atonement. While the Cross and Atonement are true, they fail to express the original purpose of why God created man in the first place.

The position of this teaching is that man is 'separated' from God and lost, and that Jesus came to earth to take the sins of man upon himself and save man and thereby get man into God's good graces. Further, that man is sinful, that God is angry with man because of his sins, and that Jesus' torturous death appeases this 'angry' God and is bound by this spiritual contract to therefore save this individual.

Thrown into the mix are the complicating elements of 'predestination', 'election', 'double predestination', Calvinism, Arminianism, and numerous other "Isms" to further confuse.

The mix is further complicated by any number of "Plans of God" based on everything from prophetic interpretations, millinialism, dispensationalism, and spiritual "visions" various preachers have "seen".

Is it any wonder that Western Theological understanding is so convoluted?

Basically all these teachings get back to the concept of 'rewards' for being good and saved, and 'punishment' for being bad and unsaved--the doctrine of Heaven and Hell as taught by ST. AUGUSTINE in the 5$^{th}$ Century A.D.

Augustine had a background in Platonic Philosophy and adopted many, if not most, of Plato's philosophical teachings on religion and the afterlife, including Plato's 'invention' of Hell. Hence the churches teaching today that heaven is the place for good people and hell is the place for bad people.

The basic teachings of the Protestant churches of today are very consistent with those of the Catholic Church since they were part of the Catholic Church until the Reformation in the 1600's. And those teachings come in great measure from Plato and St. Augustine.

Could it be that there is a fundamental error in the premise of Western Christian Theological teachings? Could it be that God is NOT angry with man? That God actually loves humanity. That God created man to be with Him forever. That God Adopted mankind into His life, redeemed man, forgave man, and saved man from the foundation of the world? ( Ephesians 1:3-14; Revelation 13:8). Could it be that in the plan of God the original purpose of Christ coming into the world as Immanuel, God with us, was to create the UNION necessary to connect mankind into the Triune God's life?

And could it be that Jesus' coming into the world really did provide the forgiveness for ALL sins of ALL people for ALL time and raise humanity to the Father's right side and seat mankind with Jesus there? ( I John 2:2; Ephesians 2:6). And, that IN Christ ALL are made ALIVE. (I Cor.15:22).

Jesus proclaimed the greatest truth anyone could know when He said in John 14:20 ( Also in John 17:20-26) that " you would sooner or later know that I am in the Father and you are in me and I am in you." RELATIONSHIP !

The INCLUSION of all of mankind in the fore ordained plan of God is the truth of scripture that Augustinian Theology has over looked and or denied in the Christian Church for over 1500 years.

For you and me the question is what Theology do we want to embrace? Do we want to embrace Greek philosophy or the Truth that is in Jesus? (Ephesians 4:21).

Numerous men in the ministry of God HAVE understood the True TRINITARIAN Theology over the ages. Men like Irenaus, Athanatius, and more recently, Karl Barth, Thomas Torrance, J.B. Torrance, John McKenna, Colin Gunton, Trevor Hart, Gary Deddo, Michael Jinkins, Baxter Kruger, and many, many others. This Neo-Reformation is beginning to sweep over the world. It is the Truth and it can not be kept from spreading over the Christian world. It is just a matter of time.

# RELIGIONS ARE NOT THE WAY TO GOD

Religions in the world have caused more pain, hurts, divisions, and war than any other cause one can think of. The religious world regardless of what faith we wish to talk about looks for THE true religion at the expense, disregard, disrespect and disdain of all other religions. Many religions are fanatical in their efforts to impose their beliefs on others. Unless one becomes a member of THE true religion one is "lost" and headed for the unpleasant afterlife however that may be interpreted.

Christianity has not escaped this microvision of religious ideology. Even within the Christian Church we find denominations and various groups which look at other Christian fellowships with judgmental condemning eyes for lack of accepting doctrine and theologies of their own.

There are hundreds of religions and faiths in the world today. There are hundreds of Christian groups and organizations extent today as well. What makes Christians right and all others wrong? What is the answer to all the questions of all religions in the world including Christianity?

Religions seek to lead their followers to a glorious after life. Some seek more noble ideals while living here in the here and now of life by serving others and all of mankind. All religions realize the temporal short-lived existence of human life with only a few short years to prepare for eternity.

Religions generally have a bunch of hoops and ladders one must jump through, rules, regulations, requirements, laws, works, etc. before one can be qualified to be given the reward of the after life—ie.,Heaven for the Christian.

And of course, there is always that threat of eternal death or torture and punishment for those who don't find THE WAY proscribed by the religion of choice.

Question? Did God purposefully put mankind on this earth along with hundreds of religions to see if man could find the exact right one so that the man could qualify in that right faith in order to be rewarded with Heaven?

And, for those who could not somehow FIND the right faith, would they just have to be punished and tortured or destroyed forever?

In other words, is God in Heaven with a giant chessboard, as it were, playing a game with the lives and souls of men with winners and losers? You found it—you win!! You did not find it—you lose!!

And last question here, Does God want all people to become members of the Christian Church? OK, then which one? Do we begin to see the problem here? Well then what does God want? Does He want ANYTHING out of mankind's thinking? I've asked enough questions. Now for some answers.

Jesus created all things for Himself. Col.1:15-17. Jesus adopted mankind as His own and took all of mankind into His life before the foundation or creation of the world!!! Eph.1:3-14. Jesus is Immanuel. God is with and in us and we are with and in God. Jesus said it this way in John 14:20. " ...you will realize that I am in my Father and you are in me and I am in you." And lest we think Jesus was talking just to Christians, Paul tells us in Acts 17:28 talking to the Pagans at Athens that THEY lived, moved, and had their being IN God.

Paul was passionate about telling the world about the Mystery of the ages in Colossians 1:26-27 when he declares that the mystery was/is Christ IN you the hope of glory.

God has always been in His creation. In His children by His spirit. No one escapes the connection with God that makes ALL humans His children.

God is not trying to save the world and get everyone to accept Jesus into his or her life. The truth is He has ALREADY SAVED the world and Jesus has ALREADY ACCEPTED all of humanity INTO His life. And through Jesus' salvation acts Jesus has saved the whole world. He is the payment, the propitiation, the sacrifice offered ONCE for ALL. Man's Savior. Jesus is the Way, the Truth and the Life. John 14:6. And He is the only name under heaven that has saved man.

This is the GOOD NEWS. This is THE GOSPEL OF JESUS CHRIST. And Jesus wants the world to know it. He wants you and me to tell it and to share it.

When humanity knows WHO they are in Jesus and that they belong to Him they can then behave and live like it. Then when that happens Peace will finally come on earth. Love will cover the earth as water covers the oceans. Joy will reign. Tears will cease. And God's children, all of them, all of us will dwell in the house of the Lord FOREVER.

The question here again is, " Will we believe it?"


# REPLACING THE 'IF' FACTOR WITH 'SINCE'!


Colossians 3:1 presents us with a view that could be read as conditional as to one's being raised with Christ. Some translations render the first word of the verse as "if" and others as "since" and others " In view of the fact".

Not to get too technical the Greek reads, "Ei oun sunegerqete to Christo, ta ano zeteite, ou o Christos estin en dexia tou Theou kathemenos." Got that? The Amplified uses, 'If then you have been raised with Christ.....' The Phillips translation uses, 'If you are then "risen" with Christ...'

The NIV states, 'Since then you have been raised with Christ...'

The NET uses, ' Since you have been raised to new life with Christ...'

And the Wuest translation uses, 'In view of the fact. Therefore, that you were raised with Christ...'

The question arises in this as to whether or not "uncertainty" is indicated in the first part of this verse when 'if' is used, and whether or not "certainty" is indicated when 'since' is used in the translation. One would apply to all humans being raised with Christ in a Trinitarian Theology, and the other making room for some not to be raised with Christ at all by their choice NOT TO BE RAISED WITH HIM. We really need to know how to understand this properly and theologically.

In Col.2:20, Paul makes the point that we died with Christ. Since is used in the NIV and other translations due to the certainty of the fact. Then in Chapter 3:1, he emphasizes the fact that we have been RAISED with Christ as well.

We need to note here a little bit of Greek language usage as regarding the word "Ei", or 'If'. NOTE: If does NOT convey uncertainty but is what is referred to as a first class conditional clause which assumes that the statement which follows is TRUE. ( again see Col.2:20). One can often substitute SINCE or IN VIEW OF THE FACT for IF.

So with this in mind, it is a better rendering in our modern understanding of scripture to translate Col.3:1 as, ' Since then you have been raised with Christ...' This is consistent with the fact that we were all ADOPTED by the Father in Jesus Christ before anything was ever created in the universe!!! ( Eph.1:3-6) We have been INCLUDED in the life of Jesus Christ and the Father by the Holy Spirit as Jesus says in John 14:20 and again in John 17:20-26. The Father DECLARED this UNION from the "start". Originally. Before the foundation of the world. It is His plan and He can do and did do exactly as He desired. Thank you very much!

It is never a matter of ..."IF". It is always a matter of "SINCE" under the parameters of this discussion. It is FACT. REALITY.

Then when we read other verses such as Romans 8:28-39, we can read them without the 'if' factor. Using the 'since' factor of understanding in vs.31 , we read , "SINCE God is FOR us who can be against us? There isn't any IF to it!!! God is always FOR us. ALWAYS!!! And it has always been this way ....SINCE the very beginning of God's wonderful plan for humankind.

The really good news, I mean, GOOD NEWS is that YOU were on The Father's mind when He formulated this 'Grand Design' before the foundation of the world. That makes you pretty wonderfully SPECIAL to our Father in Heaven who loves you JUST AS MUCH AS HE LOVED JESUS!!!!!!!!!!!!!!! Our problem is believing this Truth of ALL Truths. All we can do is declare this to you. It is up to you to believe it.

You have always BELONGED TO THE FATHER. BELIEVE IT. Then BEHAVE like it consistent with WHO you REALLY ARE in JESUS.

# REVELATION 'SIMPLY' REVEALED

Oh, the complexities of the Book of Revelation. The most debated book of the Bible of all time. In this short paper we want to 'Oversimplify' the meaning and significance of this book and avoid specifics as others have tried to do for 2000 years.

Who is the Beast? Who or what is the AntiChrist? What about the Millennium? Is this the End Time? Who are the 144,000? What are the 7 this and the 7 that? Is Revelation written from a Dispensational position? When do four horsemen ride?

Many well meaning religionists have tried to interpret this book over the centuries with specific names, places, dates, and time frames all to be found wanting and wrong. People have waited in rivers in boats, waited on mountaintops and in caves waiting on the imminent return of Christ. How Revelation was interpreted in the early church, in the middle ages, and 18th, 19th, and 20th centuries has varied with the conditions in the world extant at whatever period of time in which one lived. Is it possible that the way Revelation was written was NEVER intended to be a road map to the future by specifics and a hidden puzzle to be unraveled by a few with 'special' insight?

We do know that God inspired Revelation to be included in the canon. We may also conclude that it has relevance for all people during the last 2000 years. So what is the over riding message of this most intriguing book?

God never put this book in scripture to confuse or challenge man's ability to discover hidden meanings and in doing so come to see the future in specifics which only God knew from the beginning.

In every age since John wrote down the Revelation of Jesus Christ mankind has faced all kinds of trials, difficulties and death. In man's darkest hour including the myrtardom of precious lives in the arena of human depravity God has left a witness in the Book of Revelation for all people for all time. Regardless of the circumstances individuals have faced and will face the message of the Book of Revelation remains steadfast. The book shows bloody battles. Violent abuses. Maniacal depravity. Potential devastation. Prophetic calamities. And beautiful scenes of bliss and happiness. What does it all mean for the 'average' human who reads the book? What would it have meant for one reading it in the past who was undergoing extreme persecution in his or her life?

Now let's oversimplify! The Revelation of Jesus Christ reveals that Jesus is VICTORIOUS over all, that ultimately GOOD triumphs over EVIL, that all that is represented by Satan—Beasts, AntiChrists, Evil, Suffering, and Death—are all overcome in the Alpha and Omega—Jesus. Jesus WINS. Humans WIN in Jesus. The Future is secured in God in eternity. Joy and Happiness reign in God's Kingdom FOREVER.

No need here for interpreting years, dates, people, times, half-times, third-times or anything else. NO NEED! Just the understanding that GOD WINS and we do too!

Revelation reveals the fulfillment of God's original purpose and intention for creation. That is all that was created in and by and for Jesus Christ is ultimately completely in UNION with Him Forever. Glory. Bliss. Happiness. Joy. Heaven. Whatever you wish to call it, Revelation reveals its ultimate reality. Our God is an awesome God who has the power and will to bring it all about in His Glorious purpose born out of His amazing Love and desire to share that Love with His creation.

## ROMANS 6:23 AND MATTHEW 10:28

Without going into a lot of discussion about Greek words for 'death' , 'suffering', Strongs' number words and different translations, we want to address two scriptures which often come up whenever Adoption and Inclusion Theology is being discussed.

The two scriptures we want to look at are Rom.6:23, and Matt.10:28.

Before we go to Rom.6:23, let us see what Paul had already written in Rom.5:18. Here Paul says that All had received condemnation through Adam, but that through the result of one act of righteousness was justification which brings life for All men.

Whatever Rom.6:23 means, it is not undoing what Paul had just written in chapter 5. Chapter 6 here is describing LIFE in and with Jesus. He describes new life by coming up out of a watery grave to walk in a New Life. Vs.10, points that this was accomplished for all humanity. When you come to vs.23 Paul is just making a simple statement which we try and make too much out of when he says that "Life" is IN Jesus' and apart from Jesus there is NO life. In other words, since all are humans and sinners with no hope in and of and by themselves, the ONLY source for Eternal life is obviously the ONE who can give it and give it as a GIFT. Apart from that gift the only other option IS Death. But, In Jesus life has been given to all as the gift of God. The WAGES FOR SIN have been paid—for all!

147

So in reality, there is NO death for humans eternally speaking. All have been carried to the Father's right hand by Jesus. ( Eph.2:6). Jesus conquered Death for all. Paul is really just showing and comparing what life would be like if only we had ourselves and sin to dictate our future. But we don't just have ourselves and sin, we have Jesus and the Gift of God—Eternal Life. Without Jesus, yes, death would be final.

Next we come to Matt.10:28.

In Matt.10:16, Jesus is sending out His disciples into "Beelzebub's" world to proclaim the Gospel. From vs.16 to vs.27, Jesus is showing areas where the disciples will face difficulty and persecution and even death. But when He comes to vs.28 as a final encouragement He says don't fear those who may kill you ( or the Enemy), but fear (honor, respect, be duty bound, follow your calling, pay respect to, listen to , submit,) the one who is sending you out in the first place WHO is the ALL POWERFUL GOD who has the power over life and death and not only has the power but with His power He CAN destroy you both physically ( which they were fearing) and spiritually. It says He has the power to do this, not that He does. The point here Jesus is making is for them NOT to fear the enemy they would face. Jesus is not establishing some Theological position as to the eternal life experience of believers and nonbelievers.

# YOUR PERSONAL GOOD NEWS

Let's just cut to the chase. What you may have heard concerning Christianity, religion, and Theology aside we will look at some astoundingly good news most have never dreamed of.

The great Triune Creator God created human kind in order to share His LIFE of total love with that human family. God adopted humankind into his very life from the very beginning even before the foundation of the world ! (Eph.1:3-14). Jesus Christ created everything that exists FOR Himself and He sustains that creation. ( Col.1:14-17).

Triune God was so full of love and LIFE that it was bursting to overflow into "something" and that something was the human family God created and started with Adam.

The only way God could experience human life was to become human and in so doing was able to carry humanity into the very heart of Himself. But this union was not one sided. As humanity was carried into the heart of the Triune God, the LIFE, heart, essence, existence, spirit, being of God was imported into humankind by the Spirit of God making the connection, the union between God and man complete. All this was done through Jesus Christ's life, death, resurrection and ascension to the Father.

The GOOD NEWS of the Bible is simply this. We are God's children, with God's Life living in us by His Spirit and loved by our Father. We have an eternal future planned for us in our Father's house with the rest of our brothers and sisters. We can share in the abundance of that life now by knowing about it, knowing where it comes from in Jesus Christ, and believing it.

This is not an "IF" proposition. This is not something "to be" acquired. This is the TRUTH OF GOD. This is an ETERNAL DECLARATION AND PROCLIMATION of the WAY IT IS.

Adam's sin brought untold suffering and death into the human family. But in Jesus Christ abundant JOY and LIFE has replaced that suffering and death.

( I Cor. 15:22).

The KEY is just understanding what The Triune God's original purpose was and His POWER to bring it all about. ( I Peter 1:3-6). And He has! In JESUS CHRIST.

The really good news NOW is that……. YOU ARE INCLUDED …..in the whole plan and you have been since before the foundation of the world. (Eph.1:3-14). God has ALWAYS loved YOU!

Many QUESTIONS arise over this brief explanation of the Gospel. Some may call it an over simplification. What about this and what about that? What about sin? What about works? What about bad people? What about "Hell"? The "what abouts' are almost endless. But the Good News is Jesus. God With us. God WITHIN us. Immanuel. The answers are to be found to be sure. But they are ONLY found in Jesus. The place to start with any question is, " WHO is JESUS?" When we start there at the correct starting place the beauty of the PLAN OF GOD opens up to our understanding like a beautiful flower on a spring morning.

GOD is LOVE. He loves YOU. You are the SON or DAUGHTER God has always loved and wanted. YOU are SPECIAL to God. How good is that?

And our future as Psalm 16:11 says will be filled " with pleasures forevermore at God's right hand." FOREVER.

You are loved, liked, wanted, adopted and included in the life of God. Jesus made it happen for all of us. Believe it !

AMEN AND AMEN

## ROMANS 6:23 AND MATTHEW 10:28

Without going into a lot of discussion about Greek words for 'death' , 'suffering', Strongs' number words and different translations, we want to address two scriptures which often come up whenever Adoption and Inclusion Theology is being discussed.

The two scriptures we want to look at are Rom.6:23, and Matt.10:28.

Before we go to Rom.6:23, let us see what Paul had already written in Rom.5:18. Here Paul says that All had received condemnation through Adam, but that through the result of one act of righteousness was justification which brings life for All men.

Whatever Rom.6:23 means, it is not undoing what Paul had just written in chapter 5. Chapter 6 here is describing LIFE in and with Jesus. He describes new life by coming up out of a watery grave to walk in a New Life. Vs.10, points that this was accomplished for all humanity. When you come to vs.23 Paul is just making a simple statement which we try and make too much out of when he says that "Life" is IN Jesus' and apart from Jesus there is NO life. In other words, since all are humans and sinners with no hope in and of and by themselves, the ONLY source for Eternal life is obviously the ONE who can give it and give it as a GIFT. Apart from that gift the only other option IS Death. But, In Jesus life has been given to all as the gift of God. The WAGES FOR SIN have been paid—for all! So in reality, there is NO death for humans eternally speaking. All have been carried to the Father's right hand by Jesus. ( Eph.2:6). Jesus conquered Death for all. Paul is really just showing and comparing what life would be like if only we had ourselves and sin to dictate our future. But we don't just have ourselves and sin, we have Jesus and the Gift of God—Eternal Life. Without Jesus, yes, death would be final.

Next we come to Matt.10:28.

In Matt.10:16, Jesus is sending out His disciples into "Beelzebub's" world to proclaim the Gospel. From vs.16 to vs.27, Jesus is showing areas where the disciples will face difficulty and persecution and even death. But when He comes to vs.28 as a final encouragement He says don't fear those who may kill you ( or the Enemy), but fear (honor, respect, be duty bound, follow your calling, pay respect to, listen to , submit,) the one who is sending you out in the first place WHO is the ALL POWERFUL GOD who has the power over life and death and not only has the power but with His power He CAN destroy you both physically ( which they were fearing) and spiritually. It says He has the power to do this, not that He does. The point here Jesus is making is for them NOT to fear the enemy they would face. Jesus is not establishing some Theological position as to the eternal life experience of believers and nonbelievers.

# SALVATION, HELL AND UNIVERSALISM

For the first 400 years of the New Testament Church it preached the reconciliation of humanity and all things in Christ ( Col.1:19-20). Also the redemption of humanity in Christ, and the Salvation in Christ of all of humanity ( I Tim.4:9-10) was preached.

The church did not deal with topics such as "election" , or the "tulip", or dispensationalism, or "hell" for the punishment of the evil humans who were involved in it. (The Old Testament had NO scripture indicating punishment for evil men on the earth.)

The church had to deal with topics as they arose in a new religion. First off, they dealt with Judaizers, gnosticism, the nature of Jesus Christ, i.e., was he human, divine, created, proceeding from the Father, or a ghost. The concept of the Trinity ( to determine was Jesus God) was also debated and articulated by Tertullian in the 3rd century.

The concept of whether or not all humanity was adopted in Christ from before the foundation of the world was not in question. ( Eph. 1:3-14). The salvation of all humanity was not in question. ( I John 2:2). ( The early church leaders such as John, Polycarp, Irenaeus, Athanasius, Gregory of Nyssius, and later Karl Barth, Tom Torrance and others preached the Adoption and Inclusion in the life of God of all Humanity.)

In 325 A.D., Emperor Constantine proclaimed Christianity the official religion of the Roman Empire. Rome was the largest city of the Empire and also the largest group of Christians lived there. The church at Rome became very influential in the dictates of what would be included in church doctrine due to its size and power.

So what happened? In the 5th Century A.D. a church leader by the name of St. Augustine of Hippo, an avid proponent of Plato, introduced the concept of Plato's Hell with its divisions into the Christian Church. And it has been espoused in the Christian church since.

Even when Martin Luther contested the sale of indulgences to get people "prayed out of hell" in the 1600's to start the Protestant Reformation the idea of Plato's hell remained in the church. And, unfortunately today we still have to deal with this figment of Plato's imagination.

What was a pure teaching of the Salvation of all Humanity in Jesus Christ, and the reconciliation of all things, and the redemption of all mankind in Jesus became clouded by teachings of rewards and punishment for good and evil behavior, hell fire for the damned, a wrong interpretation of parables such as Lazarus and the Rich Man, "worms that die not" and "lakes of fire" all predicated upon the idea of punishment for disobedient and evil man. Further concepts of "election" and or "double predestination" for saved and lost souls entered the church.

The simplicity of the faith that was once delivered to the saints is still available and applicable today to humanity. God Loves humanity and He died for it. He saved it. He redeemed it. He reconciled it in Jesus. He raised humanity up to His throne with Jesus. ( Eph. 2:6) God's purpose and power will see His plan through to completion. ( I Peter 1:3-9). Jesus Life, death, resurrection and ascension ensure it.

Universal Salvation is TRUE. All are saved in Jesus. UNIVERSALISM, however is not true. Universalism says that all humans are saved whether they believe it or not and whether or not they accept and want it or not. All are just placed in the position of life with God forever. No ifs, ands or buts.

Universal Salvation in Hope is more applicable to the truth. It is possible for all humanity to sooner or later accept and believe who they are in Jesus and live forever in the Mansion of Heaven with the Father. If one refuses to accept it and believe it then this one just does not experience the abundant life Jesus offers eternally until they do accept and believe it. They are in a

"state of perishing" to quote the scripture.

The Truth is not rocket science. God Loves humans. He wants to be with all of us forever. You are the child the Father always wanted. Jesus made it happen. " It is finished". John 19:30.

The Good News really is Good News. Can you believe it?

LORD I BELIEVE, HELP MY UNBELIEF.

# SALVATION IS NOT A CONTEST!!!

August 7, 2007

This discussion starts with the only original starting point that there can be. That is with God. The Father, Son, and Holy Spirit- the Great Creator.

Much of the Christian world has viewed what God did was to create a challenge to humans to see IF they could make the grade- cut the mustard, live a life "good" enough, some how qualify for Christ to deem them worthy to be saved by proving their obedience to Him. If they could not pass these tests, then a fate worse than death itself awaited them -- FOR ALL ETERNITY, SEPARATION, TORMENT, WEEPING AND GNASHING OF TEETH, TOTAL DARKNESS—HELL FOREVER. All of this judgement pronounced on them because they did not measure up.

Christianity has been portrayed in this way somewhat by many sincere people for ages. It is some sort of Game. A contest for souls. A Challenge. Man against the world and the Devil. Of course it has been said that Christ would help them out, but "Who knows" the outcome of the marathon of life. The questions are many with too few concrete answers.

Maybe what happened originally by the design of the GREAT Creator, was not like this scenario at all. Let me pose another understanding.

The love of the Father, Son, and Holy Spirit for each other was so tremendous, that they said, " We can share this abundance of LOVE with more beings, a family, billions. Let us make man in our image and likeness and include him in our circle of love. One of us will have to go to earth and become a human while remaining fully God in order to bridge the chasm between humans and US—TRIUNE GOD. This assignment was given to the Word which was also the Son who was God from the beginning.

The plan was laid out. The Son was slain from before the foundation of the world. Human sins were forgiven in the death of the Son. Humans were reconciled and redeemed ORIGINALLY in the SON. ALL were included in this original plan and purpose of God for His purpose, enjoyment, and Glory to let His abundance of love overflow to his children. ALL of this was accomplished in Jesus Christ before anything was even created. We were known, loved, forgiven, redeemed, reconciled, resurrected, saved, and placed INSIDE the Triune God's life ORIGINALLY—Long before our personal physical birth.

No game. No contest. No struggle for the souls of men and women. No competition between God and the devil. No question as to "IF" this is going to happen. Just the plain DECLARATION BY GOD that it HAS happened and that He had/has/ will have the POWER to ensure its happening –No matter what.!!! Whew!! Awesome. Wow.

Here is the really good part. YOU were and ARE included in this Eternal Adoption by the Great Triune God. You are loved, wanted, appreciated, included, adopted, saved and Glorified by this loving Father of us all. You, yes you. YOU. Jesus Christ has made you WORTHY. He has done for all of humanity—You included—what none of us could have done for ourselves.

When one has ALL of the POWER IN THE UNIVERSE—and beyond, ALL POWER, ALL…ALL…ALL.ALL. ALL of it. All Power, then coupled with ALL LOVE, that One can do anything He wishes and can certainly bring it all about like he designs it. Are you with me.? Get the point? Are there any arguments devised by Human beings that can in anyway nullify what this Great, Loving, Wonderful, all Powerful Heavenly Father has ALREADY done for his family- His children? Any possibility for failure? No. Why? Because it HAS ALREADY BEEN DONE. IT HAS ALREADY BEEN ACCOMPLISHED!!! IT HAS SUCCEEDED IN CHRIST. GAME OVER. DONE DEAL. GOD WON. WE WIN TOO.

Only one question now remains. Can you see it? Can we put aside human reasoning and arguments and denials, and simply BELIEVE it?

That is the question. The only question. Can we say, " I believe, help my unbelief"? " Come inherit the Kingdom prepared for you from the foundation of the world!" YES, YOU!!!


# SEEING THE 'REAL' GOD OF CREATION


What is your foundation of your Theology? How do you define God? Who or what is God? And, what is He like?

We might ask ourselves the question, 'Where did Western Christianity get its Theological concepts of God?' Where did they come from and originate?

In Western Christian thought a man by the name of Augustine of Hippo, or St. Augustine, was the 'father' of much of the concepts which he imported into the beliefs and practices of the church in the 5th Century, A.D. In his early life, Augustine had been a womanizing libertine young man. Later as he studied the philosophy of the great Greek philosopher, Plato, a rank Pagan, he embraced most all of Plato's ideas of God, Hell, and the after life.

Augustine's view of God now from this Platonic influence was a God who was : Perfect, Righteous, Holy, Sovereign, moral, lawful, all by legal definition. In this picture of God, God was unknowable, unapproachable, distant, judgmental, punishing, angry with man, and vindictive. And, while all the time claiming to be Love. This approach to understanding God has led to all types of wrong headed thinking involving rewards vs. punishment, concepts of Heaven and Hell, and vengeance by a God who demands Justice. This is a LEGAL idea of God. And, it is classic Plato!

This concept sees Jesus coming to earth to die for sinners who God is angry with, and to appease the righteous indignation of the angry God. Salvation is then CONDITIONAL based on whether or not man will find out about how to be saved and then acting on this knowledge by 'accepting' Jesus. Whew!!!!

BUT, scripture reveals a far different God! It reveals a Triune God. A God of Love. An eternal God with complete love of the Father, Son, and Holy Spirit all three sharing this total love one for the other. Scripture reveals that this love was so great that this Triune God decided to create a cosmos and a humanity to share this love with by INCLUDING this creation INTO the very life of this Great Triune God.

WHAT WAS GOD'S PURPOSE BEFORE THE CREATION OF ANYTHING?

Ephesians 1:3-14, tells us that from before the creation of the world it was God's purpose to ADOPT man into the very life of God. Jesus tells us that this adoption wasn't just a matter of God looking at us as belonging to Him as a possession, but being adopted and included INTO to very life of God. ( See Jn.14:20 and Jn.17:20-26). This would be mutual indwelling of God in man and man in God!!!! This is what GOD WANTS. And folks, whatever God wants, God gets!!! And it is always based on Love. God's desire from the beginning was to have this INTIMATE relationship with His creation. How beautiful is that?

Then we come to II Cor.5:14-21, ( you have a Bible, read this passage) which points out that Jesus died and paid the price for ALL to be reconciled to God and that this reconciliation is a PAST event. We are not waiting to be reconciled, or as vs. 21, puts it, we are not waiting to become the righteousness of God, WE ARE NOW in Jesus.

Paul again emphasizes this 'past reconciliation" in Col. 1:12-22. (See text). Notice the 'presentness' of these verses. The Father HAS QUALIFIED you. He HAS RESCUED us from the dominion of darkness and BROUGHT us into the Kingdom of the Son He loves. Notice all past tense of these points and our being in the present condition of them. Continuing, He sustains all He has created, the fullness of God dwelt in Jesus, and in Jesus God reconciles ALL things to Himself whether they are in Heaven or on earth by His blood. Vs 21, says that we were once alienated ( notice—not SEPERATED) from God and were enemies in OUR THINKING and our evil behavior, but vs.22, now He has reconciled you by Christ's physical body through death to present you holy in His sight , without blemish and free from accusation. This is a DONE DEAL. AND JESUS DID IT. He said so. Jn.19:30, " It is FINISHED."

The Triune God's Holiness is not based on law. What law tells each of the three how to love the other? This Holiness is the full and complete relationship of love one for the other between the Father, the Son, and the Holy Spirit. Jesus has taken us INTO this relationship of the Triune God by raising us up with Him and seating us with Him at the Father's right hand—in other words, where Jesus is-we are as well.(Eph.2:6). Our true Holiness is living IN the Holiness of the relationship of Triune God! It is not defined by law or morality. Wow, this would blow Augustinian Theologians off of their podiums!

Now, I have described two Gods here in this little paper. Which one of these Gods do you want to believe in and worship. One will leave you in utter DARKNESS, filled with angst, wondering if you are going to make it, in pain, suffering, guilt, brokenness, and without relationship. The other:

Well that's a different story. That God will give rest, peace, assurance, hope, freedom, joy, and the realization of just WHO YOU ARE IN JESUS. Jesus said it this way in Jn.8:31-32. " You shall know the truth and the truth shall set you FREE."

# SIMPLICITY OF THE TRUTH

Why is it so hard for grownups to just believe what the Great Awesome Father, Son, and Holy Spirit ( Triune God) tells us. You can tell a little child that his mommy loves him or her, or that his daddy loves him or her, and that they want to be with them in the family from now on. Kids can understand this. Apparently grownup can not.

When you consider that our Daddy in Heaven loves us and wants to be with us from now on and sealed the deal in His only begotten Son, Jesus, you have to admit that His love is awesome indeed.

John said it this way, " I write these things that you might believe." ( John 1:7). If it were **easy** to believe then John would not have had to even say it, or write it. Since God knew that humans would find it nearly impossible to believe He sent His Holy Spirit to convict the entire world of their unbelief. Kids believe. Grownups don't. ( Seems like Jesus said except you become as little children......)

The Gospel, or Good News, is not so hard to understand. Believe, maybe. Understand, not. The Good News as I see it is this: God is love as Father, Son, and Holy Spirit. He wanted to share that love with a family so he created and adopted children into His family originally making it all possible through the Incarnation of His Son, Jesus--The Word.

Since He had/has all power to make this happen there is NO way it was not going to happen. God simply says," I created you, I love you, I want you, and I am not going to continue on forever without you." That is what the Good News is all about. It is what God **DID** and He wants to tell you about it. You nor I had a say in what God wanted to do and did.

The Good News is simply an announcement of what God did. But, for some, it is 'too good to be true', or it is 'too easy', or it is 'not fair', or 'too simple' to be understood. Whatever the reason some will **not believe.**

Education plays an important part in one's believing or not. If we are adversely affected with Greek Philosophy, Aristotelian and Platonic 'theology', as well as Augustinian paradigms it is going to be difficult to see the Truth apart from those disciplines. So Paul says not to be persuaded by those 'heresies' of philosophy. The truth of Jesus is not rocket science. A child can understand that God Loves him or her. And, that Jesus has done everything to make one's eternal life with the Triune God a reality.

Other 'stuff' just confuses the issue. So what will it be? Can we believe God, the Great Triune God, loves us or not? Is His love big enough to take care of the situation in which we all find ourselves? The Truth is not hard. Philosophy is Hard. It is confusing. The Truth of God is freeing, liberating, and joyful. It brings peace, assurance, happiness, and celebration. God never intended it to be hard or difficult. Satan confuses the issue and makes it into a game of hoops and ladders. It really is simple. It really is Good. Can you believe it?

# THE COMMANDS OF JESUS CHRIST

By Paul Kurts

Jesus Christ, during his three and one half years of ministry and teaching, introduced a new and different religion than what the Jews had historically followed. Whereas the Old Covenant had laws that were specifically laid out in the 10 Commandments and the other statutes and judgements, the commands of Jesus were given by Jesus based on God's Love and designed by Christ to lead one to be like Christ.

Since the "Law of Christ" as Paul called it is not written down in one place in scripture only, many have assumed that there is little to the Law of Christ.

Luke tells us in Lk: 16:16-17, " that the law and prophets were proclaimed until John. But since then the good news of the Kingdom of God. We will see in this sermon that the good news of the Kingdom of God has every-thing to do with Jesus and his "commands".

In I Jn. 1:2-6, we see that we have come to know Jesus IF we obey his Commands. If any obeys Jesus' word , God's love is made complete in him.

Jesus said in Lk.6:46, " Why do you call me Lord and do Not what I say?"

Jesus said in Jn.7:16-19, " My teaching is not my own. It comes from the Father.

In talking with the Jews in Jn.8:31-36, Jesus is showing the Jews who were entrusted with proclaiming the law ( Note: TILL JOHN ) that true freedom now can only come through Jesus and His teaching. Not the Law. John 14, Jesus' emphasis is on putting one's TRUST in Him. Jn.14:15, " If you love me you will obey what I command. Vs.21 , Jesus says, " Who-ever has my commands and obeys them, he is the one who loves me."

Vs.23, Jesus says , " If anyone loves me, he will obey My teaching. My Father will love him and We will come and make our home with him." Jesus is plain about the importance of His teaching. Jn.15:14, Jesus says, "you are my friends if you do what I Command."

# JESUS COMMANDS

We will begin now to look at many of the Commands of Jesus.

Mt.26:26-28. Jesus instituted the Lord's Supper. During this final meal before Jesus is taken to be killed, Jesus breaks bread, gives thanks and gives it to His disciples. Then the COMMAND: " Take and eat; this is my body". Then he took the cup, gave thanks, and said , " Drink from it , all of you. This is my blood of the covenant which is poured out for many for the forgiveness of sins."

Matthew 28:18-20. This is the COMMAND to carry out the Commission. Because all authority now has been given to Jesus, He commands his Followers to " 1) GO 2) MAKE DISCIPLES 3) BAPTIZE 4) TEACH them to obey everything I have COMMANDED you. I will be with you till the end of the age."

Mark 1:14 , Jesus commands us to Repent and believe the good news.

Mark 10:13, Jesus commands us to let little children come to Him.

Mark 11:25, Jesus commands us to Forgive others.

Mark 12:17, Jesus commands us to give to "Caesar" what is his and give To God what is God's.

Mark 12:30, Jesus commands us to love the lord your God (Him) with all Your heart, soul, mind, and strength.

Mark 12:31, Jesus commands us to love our neighbor as ourselves.

Mark 16:15, Jesus commands us to go into all the world and preach the good News to all creation."

# THE BOOK OF LUKE

Lk.6:27, Jesus commands us to love our enemies. Do good to those who hate you.

Lk.6:28, Jesus commands us to bless those who curse you. Jesus commands us to pray for those who mistreat you.

Lk.6:31, Jesus commands us to " Do unto others as we would have them Do unto us."

Lk.6:36, Jesus commands us to be Merciful ---Note: Just as your Father is Merciful.

Lk.6:37, Jesus commands us not to Judge others. Jesus commands us not to condemn.

Lk.6:38, Jesus commands us to Give.

Lk.6:42, Jesus commands us to remove "beams" from our own eyes

Lk.10:1-4, Jesus commands us to GO into the Harvest fields.

Lk.11:2-6, Jesus commands us to pray in this Manner.

Lk.12:22, Jesus commands us NOT to worry about physical things.

Lk.12:31, Jesus commands us to seek the Father's kingdom.

Lk.12:32, Jesus commands us Not to be afraid.

Lk.12:35, Jesus commands us to be dressed and ready for service And to be vigilant.

Lk.14:12-14, Jesus commands us to serve the Poor.

Lk.22:19-20, Jesus commands us to take the symbols of the bread and Wine in order to remember Him.

# THE BOOK OF JOHN

Jn.13:34, Jesus give us a New command to Love one another as I have Loved you.

Jn.15:4, Jesus commands us to Remain in Him.

Jn.15:12, Jesus commands us to Love each other as I have loved you.

Jn.15:17, Jesus command is this: Love each other.

I feel the key to understanding the Commands of Jesus is not to view Christ's teachings and sayings as "interesting " commentary to be Taken or left if one so chooses, but to view Christ's words as having The authority of Almighty God behind them. Then with this perspective They become a law to live by- the Law of Christ. ( See Gal.6:2; I Cor.9:21 and 2 Jn. 9-10 )

# THE BELIEVERS' UNBELIEF

Why is it that Christians will sin at various times knowing full well that what they are doing is sin? When we know Who we are in Jesus and that He lives in us by the Spirit we are motivated by this belief and His Grace to live our life and behave in accordance with this belief. But, sometimes the wheels run off and our belief system fails us and we fail at those times to see WHO we are in Jesus. It isn't just a matter of a lack of faith, but a temporary lapse into unbelief. I think another word we may use would be 'doubt'.

When Peter was called out of the boat during the storm in Matthew chapter 14 and he focused on Jesus he was able to walk on the water. But, when he 'doubted', took his eyes off of Jesus and suffered from his unbelief, he began to sink in the water. Jesus said to him, "Ye of little faith". Our faith is fragile. Even our belief system is fragile. Peter was looking at Jesus and **walking on water,** yet at that instant his faith wavered and doubt and unbelief took over. Jesus still reached out and saved him from drowning even in spite of his unbelief.

In Mark chapter 9 a man in the crowd around Jesus had asked Jesus' disciples to drive out the demon spirit from his son but they could not. He then asks Jesus to do so, " If you can," he said. Jesus tells him " everything is possible to him who believes." The man exclaims in vs. 24 , " I do believe, help me overcome my **unbelief.**"

In John 20, Thomas, one of the twelve disciples, is another example of one who had been **with** Jesus and yet until he could put his finger into the holes where the nails were in Jesus' hands he would not believe. Jesus tells him in vs. 27 to,"stop **doubting and believe.**" " Stop suffering from your unbelief."

Some days we Christians are on a "sugar sweet" high when it comes to belief. We are in tune with the Triune God. We are connected in heartfelt worship and communion. We believe Who we are in Jesus and we behave like it. But when we fail to see Who we are in Jesus and suffer from momentary **unbelief,** we do those things that are not consistent with Who we really are in Jesus. Paul faced the same dilemma in Romans Chapter 7. It wasn't that he lacked faith, it was at times when he failed to see himself as Who he was in Jesus that his unbelief took over and he sinned. How human Paul was!

It would be nice, indeed, if we never faltered in our belief. Jesus never does. But we are still human—haven't you noticed?—and we do. But even when we do God is still faithful as Romans 3:3 tells us. " Will our lack of faithfulness nullify God's faithfulness? Not at all. Let every man be a liar and God be true." God is good all the time even when we are not.

We are going to have days of doubt, lack of faith, and unbelief. But Jesus is always there to "cover" for us. He is **always** faithful and believing—even **for** us! Our belief does not save us or make God's plan work. His plan has **already worked** in Jesus. Our belief allows us to see where we have already been placed in God's eternal plan. Our belief allows us to experience the "abundant life" Jesus brought in John 10--Now and forever. Belief is the **only** requirement God places on us and even then we occasionally lack in belief and we suffer the consequences. Oh, Lord, I believe, help my unbelief!

And, oh yes, thank you, Jesus!
AMEN

# THE "BEST" NEWS YOU WILL EVER HEAR !

## ( It's a DONE Deal ! )

Did you know God loved **YOU** and chose **YOU** to be **ADOPTED** into His life from before the foundation of the world? **Ephesians 1:3-14.** Jesus was slain from before the foundation of the world for **YOU. Revelation 13:8.** God has never held your sins against you! **II Corinthians 5:19.** Jesus was made sin **for** us. **II Corinthians 5:21.** Jesus tasted our death FOR us. **Hebrews 2:9.** In Adam all humanity died but in Jesus the same **ALL** have been made alive. **I Corinthians 15:22-23.** Spiritually speaking, in effect Jesus 'undid' what Adam did! However, in the age of man, humanity must live life out in the fallenness of Adam with all kinds of misery and suffering and death.

The great Triune God simply loves **YOU** and His creation. Whatever was brought on by Satan and sin was overcome and reconciled in Jesus Christ. **Colossians 1:20.** The Great Rescue, the Great Price, The Great Sacrifice, The Great Debt, were paid by Jesus Christ!

Jesus lives in His creation. **Colossians 1:17.** He lives in **ALL** humans giving them life. **See Acts 17:28.** Jesus says in **John 14:20,** "in that day, sooner or later, you will know that I am in my Father, and **you** in me and me IN **you.**" You have always **belonged** to the Father. **You** are His child—the child He always **wanted!** Jesus has done everything needed giving you eternal life with Him and the Father...**NOW.** Jesus came to seek and to save what was lost. And He did!!! **Luke 19:10; John 19:30** .**YOU ARE INLUDED!**

What Jesus asks of you is to **BELIEVE** the **BEST NEWS YOU WILL EVER HEAR!** ( **I Timothy 4:10** ). You are Loved, Adopted and Included in the life of the Eternal God.

For more information on TRINITARIAN AND INCARNATIONAL THEOLOGY ( the Theology expressed by **Karl Barth, Tom Torrance and Paul Young in THE SHACK,** check out our articles and the interview with Paul Young, author of **THE SHACK,** at our web site: www.newlifewcg.org. Contact us at: info@newlifewcg.org

# THE CHRISTIAN'S HOPE

One may hear from a Christian, " I hope I make it. Or, I hope I am saved. Or, I hope I go to heaven when I die." What the person is saying is that they have positive optimism that these things will be so for them upon death. But Christian Hope is different than the normal hope one would have in hoping for a pay raise; or hoping that they would be promoted on their job. Or hoping that their favorite relative would come and visit them.

hopes may or may not actually occur. They are question marks as to whether they will happen.

Christian hope is very different than these aforementioned 'hopes'. Hope for the Christian is fully accomplished in Jesus Christ. Scripture tells us in I Timothy 1:1, that

"Jesus **is** our hope." Actually Jesus is our EVERYTHING. Hope for the Christian is a done deal. What Jesus has received for himself He has also received for us as well. We are crucified with Him, (Galatians 2:20), we are buried with Him, ( Romans 6:1-4), we are resurrected with Him, (Colossians 3:1), and we have been seated with Him at the right hand of the Father. ( Ephesians 2:6).

The life we now have is the life of Jesus. He is our life. ( Colossians 3:4). His future is assured and so is ours. Hope for the Christian is not some **potential** good occurrence happening in our life. It is a present reality in Jesus. It will be fully revealed to us and experienced by us in the life of God in the Kingdom of God. Our Hope is our eternal future reserved in heaven for us by the power of Almighty God. (I Peter 1:3-5). Our hope carries the full assurance of God by His Power to make it happen eternally for us IN Christ.

How can it be any other way? Our future does not in any way depend upon us to make it happen. It does not depend on our goodness, our success or failure as Christians, our works or lack of works. It depends on JESUS CHRIST. And, He has already accomplished all that is needed for us to enjoy the eternal relationship with Him and the Father and Holy Spirit FOREVER.

In our human vanity we sometimes feel like we have to do **something** or achieve something more in our spiritual walk to "make it so" for ourselves. But the truth is that Jesus has already **made it so** for everyone. The thing which will allow us to experience it forever is simply to believe who Jesus has made us to be in Him. He chose us from before the foundation of the world. ( Ephesians 1:3-14). We belong to Him. Can we believe this? By believing it we can experience the "HOPE THAT LIES WITHIN US" which is in us through Jesus Christ living in us—"The Hope of Glory". ( Colossians 1:26-27).

# THE GOSPEL FOR CHILDREN

## ( SO SIMPLE A LITTLE CHLD CAN UNDERSTAND )

"Hey kids, so you want to hear the Gospel of Jesus Christ, do ya?" Well here goes!

Your and my heavenly Father decided a long time ago that He wanted to add children to His life. He had always lived as Father, Son, and Holy Spirit, the Holy Trinity. His life was so wonderful that He decided to share that life with offspring so He decided to make children and give them life inside His unending life. He made the first man and woman, Adam and Eve, and wanted them to begin a human family that would have in time millions and millions of offspring for God to call His children.

Adam and Eve did not do what God asked them to do and brought misery and suffering and death on themselves and all of their children. But God had a really great solution to this problem. He sent His only begotten son, Jesus Christ, to "undo" what Adam did. Jesus would take all of the blame and sins of everybody on Himself and clear the name of all human beings so they could live with Him and the Father forever. Jesus bought and paid for the entire creation with His blood—His life. Now Jesus just wants everyone to know He loves them and did this for them and even lives His very life INSIDE of everybody on the earth. We are all His offspring, His children.

So what God decided to do in the very beginning, Jesus made happen through His life, death, resurrection, and ascension back to the Father. And, He has made arrangements to have all of us sit ( a place of honor) next to Him at His Father's side in heaven.

Our heavenly Father is such a great Dad, that He thought up every possible good gift and good blessing He could and gave them all to all of us in Jesus. Many of those blessings we will just have to wait to receive until we get to live forever in His presence in the next life. We know it will be fun and pleasant because His book says so!

What I am telling you here is what our Father and Jesus Christ want everyone to know. Once they know it they can believe it and then behave and live a full life. This is called the Gospel, or the Good News God wants all to know.

There is much evil and bad going on in the world today because we all live in the nature we got from Adam. But that is going to change one day. The time is coming when we will all live in a place where only good and fun and healthy and righteous and pure and lovely and happy things exist. Won't that be great. We have a great Dad in Heaven who says this is what He is going to do for all of His children. But there is one thing we need to do. And that is, BELIEVE. Jesus has made it all so. Jesus is GOD! He has ALL power in Heaven and on earth to make it so and He has. His love for all of us is that big. He has a wonderful life and He has put you in it to enjoy. God is Good, All the time. Believe it. It may sound too good to be true and that is how God wants it to appear. He is that GOOD. So just believe it. It is true. Jesus is True. You are the child He always wanted. Believe it.


# THE GOSPEL IS ADOPTION BY GOD


A "Neo-Reformation" is happening around the world. It pushes the envelope of Grace. It is taking place in Madison at Newlife Christian Fellowship at Dublin Park Recreation Center. It is Christo-centric Theology. It does NOT teach that God our Father is distant or disconnected and separated from us and that we somehow must "accept" Jesus into our life to get to God. Jesus has accepted us into His life. It does NOT teach that we need to or must "get saved". Jesus has done that already for us. God is not eager to send us to Hell, but has gone there for ALL of us.

This ADOPTION and INCLUSION Theology extols The Triune God's LOVE for creation. He purposed to create human beings and ADOPT them into His life before physical creation itself. (Ephesians 1:3-14). To take care of the Sin Problem Jesus was slain before the foundation of the world. (Revelation 13:8). Jesus' sacrifice applied to ALL sin for everyone. (I John 2:2; Romans 6:18; II Corinthians 5:14-15; John 3:16-17). In the fallenness of Adam All humans died. But in Jesus Christ the same All are reconciled and made alive IN Jesus. (Colossians 1:19-20; I Corinthians 15:22-23). Jesus lives in ALL humanity. (John 14:20; John 17:20-26; Acts 17:28).

The Gospel is GOOD NEWS for everyone! Jesus DIED for everyone!. (II Cor. 5:14-15). Jesus came to this earth to connect humanity to the Father by the Spirit. He did so by His life, death, resurrection and ascension to the Father's right hand—AND—He took everyone WITH Him. ( Ephesians 2:6). This objective reality will be seen subjectively one day when we awake just as Jesus IS. ( I John 3:2; Psalm 17:15).

Early church leaders including Irenaeus and Athanasius and later Theologians Karl Barth, Tom Torrance, J.B. Torrance, Michael Jinkins, Colin Gunton, Gary Deddo, C. Baxter Kruger and many others held/ hold this understanding. It says God LOVES His children. That All are redeemed and reconciled in Jesus Christ. All have been SAVED ALREADY and should know it and believe it.

The key factor for humans to experience this wonderful salvation and abundant life with God forever is to, in Jesus' own words, " BELIEVE IT". We all already belong to God since before creation. ( Ephesians 1). It has all been completed and finished in Jesus Christ who was the "Vicarious" human for all mankind. ( John 19:30). In Jesus we are all loved, accepted, forgiven, redeemed, reconciled, crucified, resurrected, ascended, and seated at the right hand of the Father WITH Jesus! Sin and Satan have been defeated. Our life with the Triune God is assured in and by Jesus Forever!

Our part is to believe and accept what Jesus has done TO and FOR us THROUGH Himself by the Spirit. He loves us and wants to be with us forever. With this truth there is no more fear.

This Neo-Reformation will be the greatest movement of the Third Millennium. It sounds too good to be true. And, it makes no difference whether we believe it or not to make it so. It is so! YOU are loved by the Father as the child He always wanted.

# THE PAROUSIA OF JESUS

It is amazing how we ( I ) have over looked some rather profound meaning in such simple Bible accounts such as the one I want to look at here. The raising of Lazarus.

When we can understand what Jesus is saying to Martha in this story, it helps us to better understand what Paul is saying in a number of places in his epistles. Since I ASSUME that all of you reading this have a bible, I will not read the entire account of Jesus raising Lazarus here, but will refer you to the story in John 11:1-44. (Please read this here.)

I will make the point that I wish to make concerning the fact that Lazarus is dead, and Martha makes the comment that she is aware that he will rise in resurrection at the last day. ( vs. 23-24).

Now for the very interesting truth Jesus informs Martha here in vs. 25. Jesus is aware of her referring to the future resurrection at the last day, but Jesus makes a powerful statement when He says, " I am the resurrection and the life." NOW.!!! In other words, You don' have to wait until the Last Day, I'm IT! " He who believes in me will live (NOW), even though he dies. And whoever lives and believes in me will never die, ( I am the resurrection and the life—NOW. Do you believe this?" In other words what Jesus is saying is this, " You LIVE in resurrection—NOW." " You LIVE in me, my Life, NOW." " You who live and believe, live in ETERNAL life-NOW.

Robert Capon, in his book, KINGDOM, GRACE, JUDGEMENT, phrases it like this to explain the ever presentness of Jesus' Salvation works. He says that, " Christ is the Eternal Contemporary of every moment of time." He then relates the Greek word, "Parousia" as meaning simply PRESENCE. ( Traditional Christian interpretation of Parousia has mainly referred to Jesus' Second coming, " His coming back to be in our presence." But it means much more than that. ) Jesus is present in every moment of time.

Therefore He is always the Resurrection and the Life. Past, Present, and Future. There is never a time when He is not. He is…..." I AM".

With this in mind, we can look at a few statements Paul makes and hopefully better understand.

Rom. 6:1-4 The presentness ( parousia ) of Jesus' death we share in through baptism,

As well as the presentness of His Resurrection we live in His resurrection

And share in His resurrected life and New Birth. It is all present for us.!

Col.3:1-4 "…for you died, and your life is…NOW….hidden with Christ in God. When Christ , who IS your LIFE appears, then you also will appear with Him in glory---why, because you are in that GLORIFIED reality NOW.

Rom.8:30. This is speaking of the presentness Jesus is in.

Eph.2:6 "And God raised us up with Christ and seated us WITH Him in the Heavenly realms in Christ Jesus" Presentness again—for All time.

Capon describes this reality on page 410 of his book.

Acts 17:28 makes sense and really is True. " For in Him we live, and move, and have Our being!"

Col.3:4 He really IS our LIFE…NOW and FOREVER. We exist IN Him. Praise God.!!!

God is WITH us. Emmanuel. And WITHIN us.

Jesus is our ALL in ALL !!!

Jesus is our EVERYTHING!!!

One last comment. We who are alive physically now are waiting to LITERALLY die. And be LITERALLY resurrected . But, in Jesus we are already dead and alive in Jesus' resurrection. Can we wrap our hearts and minds around that!! WOW. !!!

AMEN and again I say, AMEN.!!!

# THE RESURRECTED BODY

In Christ's resurrection there are a couple of dynamics which are often over-looked. These have major implications for our own resurrection. There has been much speculation over the ages as to what kind of 'body' Jesus had when He was resurrected. Let's notice a few scriptures which have impact on us.

In John 20:26-27, Jesus appears to the disciples in **bodily** form in the same body He had had but now of flesh and bone. He invites Thomas to handle Him by touching Him and putting his fingers in the holes from the crucifixion. Jesus is making a demonstration for a reason to display His human flesh and bone **body** to all of the disciples.

In Luke 24:33-42, Jesus appears to the disciples and invites them to touch Him and to look at His hands and feet and tells them He has **flesh and bones,** not ghostlike. Then He purposefully asks them for something to eat, NOT because He was hungry, but to demonstrate the fact that one resurrected with a body of flesh and bones can eat!!! Jesus wants all to understand His continuing humanity in a **body** capable of doing physical things.

In Matthew 26:29, Jesus had told the disciples that He would drink of the fruit of the vine with them in His Father's Kingdom.

When Stephen was being stoned ( Acts 7:55-56) he looks up into the heavens and sees the **bodily human form** of Jesus STANDING at the Father's right hand. I would say, "Cheering him on !!!"

Paul further states that Christ is "seated at the right hand of God" in Colossians 3:1 and in Ephesians 1:20.

We can see in these passages clearly that Jesus has a **body.** That He sits, stands, eats, and will drink of the fruit of the vine in His Father's Kingdom. In other words, HE CAN AND WILL **PARTY!** This all has implications for all of us as we shall see.

David had said in Psalm 17:15 that we would arise with His **likeness.** Later in I John 3:1-2, John writes that " when He appears we shall see Him as He is and we will be **like** Him."

**VIP:** Now when we read I Corinthians 15:35-57, we should be more keenly aware of just what kind of body we will have in the Father's Kingdom. This whole section deals with the kind of **body** we shall have in resurrection. ( Just read this passage for yourself.) Lastly, in Romans 8:11, Paul speaks of our mortal bodies being quickened or given life through His spirit who lives in you.

Things to note:

It is OUR **body** now raised incorruptible and imperishable, a spiritual body.

It is raised immortal in honor, power and glory.

We shall bear the **likeness** of the man from heaven--Jesus. I Co.15:49;

I Tim.2:5—" The MAN Jesus Christ.

It is a human body that **looks** like us. Yet spiritual ( I Cor. 15:44)

It has **flesh** and **bones.**

It can **eat** and **drink.**

It can **sit** or **stand** or **walk** or **run.**

NOTE: Jesus still has His human body which is now spiritual. The fullness of God STILL dwells bodily in Jesus. Jesus STILL remains the SON of the Holy Trinity but now and forever retains His humanity with His spiritual body which **LOOKS** physical and NOT limited physically. ( This could get confusing ☺ )

170

It will be ready for any kind of **PARTY** the Father wants to throw! And never get tired! ☺

My Personal speculation.

Since the resurrected human body can do these things listed above, it makes sense to me that it possibly could play golf, fish, swim, run, dance, and any number of other things humans do. What think ye? Wild Huh? ☺

God is Good. So let's wait and see just HOW GOOD !!!

Can I get an **AMEN** ?

# THE TRUTH OF GOD MAY NOT BE WHAT YOU'VE HEARD

The Truth is not what you may have heard!!

Religion has a concept of Reward and Punishment for doing good and doing bad. God is pictured as an angry judge waiting to hit the gavel of judgement sending sinners to an eternal torment in the flames of hell, or burning unrepentant sinners up in a horrific Ghenna fire. Jesus is pictured as coming to see if there might be some who would accept His sacrifice on their behalf thus gaining salvation and eternal life in heaven for them. Religion is seen as some kind of game or contest between God and the Devil. A GREAT CONTROVERSY if you will. Maybe God wins, maybe the Devil wins. Who knows for sure? The souls of men are at stake.

Rather than debate this subject, we will just cut to the chase and state what God did originally. THE VICTORY HAS BEEN WON!!!!!!!!!!!

Always existing, Father, Son, and Holy Spirit, Triune God decided to share His wonderful love with a creation and include humans in His life. From before the foundation of the world this was so. Ephesians 1, tells us that we were chosen in Jesus Christ Before the foundation of the world and ADOPTED into the Life of the Father, Son, and Holy Spirit. Romans 8:15-16 echoes this adoption fact for us.

God's life has been and is in ALL humans since the creation of man. All mankind has been included and adopted into the life of God by God for God. God planned and declared it this way from the very start of creation.

This was the PLAN from the beginning and would have been carried out in the Word incarnate—Jesus—even if man had never sinned in the first place.

BUT, man, Adam, did sin. Jesus then had to Redeem man back to God by forgiving man's sins and securing continued SALVATION for man IN and BY and FOR Jesus Christ. Any way it all went, God had it "covered" so that His Eternal Purpose would NOT be thwarted. God guaranteed His Victory over His Plan—and that VICTORY is in Jesus Christ.

People have been misled so successfully by religion in the past feeling that they are unloved by God, unworthy, and unsaved that they have FELT LOST, when in actual fact they have not been lost at all but ADOPTED AND SAVED in Jesus Christ all along. Their wrong perspective is because they have not KNOWN that they were the adopted children of the Father in the Son by the Spirit.!!! So people live in constant feelings of lostness, hiding, and fear ( Fear is the opposite of Love) by NOT knowing WHO they are!

The Gospel of Jesus Christ is NOT about trying to get people saved and therefore keep them from "going to Hell", but the True Gospel , the GOOD NEWS, is that God loved the creation, the world, Humanity so much that He just simply INCARNATED HIMSELF in His creation, ADOPTED mankind, and took care of the sin problem by the shed blood of Jesus, raised all mankind up with Jesus in His resurrection, and seated humanity WITH Jesus Christ IN the HEAVENLY REALMS. Even if we don't see this presently as a reality, God does and that is what counts. ( Ephesians 2:6).

Does this mean that EVERYONE will experience the Joys of Heaven in the Party of Heaven? NO. Why? Because some will NOT believe it. Hard to believe that some will not accept the gracious life God offers, but scripture shows that some few apparently will not. They will just be on the outside looking in while everyone else enjoys the "Pleasures at God's right hand forevermore."—Psalm 16:11. But, even here God will not give up trying to encourage those outside the party to come in. God is Good and they are His children too. See: Romans 8:38. This is POWERFUL.

The bottom line of Adoption and Salvation is that GOD HAS TAKEN CARE OF EVERYTHING ALREADY. EVERYTHING. Can we understand this simplicity? Moreover, can we Believe it?

Does it sound too simple? Does it sound too easy? Where is the Justice and punishment for all those "bad" people who are doing bad things and sinning with impunity? Did God and Jesus Christ take care of those situations too?

Answer: YES. And you and I can be thankful God did.

John 3:16-17…God loved the world. It was NEVER His intent to condemn and destroy the world, but to SAVE IT. Praise God, He did just that!!!

# THE TRUTH SHALL SET YOU FREE

John 8:31-32, tells us that, " you shall know the truth and the truth shall set you free." But, many, if not most, Christians do not feel free. They are burdened with thoughts that they "must" do something churchy, or religious, or righteous, or Christlike in order to be free. They must go to church, pray, forgive, tithe, and study scripture in order to be free. This is their way of knowing the truth and being set free by it. Deep in their soul they always feel there is something more they can "do" to be 'really' free. They feel unassured and insecure in their spiritual existence and future. Are they free?

All humans have been imprisoned by the fall of Adam. We have been condemned and sentenced to death by what we have inherited from Adam.( I Corinthians 15:22). Much of our human existence lived out in our fallenness from Adam and the fall is filled with misery, suffering and pain. Continually we are bombarded with thoughts of sin and evil and worthlessness. ( Ephesians 6).

Knowing the truth that is in Jesus and knowing **WHO** we are in Jesus and knowing Jesus has righted all the wrongs we experience in our fallenness-- all this is called **The Truth**-- are freeing indeed!

Jesus has taken care of everything **for** us. We exist **in** Him.( Colossians 1:17; Acts 17:28). He is our life.( Colossians 3:4). Our old man, or woman, is dead. We live in a new life. A newness of life. And that life is **in** Jesus. We are set free from sin and death. We are raised with Christ. ( Romans 6:1-4). We are seated at the right hand of the Father with Christ. ( Ephesians 2:6).

Jesus has taken us from our family inheritance in Adam, which is death, to our heavenly inheritance in Jesus which is life. Sin and death no longer have any claim on us. Through belief we have passed from condemnation and death into Life. ( John 5:24). We are not on spiritual "probation", not "paroled", but we are **eternally Pardoned!** We have been set free. It has all done been done by Jesus because he loves each one of us dearly as His child.

So Jesus just tells us to rest in Him. Glory in Him. He has done it all, paid it all, secured it all, attained it all, blessed us all and assured it all in Himself for us. Live in the freedom He has blessed us with. Rest in faith. There is no more condemnation for any of us. There is no more prison. No more captivity. Rest and enjoy the freedom Jesus has given to us all.

Believe this fantastic **GOOD NEWS.**

# THE TWO DYNAMICS

If we are going to understand certain scriptures and how they apply to us individually then we need to understand what we will call here "the two dynamics" that are currently present in all of our Christian lives. The two are what is literally fact in our present physical life what is reality in God's perspective.

We view all things from an inside of time and space perspective. Or, we look at everything from a linear time frame of reference. So we use terms such as this or that happened yesterday , or last year, or 5000 years ago. Or we look at a biblical concept as something that may happen in the future -days or years from the present. We would say that we will die someday. And we will literally. We will be resurrected someday. We will ascend to the right hand of God someday. We look at everything in a linear time perspective.

God is different. Not only is he In linear time and space, He is also Outside of time and space. Since He is outside of time and space He sees everything within time and space presently. In other words, He sees the end from the beginning. He sees everything in the PRESENT.

When Jesus tells Martha in John 11:25, that He is the resurrection and the life, He means He is the resurrection and the life Now.! He always has been the resurrection and the life. He was when He told Martha, He is today, and He will be tomorrow. Jesus, to put it in Robert Capon's terminology, " The Eternal Contemporary of every moment of time."

Jesus just uses the term, " I AM". There is never a time when He is not the "I AM".

God looks at things from His perspective and makes declarative statements not based on our perspective or understanding of time and space, or linear time. For example, when Paul says in Romans 8 that we have been predestined, called, justified, and glorified, he is stating this as a present reality—from God's perspective. When Paul says in Ephesians 2:6, that we have been raised with Christ and seated with Him in Heavenly realms, he states this with a present reality, not something that is going to happen to us in the future. We will, however, put on a new "body" in God's plan, but we will continue to be seated with Christ even then at that time.

Again, when Paul says that he is crucified with Christ, that he died, that the old man is dead, that we died with Christ, that Christ lives in us now, that our life is hidden with Christ in God, these are all present realities. (Col.3:1-4) . God plainly says that we are DEAD, that the old self is dead. That we died with Christ. It is hard for us to believe since we are still breathing! We have a new life now, and that life in Jesus' life living in us and generating new life in us which will last forever. We are presently born again in Christ. We presently have new birth in Christ. We are new creations in Christ. We are resurrected in Christ's resurrection...Now.

We can say that God looks at things from a completed standpoint. A spiritual reality perspective. The one who declares the end from the beginning. God is the one who not only can bring things about but does bring things about in accordance with His will.

The two dynamics playing out in our lives right now cause confusion for us because we only see things from OUR perspective. We have to trust God for seeing things from His perspective.( Isa.55) As far as God is concerned, this is all a DONE DEAL. He is the one who has DONE THE DEAL. He is the one on whom it all depends. Not us. It is good that we can understand biblical, spiritual, and theological concepts. But understanding them is not a requirement for all of it to be applicable to us and for us. Remember, God is the Author and Finisher of our Faith. It all rests with Him.

Understanding these concepts for most of us requires a change in paradigms. We process new information often times through the understanding, or misunderstanding, of old doctrines or old theologies. We try to mix the new wine with the old. We try to interpret the new with the old misunderstandings which we may believe to be correct. We have to admit that we all have been affected by bad theology to some degree in the past.

What a joyous ride we are on in seeing the LIGHT shine ever brighter and brighter in our hearts. We need to remember this, We have Everything in Jesus that we ever will have, and we have it NOW.

# THE ULTIMATE FUTURE

Paul Kurts

Gen.1 In the Beginning/ or in Starting, God created the heavens and the earth (Universe)

( Sin entered creation thru Satan—Isa 14 and Ez. 28

God creates Adam and Eve on the 6$^{th}$ day of Gen. 2 and places them in the middle of the Garden of Eden with the instruction not to eat of the tree in the middle of the garden, the tree of the Knowledge of Good and Evil.

Gen. 3 They both disobey God's simplest test and eat. They bring the death sentence on themselves and all of their descendents. (I Co.15:22 ). Paul calls our body a body of death in Rom. 7:24 and asks WHO will rescue him from it.

Paul further shows that death is an enemy, the last enemy to be destroyed. I Co. 15:26.

Death is a MONUMENTAL ENEMY. And, God had a plan to deal with it thru Jesus Christ. I Co.15:21-23. In Christ , all shall be made alive.

Jn.11:21-26, Jesus, " I am the Resurrection and the life."

Jn. 14:6 Jesus, " I am the Way, the Truth, and the Life."

I Jn.5:12 "He that has the Son has life, he who does not have the Son, does not!"

Ga. 2:20 " Our new life is in Jesus Christ, the old self is dead and burried.

The "formula for us humans is to repent and accept Christ as savior in order to have a part in all of the future God has in store for His Children. See Acts 3:19-21 This Restoration is started at the Return of Jesus but continues until the New Heavens and New Earth of Revelation 21 are completed.

II Pt.3:7-13 The New Heavens and New Earth where in righteousness dwells. Satan is gone into final restraint.

Back to Rev. 21. The Old Order has passed away in vs.4 and God says "I am making ALL things NEW" in vs. 5.

At Gen.1:1 and after Rev.21:5 Righteousness will fill all of creation.

I Co. 2:9 No human description can picture what God has in store for his children.

Ps. 16:11 Pleasure will be at God's right hand forever and ever.

Conclusion: From Gen.1:2 to Rev.21:5 describes the old order . The order was established to be DONE AWAY and allow all in Jesus, the redeemed, to live into the New Order which will be defined by Righteousness in God's Eternal Kingdom Forever.

Jesus is the only Way into this beautiful , newly created Heaven and Earth.

# THE "WAGES OF SIN" AND THE "GIFT OF GOD"

Romans 6:23 is cited by most as demonstrating the fact of a person's individual sins resulting in death and then offering the gift of God to the individual for eternal life. It is reasoned that the individual is in sins and sinful and with the proper repentance then the gift of God or eternal life is then given through Jesus Christ.

But, is this what this verse is really saying. First off, it does not say the wages of a "person's sins" are death; it says the wages of SIN, all sin, is death. That death is death for ALL humans due to the sin of the first Adam. ( I Cor. 15:22 ). The condition of death is the state all humans have found themselves in since the first Adam. The next part of the verse 23 is not an invitation to individuals to come to Jesus and accept Him into one's life and thereby receive the gift of God which is eternal life. But, it is a declaration of God, that although death was brought upon all through sin entering the human race through Adam, that the gift of God which is eternal life through Jesus Christ replaces the death sentence which was upon all. I Corinthians 15:22, " as in Adam ALL die, in Christ ALL are made alive" —not just physically alive since they already are that but eternally alive through Jesus Christ.

The whole purpose of the sacrifice of Jesus Christ is so that all sin of all time would be paid for by His precious blood of Redemption. Through this act of sacrifice all things in heaven and in earth, humans and the whole cosmos are Reconciled in Jesus Christ. In effect what we see happening is that what Satan, Sin and Adam did were UNDONE in Jesus Christ as ALL things were RECONCILED in Jesus. ( Colossians 1:19-22).

This act of Jesus' Reconciliation applies to all human beings who the scriptures call "The Elect". ( Rev.13:8). When we look at Ephesians 1:1-14, we see that Triune God purposed this election and adoption in Jesus Christ before the foundation, or creation, of the world. John 3:16 tells us that "God so loved the world"—the elect—all humanity—everyone "that He sent His only begotten son" to make all the provisions and THE SACRIFICE to seal the deal for God. For us it is matter of Belief.

Man never had a say in this plan. The plan was a done deal in Jesus Christ before man was ever created. We all were adopted and included in the life of Triune God --through Jesus by the Spirit -- before we were even born of our physical mothers. We were "born from above" before we were " born from below"! Here is the "mathematical" equation of sin and salvation.

Satan+Adam+Sin=DEATH

+ JESUS CHRIST = ETERNAL LIFE

The plan stands completed in Jesus Christ. It is Finished. Triune God is Victorious.

The Father's Power will continue to see this plan fulfilled in Jesus for ALL.(I Pet.1:3-5).


# THE "WHAT IF" FAITH


You are a child of God! What if you embraced a faith that did not allow for your Father in heaven to 'punish' any of His children for their lack of performance as followers? What if it had no set of confining rules and regulations or laws for you to adhere? What if it had no concept of a fire-breathing 'hell' fire of torture and punishment for anyone? What if it proclaimed that ALL humanity was loved and chosen by the Father in Jesus even before the creation of the world? What if it taught that ALL were the elect and therefore saved by Jesus Christ and were raised to the Father in Jesus in His resurrection and ascension?

What if God were so unconditionally loving that He respected no one or preferred no one over another and secured everyone's eternal existence through Jesus making it happen for all? What if all sin of all time of all people was totally taken care of by Jesus and His blood.

What if there were no buildings, no pews, no candles, no robes, no pulpits, no liturgy, no formalities, and no requirements to embrace your faith?

What if life not only with the Triune God forever but INSIDE the very life of God forever was celebrated for all of God's children.

What if humans who were not Christians or people who met untimely deaths and children and infants who died as little babies were NOT consigned to some indefinable place but were also taken to the Father's side and included in the eternal life of the Triune God just like Christians?

What if your Father realized that the only way He could count on His plan working out was to "do it Himself" in JESUS as the vicarious man for all ?

If you saw all these evidences in your faith you would be seeing the faith that was once delivered to the saints. You would see the faith of Jesus. You would see the faith of the early church for the first 500 years of its existence. By Grace you would see the Truth of God expressed through Jesus.

# WORSHIPPING GOD AS THE PAGANS DID
## ?

In Deuteronomy 12:29-32, God said not to worship Him the way the pagans worshipped their gods. True enough. Fundamentalists have used this scripture for years to uphold whatever aberrant "truth" they may hold to in order to stand alone as the sole beacon of light on said subject.

When the LORD made this statement in Deuteronomy 12 it was at a time when He was bringing the Israelites into pagan lands where they would set up His way of life based on His 613 rules and regulations— laws. These Israelites would be replacing people who practiced every conceivable manner of wickedness involving their "worship" of their gods imaginable. Much of their worship included indiscriminate sex worship of the pagan gods. He lists various things in a few scriptures near. Dt.14:1,

" don't CUT yourselves or shave the front of your heads—resembling a male organ". Dt. 18:10, " don't sacrifice your children in FIRE , or seek DIVINATION, or, SORCERY, or, INTERPRETERS OF OMENS, or , engage in WITCHCRAFT, or, CAST SPELLS, or, seek a SPIRITIST, or , one who CONSULTS THE DEAD. God wanted Israel to be separate from these practices and gave them the law which would do this. The heathen's superstitious practices could not be included in this God given new way of life.

In John 4:21-24, Jesus talks with the Samaritan woman at the well and tells her that her past forms of worship and even what was practiced in Jerusalem would pass and indeed had passed as correct ways to worship God. Jesus clearly says that not the physical or superstitious practices would be acceptable, but that true worshippers would worship God in "Spirit and in Truth."

What Jesus is saying is that no legally formatted worship or superstitious worship would be of value. But, that worshipping God in Spirit and in Truth involved an intimate, personal RELATIONSHIP with the Father.

When we see in Colossians 1:20 that ALL things have been reconciled in Jesus Christ, all things take on new meaning for us. Activities take on new meaning. Practices take on new meaning. We see through the "eyes of faith" now. And live through the eyes of faith as well.

We obviously do many things the pagans did due to the fact that they were human and lived on this earth. Those things are not wrong for us to do! The pagans married, had children, wore rings, ate food, sang songs, played music, danced, laughed, loved art, built houses, had places of worship, kept harvest festivals, used greenery, holly berries, crosses, candles, bells and other things in their worship, and the list goes on and on. Just because the heathen or pagans did something or used something does not make it wrong for us to do or to use the exact same things!!! After all there are only so many things humans can use in our physical existence.

The Great Triune God wants us to realize who we are. We are His kids. He created us and Adopted us INTO His very life through the life, death, resurrection, and ascension of Jesus Christ. He wants us to know it and believe it and live it in RELATIONSHIP with Him.

In all honesty, however, I am sure this little paper will not convince some people that some things are still wrong for Christians to do today. I can only say that their "Spirit and Truth" has not grown to maturity just yet. But, then again, we have an eternity to grow inside of God's great love for us.

# THE WORD AND JESUS MAKE IT SO.

For us it was a long time ago. For The Great Triune God, Father, Son ( Word) and Holy Spirit, it was just like yesterday or today. Time flies when you are not limited by it.

In beginning ( not 'The' beginning), Father, Word, and Holy Spirit looked around and there wasn't anything around. It was they. And They was it. Nothing else. Nothing. They all three had been thinking the same thing when the Word spoke up and said, " Let's make a human being— man in our image." We have never been human, we don't know what it would be like, and we can experience humanity only through a human if we make one. Not only that, man, humanity can live inside of our life forever and the rest of eternity can really be unique. (Gen. 1:26-27). We will make a great Cosmos for humans to inherit some day. ( Heb.2:8). And an earth for him to live in.

We can adopt all of humanity into our life thereby bringing them into our Triune relationship forever. We will include them in our life. ( Eph.1:3-14).

The way we will do it is to send you, Word, down into man's life as a physical man with Holy Spirit as your father and Mary as your Mother. You will be both God and man. But, you have to be a baby first!!!

So far so good. But, we have a problem, 'Houston!'. Adam is going to pull a boner and fail to do what we ask him to do and this whole plan is going to jump the tract. But, we will still make it work. After all, we have all power to do anything we want, right?

Word, you are not only going to be the one to be incarnate and bring all mankind to the Father, but you are going to have to also step in and become the Atonement for humanity, redeem humanity, reconcile the cosmos and humanity, and save what became lost through Satan and Adam. " I have great confidence in you and I know you can do it." " I will be well pleased in you."

Now for the rest of the story. Word did just that. He came incarnate, sought what was lost and saved what originally started out in God's plan in a saved state originally.

Word's new human body suffered as no one ever has or will. Every day of His life was a living sacrifice for His brothers and sisters—the Children of God. Word lived a sinless life. Word suffered torture, was killed, was raised from the grave on the third day and ascended to His Father in

Heaven taking us with Him and accomplished what He set out to do originally. ( Eph.2:6).

What The Great Triune God originally planned and purposed, is now complete and completed in Word. It is final. It is finished. Word said so. (John 19:30). It is accomplished for everyone. All of Adam's descendents who inherited the death penalty from daddy Adam, are now made new and alive in Big Brother Word. Cool story. Huh? The only thing Word asks for us to do is to believe what He has done to us and for us.

Oh yes, Word has a name , a name above all names in heaven and in earth. We just simply call Him........ **JESUS.**

# TRUTH FOR BELIEVERS AND UNBELIEVERS

I want to share with you the 'Best News' you will ever hear in your life! This won't take long to read so please continue on.

The world is filled with religions of every description and so it is no wonder that many people feel no need to be connected with a particular faith group. Whether you believe in God or not what follows is still the BEST NEWS you will ever hear in your life. Believing it does not make it so or not so and whether you know it now or not you WILL know it sooner or later. So, why not now?

Here it is: God Loves YOU. He does not even want to be God forever without you! He even chose you to be His child before He created the universe. Your life with Him forever has never been a question since He made all the arrangements for you. God's only purpose in creating you was so that He could spend eternity with you!

Jesus "Qualified" all of humanity to live with God forever. Mankind became "lost" through sin (attempting to live life apart from who we really are). But Jesus came to seek and save what was lost and He did just that through His life, death, resurrection and ascension back to heaven.

You may think that you are sinful, not worthy, unacceptable, unloved, or not wanted by God. This is exactly what the Devil – the arch enemy of God and man – wants you to think!

But the truth of God is that you ARE loved, you are wanted, you DO belong to God and Jesus Christ has connected you in UNION with God now and FOREVER. The Bible makes it very clear that God is not going to let anything separate you from Him and His love for you. He has ALL the Power in Heaven and earth to ensure it all happening just the way He planned it originally. The question is, "WILL YOU BELIEVE IT and begin experiencing it?"

# TRUTH FOR BELIEVERS AND THE "UNPARDONABLE SIN" WHAT IS IT ?

The "UNPARDONABLE SIN". What is it? Jesus said that all sin is forgiven and even blasphemy is forgiven.. He says that one who blasphemes against the Holy Spirit will not be forgiven in this life or the **next.** The account is found in three places, none of which use the term 'unpardonable sin." They are, Matthew 12:31-32; Luke 12:10; Mark 3:28-29.

To answer this question we need to look at a few of the scriptures which state that ALL sins are forgiven in Jesus Christ. I John 2:2, states that Jesus is the propitiation or payment for all of the sins of the world. None excluded. All included. I John 1:7, says that the blood of Christ cleanses us from ALL sin. There are numerous other verses which say the same thing. For brevity's sake we will stop with these.

Jesus' sacrifice was in effect from before the foundation of the world. Revelation 13:8;

I Peter 1:20. Humanity was chosen and adopted in Christ before the foundation of the world. Ephesians 1:3-14. Jesus came to seek and to save what was lost and He did. Luke 19:10. The sin problem and question has been laid to rest in Jesus Christ.

A person is forgiven in Christ whether he or she knows it or not. Man does not have to "know " it to make it so anymore than one must know that Jesus lived and died and became the saviour of the world to make that so. It is so. And it is so for everyone.

God is not going to 'force' anyone to believe what He has done for them. Man can continually reject belief in Christ not only in this life, but in the life to come. For man to **experience** the abundant life in Jesus he must believe **WHO** God has made him in Jesus from the very beginning.

According to John, man loves darkness more than light. Some people just refuse to come to the Light for Life. Blaspheming the Holy Spirit is not a particular individual sin per se, but it is a continual denying the work of the Holy Spirit in one's life and who they are in Jesus. It is an on going process. And, as long as it goes on or continues the person is not able to experience the abundant life Jesus holds out for them. And, this can continue on and on, and theoretically could go on forever. If that were to happen, then the person's lack of experiencing the party of Heaven and their being alienated from God would leave them in the perishing condition the **same as being unforgiven.** The experience would be the same. But, They simply **are** forgiven like everyone else.

There is no way the Triune God can pour out His blessings and benefits eternally on an individual if that person rejects and refuses to believe what God has ALREADY done to them, for them, and in them through Jesus Christ.

The point is that it is their **choice** whether or not they want to live and experience the abundant life IN Christ, or to continue alienated from God through UNBELIEF.

# WALKING IN THE FLESH AND SPIRIT

We as Christians live in the fallenness of Adam. We live with sin within by our very nature. Sin dwells in our flesh and humanity. There is no escaping this fact. We exercise all the pulls of the flesh so often giving in to these base impulses. And we are Christians.

The Apostle Paul faced this war of the flesh and the Spirit articulated in Romans chapter 7. It makes one wonder just 'how' fleshly, physical, carnal and human Paul really was. In facing this dilemma Paul was honest in admitting his 'evil concupiscence ' that welled up inside of him. Although he did not want to do or think or perform sinful and evil actions at times he simply did. And, when confronted with things he should have done he did not do those things as he wished he could. Sound familiar? So what was and is the answer? You and I face these same conflicting circumstances in our daily Christian lives just as Paul did.

Paul, like all of us, admitted that sin dwells in all of us from our ancestry from fallen Adam. And with that nature we not only sin, we **want** to sin. The natural mind of man is simply hostile or against the law and nature of God. It **can not be subjugated to the life and law of God.** There is an old saying that, "you can not make a silk purse out of a sows ear". This is true with the hostile mind of man. So Paul asks, "Who shall deliver me from this body of death? I thank God that it shall be through Jesus Christ" Rom. 7.

The comforting thing for all of us is that now there is no condemnation for any of us in Jesus Christ. Rom. 8:1. There is NO sin in Jesus as he has taken away all of our sins. I Jn.3:5. All of our sins are forgiven in Jesus, past ones, present ones, and future ones. All forgiven. No matter how big!

One may ask, "Well if this is true, then I can go out and sin all I want to." I have a couple of answers for this. One, how much do you want to sin? And why? We do not obey God because of law or a written code or a list of do's and don'ts, but we do desire to obey from the heart by the Spirit of God living in us and all of this by Grace.

I John 1:7 tells us that if and when we do sin, and we do often, that the blood of Christ covers us of all the sins we can and ever shall commit. Romans tells us that when our sins abound that the Grace of God abounds MORE. See Romans 5:20. I John 2:2, tells us that the desire of God is that we do not sin, BUT, if and when we do we have a Saviour who is the propitiation for our sins and for the sins of the whole world. Our sins can never catch up with the Grace that God continues to extend to us in Jesus. God says, " I am saving you and forgiving you no matter what whether you like it or not."

So what is my reaction when I see and experience sin in my life? Here is my response.

1. Thank you Jesus for covering my sins.
2. Jesus, live more and more fully in me as you and your Spirit replaces my fleshly desires from my fallenness in Adam.
3. I release ALL of my Guilt to you Jesus knowing you have taken it all.
4. I look forward to my change from mortal to immortal someday.
5. Thank you for declaring your life, holiness and righteousness to me.
6. You get the point here.

For Christians Paul goes on to show in Romans chapter 8 that we are no longer controlled by the human flesh **ONLY**, but now can exercise the Spirit living in us as well and experience the abundant life Christ came to give. We are not led by the flesh **ONLY**, but we also can walk more and more in the Spirit as we truly are the Sons and Daughters of God. Assured. Adopted. Included. Purchased and loved by God.

Thanks be to God for EVERYTHING.

Blessings,

Paul

# WE NEVER DIE IN JESUS

Upon one's physical death, does the person continue to live in the presence of God? Some say yes and some say no. Some posit that the person is in the grave in a state of "sleep" awaiting a future resurrection. While scripture is not 'specific' on this subject, there are theological implications which may help us answer the question.

Let us remember that time and space were created by the Triune God. God does not operate confined to His created time. Past, present and future are terms we use to define events in linear time by which God is not governed.

In God's economy of existence He simply is involved in His creation as everything being in the present. Subjectivity and objectivity of understanding obviously are operative here. Without confusing the issue here, Einstein demonstrated that in timespace, with time and space being the same thing, that past, present and future were all the same...present. Do I understand that, quite honestly...NO. But then again there is much about the great Triune God I do not understand. Back to the original question.

We see in Genesis 1 that God did not intend for man to die but to continue living. Sin brought the death factor upon Adam and all of his descendents. Now it is appointed man ONCE to die. (Heb.9:27). And humanity has lived in the fear of death since Adam. ( Heb.2:14-15).

Jesus shows, however, in John 5:24, that those who believe Him and the Father HAVE ETERNAL LIFE and have crossed over INTO LIFE! Jesus IS their life and the person's life is now hidden with Christ in God. ( Col.3:3-4).

Paul mentions this operation in II Cor.5:1-8, as we who are mortal in our earthly tent may be swallowed up by LIFE. He says to be away from the body is "to be home with the Lord." Then, in Philippians 1:21-24, Paul points out that to die is gain, or an improvement that is much better.

Paul does not indicate that this would be anything other than immediate. Simply a change from mortal at death to immortal and life which is in Christ.

We know that we live and move and have our being in Christ.( Acts 17:28). And we know that Christ is our life. And we know that we have passed from death into life. And we know that Jesus conquered and defeated death. And we know that we are resurrected in and with Jesus who is our resurrection. ( Col.3:1). Now what Jesus tells Martha in John 11:25-26 has a much clearer meaning. " I am the resurrection and the life, he who believes in me will LIVE ( Gk. " Zesetai" is live here and carries the meaning of 'shall continue to live' ) even though he dies. And whoever lives and believes in me will NEVER die. Do you believe this?" What Jesus is saying, I believe, is that at our mortal bodies death we CONTINUE to live in our new existence since Jesus is our life and we participate in His resurrection. ( I Peter 1:3). And, therefore, objectively speaking, we are seated at the Father's right hand with Jesus. ( Eph.2:6).

I think we have confused in the past our resurrection as being "OUR" resurrection and not the fact that we have been resurrected in Jesus already. What we are awaiting is the "resuscitation" of our mortal bodies to meet up with our resurrected spirit and thereby live in and with God in the heavenlies forever in our new spirit body which will be like Jesus' body now. (ICor.15:49, I Jn.3:2)

In Jesus there simply is no death, no cessation of life. We live and move and have our being IN Jesus Christ and therefore we live eternally with no possibility of death. Death itself does not even separate us from the love of God . We and that love continue on. ( Rom.8:37-39).

How we may have looked at scriptures before concerning resurrections (plural) and other events as well was from a linear time and dispensational stand point. We put things in 'order' and sequenced events based on our timeframe as we interpreted past events and prophetic writings. While those may seem to have fit, we simply can not ignore the very words of Jesus Christ as He encourages us with the fact of our NEVER dying again in Him. We have passed from death into life....Forever.

AMEN
Blessings,
Paul

# WHAT DO CHRISTIANS, JEWS, BUDDHISTS, MUSLIMS, HINDUS, ATHEISTS AND ALL OTHER RELIGIONS HAVE IN COMMON?

What Christians, Jews, Buddhists, Muslims, Hindus, all other religions and even Atheists have in Common might surprise you. For one thing they all have in common a concept of a god that is flawed. They see God as distant, unapproachable, unknowable, disinterested, holy and not connected to the activities of humans. (Atheists would argue with this assessment.) True nevertheless.

Even in the Western Theological Christian World within the various denominations there is the thought often times that unless one is or becomes a member of "MY" specific group or denomination then he or she is lost, damned, condemned, and consigned to the ever torturing flames of Hell to suffer eternally. Sound familiar? It did to Jonathan Edwards the great preacher of the 1700's in America.

So we see a lot of consistencies or commonalities among and between various faiths and religions. In addition we see most of these same faiths with a "Holy God" who is so Holy that for anyone not to aspire to His Holiness and become saved in His Grace that they are " in His Great Love " cast into the flames of hell to be punished forever. More commonalities. Is this God loving, Great, and Cool, or What???

Now let's leave all of this "bull caca" behind and move on. The question was in the beginning what do all of these peoples have in common. COMMON! Let's see what they do have in common.

God Loves ALL of them. No exceptions. ( Jn.3:16). They all were chosen in Christ BEFORE the foundation of the world. ( Ephesians 1:3-14). They all were created IN Christ, BY Christ, FOR Christ and THROUGH Christ. ( Colossians 1:14-15.) Here comes the good part, they all were Saved by Jesus Christ at the Cross 2000 years ago along with ALL other humans who have ever lived or will ever live. Cool huh?

Not only were they saved 2000 years ago they were adopted into the life of God to be HOLY and without blame in Christ BEFORE THE WORLD WAS EVER CREATED.

They all were created IN God's image and placed inside of God's life by Jesus Christ. Remember Jesus was slain from before the foundation of the world. ( Rev. 13:8). What Adam did was undone for all of humanity by Jesus Christ and He is the Saviour of the whole world and ALL people. ( I John 2.1-2).

The question remains, do all people from Adam forward know this reality? And the answer is NO. Whether they know it or not does not make it so or not so. It is SO! Some will come to know it in this physical life in the fallenness of Adam. However, most humans will come to know it in the resurrection standing before the judgement seat of Christ AFTER their death on this earth. ( Remember some 100 Billion people have lived on this earth over the ages.)

The Great Triune God has it all under control. His control. Many will come to know this truth during this physical lifetime, but many others will only come to know it in the "afterlife."

There are no children God ever created who He does not want with Him forever. He has made all the arrangements to make it so. Jesus Christ took care of all of that.

The commonalities of all humans are these:

God loves all of His human family.

Jesus died was resurrected for all and ascended to heaven with ALL humans. ( Eph.2:6)

God wanted all of us as His children before the world was ever created in the first place.

No "RELIGION" is the "right" one. No religion gets humans to heaven. No religion takes the place of the only begotten Son of the Father who He loves dearly. Good pagans, good Hindus, good Buddhists, good Baptists, good Methodists, good Lutherans, good SDA's , good JW's, **NOR** any other "good religion" is going to get anyone to the Father's right hand. Period. Why? Because it has all been done already in Jesus.

We all have much in common for which we may be thankful-- GOD'S LOVE!

The question is , Will we believe?


# WHAT DO YOU MEAN, "ENDURE TO THE END"?


He that "endures" to the end. The doctrine of "Perseverance". And other similar doctrinal postures which say in order for one to be saved one must

Persevere or endure to the end of one's life through the individuals personal faith. Loose faith, loose out!

While this may sound reasonable to our pragmatic minds we need to take a look at a few non-negotiable facts regarding salvation in the plan of God.

No one would argue that the original creation of God was perfect in every way. It existed in a state of wholeness with God. Man was created by God and placed in a world created FOR man in which to live and be adopted and included in the life of God forever. This creation and man— humanity—became "lost" or disconnected from God's original purpose through sin. Jesus came to seek and to save what was lost—and He did just that. ( Luke 19:10). In Jesus the Cosmos, man included, moved from 'lostness' to 'savedness' or into Salvation through Jesus and HIS Faith.

This whole creation has been redeemed, reconciled and saved in Christ. ( Colossians 1:20). This because of God's great love for us even when and while we all were yet sinners. Whatever work was required to be done by Christ was done through His life, death, resurrection and ascension to the Father's right hand. Jesus said, " It is finished." (John 19:30).

Paul points out in Ephesians 2:6 that humanity has been taken to the right hand of the Father and seated there with Jesus Christ. While we may not understand this from our subjective viewpoint, nevertheless God sees it this way from His Objective viewpoint in His eternal perspective.

Again in Ephesians 1:3-14, Paul makes the point that this salvation and Adoption by God was planned out for ALL mankind even before the creation of the world. Jesus MADE IT SO.

When it comes to us individually to "persevere" until the end of our physical life in order to be saved, how could that possibly affect our salvation when we were saved already by Christ and His completed work for us before we were ever born?

Our salvation is complete in Christ. It is not a matter of us 'enduring to the end' or 'persevering' until the end of our life to be saved. The Gospel of Jesus Christ is not a life on trial to see if we can make it. The Gospel is that we HAVE made it in Jesus. We are safe and secure in His hands forever. (John 10:28-29; Romans 8:38-39).

Salvation is not a matter of us 'accepting Jesus into our life.' The Great Triune God ACCEPTED us to include us into His life originally. Jesus made it SO! Paul further states in Ephesians 2:8 that our being saved is through faith—BUT THAT FAITH IS NOT FROM YOURSELF OR NOT OF YOURSELVES. Paul continues, It is GRACE you are SAVED by and this is the GIFT of God. God gives the Grace. God gives the salvation. It is God's perfect and eternal Faith which saves us all. Whatever faith we personally have in all of this comes from the Faith of Christ which He extends to us to see and understand His plan for us. This then promotes our BELIEF. We come to see it. We come to understand it. We then know WHO we are IN Jesus. Then we live the abundant life Jesus calls us to.

We rest in the eternal arms of Jesus. As time unfolds and the future becomes the present what we now can only see through a glass distortedly will become crystal clear in the ETERNITY God has prepared for us.

I believe, Lord help my unbelief.


# WHAT DO YOU MEAN INCLUDED ?


The true Gospel message of Jesus Christ is that of Adoption into the very life of the Father through Jesus by the Spirit. In conjunction with this understanding we use the word "included" -- that we are Adopted by the Father and Included. We even hear the wording that, " We are included." My point in this paper is to explain a little further what "included means."

Jesus has indeed included us in His life. He **is** our life. ( John 14:20, John 17:20-26, Colossians 3:1-4). Does this mean that now we have been added to His life and given eternal life since He has the power to grant eternal life to us? In other words is it a going forward thing for us?

Paul says in Galatians 2:20 that we are crucified with Christ . And that we are buried with Christ, ( Romans 6:1-4), and Paul says in Colossians 3:1 that we have been raised with Christ. Ephesians 2:6 tells us that we ascended **with** Jesus to the Father's right hand and are seated there **with** Jesus. Other verses tell us that Jesus became sin for us, ( Heb.10:10, II Cor. 5:21), Jesus "tasted" death for us ( Hebrews 2:9), and that we are resurrected in Him in New Birth, ( I Peter 1:3).

There is an intimate interaction between humanity and Jesus. So intimate in fact that Jesus literally enters into our life and gives us life, but, we all also **Enter** into His very life by His choice to **place or include us in His life** and thereby we are involved personally in everything that happened to Jesus. So we say that what happened to Jesus happened to us. The word we use to describe this Theological principle is **INCLUSION.** It means that we all are included in the events of His earthly life and also we are included in His eternal life as well. We now are included in the life that Jesus shares with the Father and the Spirit by our Adoption and our Inclusion in Jesus' life. He **IS** our life now and forever. When Jesus said in John 14:6, " I am the way, the truth and the **LIFE**," He meant exactly what He said. When John 10:10 refers to Jesus coming to bring **LIFE** and that we might have it more abundantly He is referring to HIS life that we are included in.

God's purpose from the "very beginning" was to adopt us as His children and to include us in the life of Jesus who became Incarnate for that very purpose. ( Ephesians 1:3-14).

We are not just "included" generically in the plan of God somewhere in the lostness of eternity somehow. NO, we are Included **IN** the life of Jesus, " the only begotten son of God." The relationship Jesus has with the Father and the Spirit **IS** the relationship we have with the Father and the Spirit. Jesus shares it with us. We **exist** in Jesus. He is our life. It is what Triune God desired from the very beginning. To share His divine nature with us. Adoption and Inclusion is the way He purposed it.

# WHAT GOD HAS DONE FOR US ALL

In order to discuss Theological postulates, there are a few questions which must be addressed and answered thus assuming a foundational premise for the logic of the argument.

These are the ones I feel are needed most to be answered, and established up front.

1.  Has God, Father, Son, and Holy Spirit Eternally existed. Yes
2.  Is This God Love, and does He exist in love one of the persons of the Trinity for the others ? Yes. I Jn.4:8. God is Love.
3.  Are ALL things created BY and FOR Jesus Christ? Co.1:16-17.
4.  Does God say He/They Let's make man in our image and likeness? Yes. Gen.1:26-27. Why? Does He want to share His/Their deep, total love with a created family? In a reciprocal love situation.? Scripture obviously says this. The Great Commandment. Love God.
5.  Does God choose a human family for his children before the foundation Of the world? And Adopt them/us to Himself by Jesus Christ? Eph.1:3-14.

6.  Did Death come upon all Humanity by the sin of Adam? Yes. I Co.15:22

7.  Are ALL made alive in Christ? I Co. 15:22. Did Jesus die for All? II Co.5:14.

8.  Does EVERYTHING exist, live , move, and have its being in Jesus? Yes. Acts 17:28; Col. 1: 17. Is Jesus In the Father and We in Jesus, and Jesus IN US? Jn.14:20.

9.  Have we ALL been made HOLY through the sacrifice of the body of Jesus Christ one time FOR ALL—EVERYONE.? Heb.10:10.

10. Since these passages refer to ALL ,(also see I Tim.2:4-6) Has Christ saved us by his grace And raised us up with Him and SEATED us in the Heavens WITH HIM.? Eph.2:6-8.

11. Is belief of this essential for our enjoyment of it? Yes. Jn.5:24, I Jn.5:13.

12. Those who do not believe will simply not enjoy the Good Life of Eternal Life.

Much may be said on this topic, however, these points are a good place to start .

Blessings !!!

# WHAT IS THE "HELL" OF II PETER 2:4 ?

II Peter 2:4-9, poses an interesting question for those who believe in a hell fire stance on hell for humans. But, what are these verses actually talking about? Well, let's see.

Peter is at the end of his ministry. He knows he is facing martyrdom. ( II Peter 1:14-15). He foresees in the future trouble for the church and warns the church in a number of areas. False prophets, departing from the faith, remaining unentangled from the world, etc. He gives the illustration in II Peter 2 of how God did not "spare" or overlook or ignore it when the angels sinned, but cast them down to "hell". A note here on the words hell is translated from. There are four words in scripture translated by our one word hell. Sheole in the Hebrew meaning **grave** or **pit** appears 65 times in the O.T. Hades meaning **grave** in the Greek appears 11 times in the N.T. Gehenna in the Greek is a trans-language word for the Hebrew word "Hinnom". The valley of Hinnom was a garbage dump outside of Jerusalem where refuse, dead carcasses of animals, garbage, dead derelict humans were thrown, the fires were kept burning, where the smoke continually billowed up, and where flies continually bred with maggots or worms that never died out. The stench was beyond description. Now the last word translated hell.

The word translated hell in II Peter 2:4 is none of these. It is "tartaroo". It means a place of restraint, or imprisonment, or dungeon, or a chaining up. Peter uses the word to explain that this imprisonment on the earth of the angels that sinned was their place of restraint until their judgement time came ( vs. 4 and vs. 9 ), and that **their** punishment would continue until that time. What Peter is saying in the context of II Peter 2 and II Peter 3 is that God is not going to "spare" or overlook the deeds of evil men and false prophets anymore than He overlooked the angels that sinned. Their judgment is sure as well. Peter also is saying through these verses that God knows how to deliver Godly men from the snares of evil influences and heresies also.

A key factor in understanding II Peter 2 is to realize that II Peter 3 must be read in conjunction with it. Peter concludes II Peter with the encouragement in II Peter 3:17-18, ".. . now you know these things so don' t be carried away with the error or heresy of lawless men and stumble, but, Vs. 18, ' Grow in the grace and knowledge of our Lord and savior Jesus Christ.' ".

II Peter 2:4-9 then has nothing to do with any humans being cast down into "hell" or tartaroo or restraint until they are judged, but is referencing angels which left their first estate and are imprisoned on the earth until their judgment.

# WHAT IS YOUR VIEW OF GOD AND HOLY?

Do we need to rethink our view of God and His Holiness? Whether we know it or not Western Christian Theological thought and understanding about God came from a source most of us are not familiar with.

Most Christians would define the existence of God in terms such as All wise, All knowing, All powerful, everywhere present, as well as Distant, separated from man, unknowable, unapproachable, detached, sovereign, and Holy. Hardly a "Relational" concept at all. Where did we get this idea of God? And what does the scripture reveal that God REALLY is like?

The church's concept of Most things goes back to the 400's A.D. ( the Fifth Century) to a giant of a figure in Christian circles, the man Augustine. Augustine was an avid student of the Greek Philosophers, namely Plato, as well as a student of Roman Civil Law stemming from the writings of Tertullian, a Roman Lawyer ( 160 A.D.—c 225 A.D.).

Augustine developed his image of God based on Pagan concepts and Legal descriptions of morality. LEGALISM. GOD became known as this distant figure who was unknowable due to his perfection and Holiness which were defined in terms of moral law. This vast gulf between God's Holiness and man's sinfulness kept man separated from this God creating the idea that while God could be worshiped He was NOT 'Intimate' with His creation and especially man.

So God came to be described in Legal terms, Moral terms, and Holy terms which did not reflect the RELATIONAL BEING He has always been and continues to be. The intimate connection between God and humanity was lost in the misguided ontology Augustine introduced into the church.

But the true Triune God is very different than what has been thought by the perpetuators of Augustinian Theology. And God REVEALS Himself to be so in scripture and in sound Theological thinking.

The tripersonal God has always been in relationship in His threeness with Father, Son and Holy Spirit. They have always been face to face in their relationship of love, respect, agreement, purpose, plans, appreciation, and honor one for the other. So much so that the Three are One! ( We may not understand this, but scripture supports it as so.).

God's purpose in creating man in the first place was to share His life with man in His expanded family. God said, " Let us make man in Our Image". ( Genesis 1:26-27). God desired a created being who with Godly attributes could SHARE in God's life and Divine Nature. Even before the creation of ANYTHING God planned to Adopt and Include mankind INTO His very life through Jesus Christ. ( Ephesians 1:3-14; Colossians 1:20; John 14:20; John 17:20-26).

God is Holy, to be sure, but His Holiness is not defined by legal or moral dictates. It is holiness because of the RELATIONSHIP that has ALWAYS existed between the Father, Son and Spirit. When God shares this relationship with man and Adopts mankind as His children and Includes mankind into His life then mankind enters into God's Holiness and God's Holiness enters into mankind through   this RELATIONSHIP.

What this does for us Theologically is to demonstrate that God is NOT far off, not separated ( Augustine), not unknowable, not untouchable, and not distant but here with us, close, walking with us, living with us, being with us, communicating with us, and being INTIMATE. God loves us and He will NOT be God without us. He is that emphatic about it.

The Father sent Jesus Christ to this earth to make it so!!! Salvation is simply the DECLARATION by God of the absolute VICTORY of His Plan for all of mankind through Jesus Christ.

Salvation is not a contest. It is a FACT. Salvation is not in question. It is answered in God's Love and in Jesus Christ who will complete what He started!!!

Maybe we all need to do a little rethinking, not about a Distant GOD, but about a loving, sharing, personal, RELATIONAL Father of Creation who will love us FOREVER.

# WHAT KIND OF THEOLOGY DO YOU WANT ?

What kind of doctrine and Theology do you want? Do you want the Truth that is asked when defendants are told on the witness stand to speak the "truth and nothing but the truth'?

The choices we have are actually quite limited. We can believe in Calvinism, which states that God originally selected some individuals to be lost eternally and damned to Hell; and, He selected some in His Righteous Wisdom to be saved and go to Heaven and be with Him forever.

Then there is Armenianism which says basically that individuals must come to 'accept' Jesus Christ as their personal savior and be saved at that time, but if circumstances change in the future and the person "falls from Grace" , then that person goes back to being unsaved, loses their salvation, and is lost and is consigned to Hell. ( Reminds me of a rat running in a maze trying to figure out how to get out of the thing ).

Then there is the D.James Kennedy teaching that we must get to all individuals with the Gospel message and that they CAN be saved if they will believe and accept the salvation Jesus offers. If we can not get to them before they die, then they are LOST and burn in Hell forever! Whew.!

We could go on and on with differing approaches to salvation and damnation which various groups teach. But we won't. Let's just go to scripture and make it really simple.

The Triune God is love. Before the creation came into being, Triune God decided to share His loving relationship with mankind who He Adopted into His very life. (Eph.1:3-14).

The Word was coming into the world of humans from the beginning to connect and create a Union between God and man so that each could live in the other. This is Plan "A".

When Adam sinned he side tracked the plan temporarily and brought the death penalty on all mankind through his disobedience. (I Cor.15:22). Now Jesus' coming to the earth as Immanuel not only would connect humans to God, but Jesus' now had to be the payment or propitiation for the sins of all mankind so that what Adam did to all mankind could be reversed or undone by the righteous act of the one man Jesus thereby placing the plan back on the right track. ( I Cor.15:22; Rom.5:17-18 , I John 2:2).

God's original purpose in creating man was to give man EVERY BLESSING of the Treasures of Heaven—the intimate relationship with God inside the Trinity—and every Spiritual blessing in Christ. Since EVERY blessing of the Treasures of Heaven and EVERY spiritual blessing have been given to man what more blessings could possible remain for God to ever give to His children? ( Eph.1:3).

This Adoption of man into the life of God occurred BEFORE THE CREATION OF THE WORLD. What this Theology does pictures Triune God as Love. Love for all . Not a respecter of persons. Not "electing" some to be saved and some to be lost. Jesus said in Luke 19:10, that He came to "seek and to save what was LOST". And He did just that!!!

John 3:16, makes it clear that God LOVED the world, all humanity, that He sent Jesus into this world that WHOEVER would believe what Jesus had done for and to them would EXPERIENCE the joy of the salvation already procured for them from the foundation of the world. Those not believing this truth would just continue in a state of suffering or perishing some would call 'Hell'. The price has been paid for all humanity. We have been 'bought with a price'. Jesus has a place already prepared in His Fathers house for us all. There is a mansion for everyone who will believe this truth of Who they are IN Jesus Christ. ALL can go. ALL are invited. The tickets have all been purchased in advance.

Will EVERYONE go? Scripture seems to indicate there will be some who will not get on board. Their unbelief or their refusal or for some unknown reason of theirs they just simply will NOT go to the party. If they continue in this mindset they can stay outside of the party indefinitely until such time that they decide to believe who they are in Jesus and come into the party.

Just like the two sons of the Father in Luke 15 in the Parable of the Prodigal Son, EVERYONE, just as were the two sons in the parable, are the Father's children no matter what. And God is LOVE. Forever Love.

# WHAT THE LAST JUDGEMENT IS AND IS NOT

The Last Judgement, or Judgement Day when understood properly gives great relief and encouragement to all. Many, if not most, people have a great fear of being judged by their acts in this life when they give "account" of them at Judgement Day. Most religions have a type of judgement day in their beliefs. Bottom line: If one is judged good enough then reward/ heaven; if one is judged bad/evil enough then punishment/purgatory/ hell.

It is true that Nineveh, the Queen of the South, and Sodom and Gomorrah will rise in the Judgement of the final day. This of course requires resurrection at some future time. Jesus says in John 12:31, that " now is the time for judgement on this world." Peter says in I Peter 4:17, that "judgement has already started with the family of God."

We know that ALL men/women have been judged guilty in Adam and have received death as a sentence. But, we know that in Jesus Christ those same **ALL** will be made alive in Jesus Christ. We know that all humanity was **chosen** in Christ before the foundation of the world and predetermined to be adopted as sons/daughters through Jesus Christ. ( Ephesians 1:4-6). We know that all are included in this plan as John 3:16-17 shows—along with many other verses as well. Titus 2:11 points out that the Grace of God which bequeaths salvation has 'appeared' or is 'applied' to **ALL** men—humanity.

With these realities in mind what can the "Last Judgement" **possibly** be? First, all of humanity has **already** been judged!!! All humans are judged guilty. The wages of sin, which all have committed, is death! (Romans 3:23; Romans 6:23). Now this is where it gets really good. "But the **GIFT** of God is eternal life through Jesus Christ." This eternal life has been given to **ALL HUMAN BEINGS.** This gift extends all the way back to Adam—for ALL. Jesus was slain from the "foundation of the world". (Revelation 13:8). Jesus' sacrifice applies to ALL. ( I John 2:2).

So, for humanity, there is no escaping what Jesus has done for all of the sons and daughters of Adam. He has, hold on, **adopted, redeemed, reconciled, forgiven, accepted, liked, loved, saved, included, justified, predestined, glorified, resurrected , and seated at the Father's side ALL OF HUMANITY.** ( If you can think of something I left out here, just add it !)

Now back to the "Last Judgement." Whenever in resurrection one stands before the judgement seat of Christ he stands guilty, guilty, guilty. But, he also stands completely forgiven. If he does not know this, then the last judgement is to declare to him that yes he is a sinner and guilty, but that Jesus has taken care of that and forgiven him and provided an abundant eternal life with Jesus if he wants to accept it and believe it.

This will be the "last" time that this eternal offer will be made to all of humanity who have not known it before and accepted and believed it to now know it and believe it.

The Last Judgement is **NOT** a judgement to hear a court proceeding to determine if the person is worthy or not to be accepted into God's Heaven. No one is!!! It simply is to inform any and all that in Jesus Christ they have been loved, forgiven and accepted into the life of God and now by knowing it they can choose to believe. They can now choose to have "metanoia"—a change of mind and understanding—**REPENTANCE.** This is not a second chance, this will be their first opportunity to believe. This Last Judgement will include the 'approximately' 94 billion, or so, humans who have already lived and died on this earth not knowing who they were in Jesus nor the salvation and life He offers.

What a great day!!!! What a Good Deal!!! What **GOOD NEWS** this will be for all of humanity to find out at last. At the Last Judgement. Wow!!! God really is **GOOD** after all.

Lord I believe, help my unbelief.
**AMEN**

# WHEN GOD'S TIME CAME

With the Incarnation of God as the child Jesus God was making a statement He had waited for 'ages' to make. False religions under the direct influence of the 'liar from the beginning,' Satan, had filled the world with doctrines and philosophies based on works and legalism. They were based on rewards for the few who could somehow manage to 'discover' the secrets of the particular religion. So, some were rewarded in these philosophies and some were cursed.

God allowed all these religions to flourish until the time He determined that He would reveal the truth of His Gospel in the person of Jesus. Eph.3:7-9, Col.1:24-29, and I Pet.1:20, all point to the fact that the MYSTERY that God hid from mankind was now being revealed in Jesus.

The Incarnation was astounding. God's time had come to demonstrate His Great Love for the creation and the human family. The Incarnation was no little accomplishment. Religions up to this time had been selective in who they engaged. There had been something for everyone's preference in religion. And, all of them false and wrong. ( This does not include Israel the 'church in the wilderness.')

It is hard for us to understand the excitement God the Father must have had when anticipating for nine months the birth of His Son, Jesus. This was not just another miracle. Not just another birth of a child. God was stepping into the human experience as Immanuel, God with us—and in us. It is no wonder that the Heavenly Host of angels sang at the top of their voices in the great choir of Heaven when Jesus was born.

The really remarkable thing about this birth and Incarnation of God was the fact that now this reality hidden from past ages was an event ( the GREATEST MIRACLE OF ALL TIME) that would not just be for a select few in some small middle eastern religion, but an event that was for ALL MEN as the story of Christ's birth in Luke 2:10-14, points out. "........FOR ALL MEN.

In Col.1:24-29, Paul echoes the fact that now the Gentiles are included and that the Mystery applies to them as well, " Christ in you the Hope of Glory!"

John writes in I Jn.2:1-2, that Jesus is the propitiation for Our sins, but not only our sins, but for the sins of THE WHOLE WORLD.

God's time had come. This was it. God had patiently waited until the last times to accomplish this Eternal Purpose of His. Today was the day.

The angels said so. " For unto you this day in the city of David a SAVIOUR has been born, who is Christ the Lord."

John 1:1-9, says that this Word which came to man was very GOD! That in Him was life—a fact only applicable to God. That He was Creator of all things. That through Him ALL men might now believe. And, that the true light that gives light TO EVERY MAN was coming into the world.

Yes, the Incarnation was no small event!!! The birth of Jesus as Immanuel. The Word made flesh. God with us. The Salvation of ALL mankind was truly something to observe and celebrate.

# WHEN WAS / IS MAN ADOPTED BY CHRIST ?

Concerning 'Adoption' Theology, let's examine a few points which MAY make this subject more clear to us all.

Often the claim is made that not "all" humans were Adopted by Jesus Christ before the foundation of the world. Those who take this position say that those who are not presently saved are 'lost' unless and until they 'accept' Jesus as their personal savior. In other words they change their mind (repent) and come to belief and this is what saves them. Up until this point they were NOT saved but lost.

For the sake of this discussion, let's assume that this is true. That this is the way it really is for humans in order to be saved. With this in mind, let's go back and ask ourselves the question, " IF God did NOT Adopt them and Include them in the life of God before the foundation of the world and NOW they are accepting Jesus as savior, then WHEN DID or DOES He Adopt them and include them in the life of God? And, what if they don't now or later 'accept' Jesus as their savior is their lack of acceptance to mean that they were NEVER intended by God to be Adopted, Included, Redeemed, or Saved in the first place.? And what if they later change their mind and decide to accept Jesus WHEN and HOW does their Adoption occur? In practical fact is humanity then responsible for their personal Adoption, Inclusion, Redemption, Reconciliation, and Salvation and does this by their CHOICE dictate what God did ORIGINALLY? Do we begin to see a problem with all of this?

Without going into the discussion of "objectivity ( what actually is) and subjectivity ( what a person thinks is) at this point, let's look at another facet which may be worthy of consideration.

I think this all boils down to terminology and a definition of terms. For those who feel that a person "gets saved" when he accepts Jesus as personal savior, and that the person is "lost" until he accepts Jesus let's look at it from this point. A better way of phrasing it, I feel, would be to say that this person "COMES TO BELIEF IN JESUS". They come to believe what was done FOR them and TO them in Jesus from before the foundation of the world. In their mind they call it being saved, becoming saved, getting saved, etc, and Trinitarian Theologians would call it seeing, understanding, believing, and now 'EXPERIENCING' the salvation and Adoption that was there all along in Jesus from the foundation of the world. For the individual the REALITY is the same. They are saved and now they know it. Now they can live their life knowing it. They can EXPERIENCE it—FOREVER.

When you think about it God's Adopting, Including, Redeeming, Reconciling, and Saving the whole of Humanity from the foundation of the world is in reality the ONLY WAY THAT HE COULD HAVE DONE IT thereby being fair to all. Therefore, objectively, it is so. It is the Truth. It is the way it is.

This way it allows God "not to be a respecter of persons"; it allows God "not to be willing for any to perish but to come to repentance" (belief); everything needed to be done in Christ occurred once and for all from the start; all humans are on the same footing ; no other HUMAN FACTOR of all time enters in except the factor of BELIEF; the playing field is leveled; and Spiritually God does not do for one that He does not do for another. There is no respect of persons with God. No partiality. We humans are all God's children. Loved, Accepted, wanted, provided for, provisioned for, Adopted, included, and Saved by a loving Father who designed this plan of His originally for us all to be with Him forever because HE LOVES US !!! And He Likes us too.

With THIS perspective EVERYTHING for the Salvation of Humanity rests squarely on the shoulders of Jesus Christ. Man has no part in his own personal salvation. He doesn't acquire it. He doesn't maintain it. He doesn't loose it. The reason being that it is ALL done IN, THROUGH, AND BY JESUS CHRIST from the beginning. In truth, Jesus doesn't NEED man to help him out in the Adoption and salvation process at all. None. NADA.

Zip. Zero. The reason being that it was all done in Jesus before man was ever created in the first place.

So, what does this picture mean for man? It means that man has the freedom to choose to believe it or not. This is the ONLY thing man CAN do. But, the Good News is, that is ENOUGH !!! And YOU get to believe it too.

# WHERE DO YOU GET YOUR TRUTH ?

"I am the Way, the Truth, and the Life." Jesus proclaims in John 14:6. Most all Christians can quote this verse. But most all of us are not aware of the RADICAL nature of this statement of Jesus.

By way of comparison this would compare today to some Professor of Logic or Philosophy stating that EVERYONE else is wrong in their philosophies and logic and that ONLY he now has the true understanding of the way things are, the nature of God, the beginnings of the Universe, the final resting place and state of the dead, and essentially ALL other questions of life and the existence of the Cosmos.

In reality he would be saying he is the light of the world. He is the ONLY one in which TRUTH rests. Radical! Yet, when we look at the life of Jesus and His claims this is exactly what He did in his earthly ministry.

A little back ground. By the time Jesus came onto the scene there had been literally hundreds of philosophers and teachers parading through history with any and every kind of doctrine, philosophy, and "truth" imaginable. Everything from why the Cosmos was made in the first place, how it was made, from what it was made, the inception of evil into the creation, the afterlife of those doing good and the afterlife of those doing evil during their lifetime.

There was no shortage of "thinkers" the world had produced in the thousands of years before Jesus. There was one philosopher, however, who in his education and mental brilliance embodied the composite teachings of the 'best' of the ancient philosophers.

He wrote on just about every subject imaginable. The Western world patterned its thinking after the elements of this man's teaching. He wrote numerous treaties dealing with all aspects of life. He introduced the concept of "hell" as a place of eternal infernos of punishment for evil. His works included, Protagoras, The Republic, Apology, Phaedo, Timaeus, Symposium, The Laws, and Gorgias. This was a brilliant man. Respected. Admired. Followed. Revered. Acclaimed. And mostly WRONG. The man was Plato of Athens Greece who lived 400 years before Christ.

Plato's teachings were just accepted as the way things are. They were considered the map and highway to a positive after life experience. Heaven if you will. A state of eternal bliss. Plato was considered a teacher of truth.

Jesus comes on the scene in His ministry in about 30 A.D. and with His teachings explodes the concepts of ALL philosophers before Him including Plato when Jesus says, " I am the Way, the TRUTH, and the Life. No one comes to the Father—or gets to the heavenly afterlife—but by and through ME." Talk about radical. In this one statement Jesus repudiates EVERYTHING in the entire society they had come to believe. He is not making friends to say the least. Paul later does the same thing in Athens—Plato's home town—in Acts 17.

Paul further warns us concerning philosophy which mitigates against the Truth that is in Jesus in Colossians 2:8, ""See to it that no one takes you captive through hollow and deceptive philosophy, which depends on human tradition and the basic principles of this world rather than on Christ."

Why is all this important for us today? There are only two ways anything can be understood and explained when it comes to the Bible, doctrine, or theology. The first way is what Paul calls 'the BASIC principles of this world' which starts from the wrong premise of human reasoning. The second way to understand these principles is to begin with the TRUTH. The Truth is in Jesus. ( Ephesians 4:21). We must start with the Creator God. The Triune God. Father, Son, and Holy Spirit. With His overflowing Love. With the fact that All things were created by , through, and for Jesus Christ and that He upholds and sustains ALL Creation. (Colossians 1:16-17). That He is LOVE. That He Adopted mankind and redeemed mankind and included mankind in His life before the foundation of the world. Before creation of the cosmos. (Ephesians 1:3-14). Take your choice. Take God or man. Who's your daddy?

Philosophy of the world is complex and convoluted. The TRUTH that is in Jesus is simple. It is not rocket science. Paul says it this way in II Corinthians 11:3, " But I fear, lest by any means, as the serpent beguiled Eve through his subtlety, so your minds should be corrupted from the SIMPLICITY that is in Christ."(KJV).

This is all important to us because modern Christianity has taken many of its concepts from the pagan world, especially from Plato. The truth is not in Plato. It is in Jesus.

The world has been redeemed and reconciled in Christ. Salvation for all mankind is a reality not a possibility. The Kingdom was prepared from the foundation of the world for **ALL** to enter. The question is: "Will you believe and choose to enter?"


# WHERE IS JESUS WHEN WE SIN ?

( Does Jesus go away and hide when we are sinning ? )


The Holy Spirit has been poured out on all flesh. Jesus lives in all humans. That is fine to understand as long as we are doing good and right things. But, when we sin and do evil things where is Jesus then? When we lust, or hate, or belittle, or get drunk , or fornicate or commit adultery, where is Jesus THEN?

Let's look at some scriptures first. John 14:20 tells us that Jesus is IN the Father, the Father is IN Jesus and that Jesus is IN you ( us ). In Hebrews 13:5, Jesus has said that He will never leave us. Everything that happened to Jesus also happened to us. We were baptized when Jesus was baptized; we were crucified when Jesus was crucified ( Gal.2:20); we were resurrected when Jesus was resurrected; we ascended when Jesus ascended to the right hand of the father and we are seated there with Him.(Ephesians 2:6)

We know that we were chosen and predestined and adopted in Christ before the foundation of the world. ( Ephesians 1:4-6; I Peter 1:20). We know we have been raised with Christ and that He is our Life. ( Colossians 3:1-4).

SO, the question is WHERE is Jesus when we are in the middle of some sin—no matter how big or little it is? The Apostle Paul said that the mystery of life is that Jesus Christ is IN usThe Hope of Glory. We live and move and have our being in Jesus. ( Acts 17:28).

So, to answer the question here. Jesus is IN us and right IN the middle of what ever we are doing—sin included—right there WITH us. Not gone. Not leaving us. Not forsaking us. Not abandoning us. But right there IN us. We can no more get rid of Jesus IN us than we can separate ourselves from our own shadow.!

With this in mind look at II Corinthians 5:19-21. Jesus is not counting our sins against us. We are Reconciled in Jesus and we should live reconciled. Be reconciled! Jesus was MADE our sin for us. We are not given permission to violate a principle of love and commit adultery, but when and/or IF we do, Jesus is STILL right there IN us just as before. He doesn't leave. By His being there in the sin with us, we are motivated by Grace to NOT do this kind of thing in living out WHO we ARE in Jesus. We can still love Him though knowing He still loves us and made ALL payment for this present sin of ours and all other of our sins as well. We are told to flee fornication—and adultery.

With Jesus living in us and our KNOWING it, the Holy Spirit is continually leading us to the Godly behavior He wants us to exhibit and our desire is to NOT be sinning in this way.

So Jesus is still there. He still loves us. We are still saved. We still belong to the Father and always will. We are still seated at the right hand of the Father FULLY FORGIVEN for ALL sins we ever committed and for all the sins we shall commit in the future. Grace is NO license to sin! Freedom in Christ is NOT being free to DO anything we want. We were bought with a price, the blood of Jesus, and He wants us to LIVE knowing WHO we are IN Him and NOTHING can ever separate us from that Love of God He has for us.

# WHERE THE HELL DID THAT COME FROM?

One of the big questions which comes up in discussing Adoption, Inclusion, and Salvation Theology where all mankind is included in the original plan of God before the foundation of the world is the concept of "Hell" and what happens to wicked people. Are they not going to burn forever in Hell fire? Are they going to be annihilated? While we are not going to try and discuss all aspects of the Hell question, we would like to address certain facts about the concept of an ever burning and torturing Hell.

The concept of a punishing, torturing, burning, eternal place of torment is common to most all world religions stemming back to the first recognized religion of the world called Zoroastrianism after Zoroaster from about 6000 B.C. The punishment after death would be for those whose bad deeds outweighed their good ones in this first world religion.

The Pagan Plato, a student of Socrates, introduced the concept of a tormenting Hell fire in his writings in 400 B.C. in the famous work Phaedo. Then in the fifth century A.D. ( See the Catholic Encyclopedia article on HELL and LIMBO) Augustine refined the idea in the Christian Church where it took root and became a common teaching. Then between 1302 A.D. and 1321 A.D. Dante Alighieri wrote the poem, The Divine Comedy, in which he described his imaginings of a torturous, burning hell punishing wicked people. His three part poem consisted of Hell, Purgatory, and Paradise. Hence, the imaginings of this type of hell are from the minds of pagan men and perpetuated through the centuries by others who wanted to keep Christians "in line" with this fear tactic doctrinally.

For the first five hundred years of the Christian church, the theology of God's love which was demonstrated in His adoption and inclusion of all mankind into his Triune Life and the salvation of all mankind through the atoning and redemptive work of Jesus Christ was the message of the early church leaders.

The concept of a torturing hell was not disputed during the Protestant Reformation in the 1600's since the primary protest of the reformers, Martin Luther and others, was the sale of indulgences by the Catholic Church.

Western Christianity has just bought into the torturous ever burning hell of punishment for the wicked out of ignorance of where the idea come from in the first place.

Gehenna Fire is one of the common names for Hell fire. The name comes from Hinnom or the Valley of Hinnom which is located Southwest of Jerusalem. The area was historically used for the tossing of dead bodies of animals, garbage, and even people who died who were not members of any particular family and who had no one who cared anything about them for any kind of "proper" burial. This place represented a very bad ending of any human who was dumped—cast—there because it showed that they were not connected to any family who cared for them or loved them.

Jesus uses this comparison of one being thrown into this Gehenna Valley, ie, valley of Hinnom, to show that not being inside of the "Party of Heaven" was a terrible end. Fires were continually burning up the carcasses and other debris that was thrown into the valley of Hinnom. People in

Jesus' day would have understood better than we what He was trying to say using this analogy. Jesus was not trying to establish a doctrine of an ever burning torturous fire to forever punish the lost.

Lastly, in the Book of Revelation, we read that death and HELL both are to be cast into the lake of fire.

My purpose here is not to try and establish any doctrinal position on the doctrine of Hell, but to show some perspectives on the subject which many of us have not considered before.

We can say with assurance that God is Love and that all things can and will be made right in Jesus Christ and that all things have been reconciled in Jesus Christ and that God will conclude His plan for creation in His way and in His will based on His unending LOVE.

# WHO COMES INSIDE THE "PARTY" ?

Revelation poses for us a real problem between Chapter 20 and Chapter 22. For any looking for a literal interpretation of Revelation or a dispensational view of prophecy, there is a situation going on here which is obviously contradictory as far as the eternal fate of some goes.

In Revelation 20:15, " If anyone's name was not found written in the Book of Life, he was thrown into the lake of fire." In verse 14 this is called the "second death". Then in Revelation 21:8, we see a group of individuals which here says they will have their place in the lake of fire, the second death."

Now let's come to Revelation 22:14, " Blessed are those who wash their robes that they may have the right to the tree of life, and may go through the gates into the City ( New Jerusalem)." Then verse 15 says that **Outside the city are the dogs, those who practice magic arts, the sexually immoral, the murderers, the idolaters and all liars."**

Revelation 22:12, Jesus says He is going to give to **everyone** according to what he has done. The question here is what is meant by what he has done? Is it what the individual has done in his earthly life? If that is true then entrance into "heaven" or the City of Heaven is based on works!!! What the person did. Then its "here we go again" with the works / grace controversy. Could it be that what Jesus is referring to here in vs. 12 when He says, " I will give to everyone according to what he has done" is a reference to **BELIEVING** Jesus and **Who they are eternally in Jesus.**

Here I refer you back to John chapter 3:18. Belief is connected to not being condemned and unbelief is connected to standing in condemnation—or continued suffering and alienation in their unbelief.

If grace is true, and it is, then what Jesus is saying to **ALL** is that the good thing to do in order to participate in the Eternal Life in the joys of heaven is **TO BELIEVE.** By not believing, ie, not washing their robes **IN JESUS** and believing, they simply remain "unwashed", alienated, perishing, in suffering torment, "outside the city" in what the scripture calls the state of "second death" or lake of fire. Not pleasant to say the least!

When you stop to consider what those INSIDE the City are experiencing compared to what those OUTSIDE the City are experiencing the comparison between **Heaven and Hell** seems to become quite a bit clearer.

In conclusion, the place to start in answering any question concerning any scripture is to begin with **WHO IS JESUS?** When we see that the purpose of God has always been **Adoption** into the Triune life of God through Jesus Christ, the scales fall off of our eyes, our vision clears up and we see the glorious Eternal future of **ALL,** both the living and the dead, who ultimately come to see the **TRUTH THAT IS IN JESUS** and **BELIEVE IT.**

God is patient, not willing for any to perish, but for all to come to Repentance or in the Greek , " **METANOIA" Gk —A CHANGE OF MIND AND THINKING--BELIEF. A**nd God is ready to spend an **ETERNITY** helping humans, who have of not yet done so, **wash their robes in Jesus** and enter into the glories of the Father's House and into the party of Heaven.


# WHOSE FAITH REALLY MATTERS ?


Just whose faith is it anyway that makes the difference in our salvation, adoption, inclusion, redemption, reconciliation, new birth, resurrection, and ascension and future change from mortal to immortal? Whew, what a mouth full!

We have all probably heard preachers in the past, and not so past, emphasize the need for us to "have more faith". We have read of those of 'great' faith and those of 'little' faith. It is as if faith were an elusive commodity Christians seek for but somehow always seem to fall short of when the chips are down. Some worry if they have "enough" faith for their eternal future to be secured as if THEIR faith somehow were the determining factor as to the outcome of The Eternal Father's eternal plan for them.

Some question their faith in all areas when things don't seem to come together the way they have petitioned God. Some are told that if they 'just had more faith' they would be healed, have more money, get a better job, or ..............you can fill in the blank here.

The real question boils down to two and only two things. 1. What does it mean for you to have faith IN Jesus Christ? And, 2. What does the Faith OF Jesus Christ do? Here again this is not rocket science.

We can ask these questions. Before all things were created in, by, through, and for Jesus Christ AND You were thought of , adopted, redeemed, and chosen by God IN Christ WHAT part did YOUR faith play in the original 'blueprint plan' of God? Next, when Jesus was on the Cross reconciling you and forgiving you all of your sins, WHAT part did your faith play in the success of that death , resurrection, and ascension of Jesus? WHAT part did our faith play when Jesus came to seek and save what was lost? And make no mistake, what was LOST was found and SAVED by Jesus Christ. When Jesus cried from the Cross, "It is FINISHED", WHAT part did your faith play in the finishing of what Jesus came to do? When Paul declared in I Corinthians 15:22, that as in Adam all die, in Christ ALL are made alive, WHAT part did your faith play in what made that a reality in the first place.

The Triune God, Father, Son, and Holy Spirit, has/have PERFECT faith. Jesus Christ has perfect faith. It is ONLY He who can be the author and perfector , the beginner and the finisher of our faith. But, our faith DOES NOT MAKE GOD'S PLAN WORK! God's plan works because He MAKES it work. He is TRIUNE GOD. He is Lord God Almighty. He has the Love and Power to make it work for His Pleasure. And NOTHING can stop Him. ( Romans 8).

Maybe the question to ask of ourselves is NOT how much faith we have, because it really does NOT amount to a hill of beans in the grand design of things. But, the question to ask is do we BELIEVE by our limited personal faith what ALL it is that Jesus has already accomplished in us, for us, and to us.? Also, do we believe who we are IN JESUS? When we answer these questions in the affirmative then all other things we erroneously credit to our 'personal' faith will fall into place. Then Jesus Christ is the one who gets all the praise, honor, and glory. He is exalted. It then is not by any 'works' of ours that anything is accomplished spiritually in our life, but it is by Jesus Christ's love and grace and ....oh yes, FAITH, that DOES IT ALL for us ALL.

I believe, Lord help my unbelief!

Amen

# WHY CHRISTIAN LIVING ?

## ( REPLACING THE 'IF' FACTOR WITH 'SINCE'...Part II )

This paper is a follow up to "Replacing the 'if' Factor with Since". It deals with the position that Colossians 3 is not a prescription of how to 'get' saved, but that Col.3 is a description of how one whose identity is in Jesus Christ behaves.

Colossians 3, along with Ephesians 4 and Romans 12, are three chapters of scripture called 'Christian Living Chapters.' These chapters were never meant to be requirements for one to live up to in order to become a Christian, or to gain the love and approval of Jesus Christ. As some would say, individuals are 'separated' from God and 'unsaved' and that these 'requirements' – if lived out by the person- would place that person in a position for Christ to accept, love, and save them. Do we hear "WORKS" screaming out of that position?

What these chapters ARE dealing with is the description of behavior that reflects the life of Jesus Christ living in the person. This is how we are to live our life knowing WHO we are in Christ. These are descriptions of how Jesus lives. How He thinks. How He acts. They are reflections of the mind of Christ Paul mentions in Phil.2:5. "Let this mind be in you which was/is in Christ Jesus."

A person who walks in the flesh, who is motivated by selfish interests, vanity and by their carnal mind finds it impossible to employ these godly characteristics in their life. (Romans 8). BUT, when a person sees WHO they are in Jesus Christ and that Jesus lives His life in them and THROUGH them, then these elements of behavior will be manifested in their life. It really is not them doing these things and living in these ways, but it is Christ living in them who is the motivation for their life. He IS living this way and it is observed in the person through their actions.

Jesus is not some metaphysical mysterious magician who says the magic words "hocus pocus" over an individual and that person is now changed into the person described in the Christian living chapters of the Bible. No, Jesus along with the Father and the Holy Spirit INVADE the person's mind, heart, soul, being and life. The person lives and reflects this New Life empowered by the Triune God. The person grows in the Grace and knowledge of our Lord and Saviour, Jesus Christ. (II Pet.3:18).

All of this is a description of the Union between God and man, which Jesus came to complete. This Union produces relationship. It is promoted by love. First God's love for us and then in response to God's love our love for God. It is a way of life which God our Father desires for ALL of His children. He has secured it in Jesus Christ. It is available to and for all of mankind. This is the GOSPEL. This is Life.

# WHY IS BELIEVING ENOUGH?

WHY is believing enough? Surely there is more to our being saved than "just" believing. Surely there are "things" we must DO in order to "get" saved. "I believe in Grace, but let's not take this Grace thing too far!"

We may be familiar with the NUMEROUS scriptures which say, "believe or believes". Some of those would include: Acts 16:31; I Timothy 4:10; John 1:12; especially Romans 1:16. In fact the words believe or believes in context of believing Christ and in Christ occurs over 110 times in the New Testament. Interestingly enough in not one of those places is anything ELSE mentioned which needed to be done. None say believe AND do this or that or obey this or that. No other stipulation or work or duty is added to "just believing" in Christ or on Christ, or just believing Christ.

You would think that IF anything else were required that at least it would be mentioned in at least ONE scripture—but it is NOT. The purpose of this paper is not to 'prove' that we should believe, but to show WHY believing is ENOUGH.

Well for starters the numerous scriptures on "believe and believes" sited above say so! God never intended to make our life with Him forever contingent upon our human ability to do ANYTHING. He put ALL that responsibility on Jesus Christ through the INCARNATION. The whole world, humanity and the Cosmos are reconciled in Christ. Since this is true, what possibly can I do to make it "more" reconciled, redeemed, or saved? (Colossians 1:19-20).

God's original purpose in creating man was to Adopt him and include him in His very life ( Ephesians 1:3-14) and to do it through Jesus Christ, the WORD. In Jesus was LIFE. (John 1:4). He is the ONLY source of life. The Incarnation is ALL important.

Through the incarnation Jesus' life, death, resurrection, and ascension to the Father accomplished far more than just Jesus "making" it back to Heaven! Jesus became EVERYTHING for us! As the Vicarious human, (See Irenaeus, Athanasius, Barth, T.F. Torrance, Jinkins, Gunton, Kruger, and others), Jesus became our life for us and did everything to us and for us needed to accomplish God's purpose. So the BIG QUESTION IS: What is left for man to DO?

We even sing the songs, "Jesus Paid it ALL", and "Jesus Did it ALL" , and " I Surrender ALL". Ephesians 2:8-9 plainly tells us that we are saved by Grace and that there are NO WORKS which enter into the equation. It is all done, accomplished and finished in Jesus! ( John 19:30). So, scripture tells us plainly to believe this.

The Great Triune God, Father, Son and Holy Spirit never intended life with them to be any type of maze or contest or trial on humans behalf. If that were so, the Plan would

have failed from the start. God never intended for humans to "make it so", but He intended IN Jesus to "make it so" and Jesus DID.

The problem with this for most people is that it says we get something for nothing on our part. We all grew up with the concept of payment for goods and services rendered. That we have to do SOMETHING in return to make it fair. The point here is there is nothing we CAN do to add to what Jesus has already done for us as the substitutionary or vicarious life He lived for us. He is our LIFE. ( Colossians 3:4). He is our SIN. Let me repeat that, HE IS OUR SIN! And in Him all our sins which are now His sins are FORGIVEN AND FORGOTTEN and we have become in Him the Righteousness of God. (II Corinthians 5:21).

It is nice and appropriate for Christians who are in Jesus and know it to live like it. It is good not to sin. It is good not to lie, steal, cheat, over indulge, judge others, belittle others, and do any number of un-Christ like things. But the good news is that all of those things and all other sins now belong to Jesus and His blood and no longer are OURS.

( I John 2:2).

Does this sound unfair? Or, too good to be true? Probably so. But it is the GOOD NEWS and it is GOOD NEWS for all of us weak, carnal, selfish, human descendents of fallen Adam in whom we all died but who all are made alive in Jesus Christ! ( I Corinthians 15:22-23).

If we insist that this is NOT fair-- when it comes to this Great Salvation God determines what is fair and what is not-- then we are just going to have to get a grip on it and deal with it. God is not going to change to accommodate our incomprehensibleserindepityoustransliteratpersonaldeterminationalignorance.! Period.

I made that long word up to show the foolishness of not believing!

Can we just believe and trust and rest in Jesus and His Adoption, Inclusion, and Salvation for us All?

Lord, I believe, help my unbelief.

AMEN


# WHY MAN AND THE INCARNATION?


Why? Why did God create man in the first place? Why did the Word become flesh and dwell among humans? Or, asked another way, did Jesus come first and foremost to 'save' sinning mankind? What was the original purpose for Jesus to come into the world? The answer to these questions tells us WHY we are here and where we are going!

In answering these questions let me say what most Christian writers and Theologians state as to the reason Christ came. Their reason for the incarnation of the Son of God....

These writers say that the reason Christ came into the world was to Save sinning humans and make salvation possible for those who believe. The Atonement is the reason Jesus was born into the world in order to be the propitiation for the sins of the whole world.

NOW: Let's go back to a time BEFORE time into the mind and heart of the Great Triune God. Look at Ephesians 1:4. This is before the creation of the world. Before Adam. Before Adam's sin. Here we see in this verse that we, you and I and all humans, were chosen—by name I might add—by God IN Jesus to be Holy and without blame of any kind before Him in love. The next verse, :5, tells us that this PREDETERMINATION for the **Adoption** of all will be in Jesus Christ according to the desire, the will, the pleasure of the Great God. Verse 3, tells us that we have been blessed with EVERY spiritual blessing in heavenly places in Christ. So it is all laid out from a beginning before the creation of the Cosmos for man to be with God forever.

Backing up let's go to that divine meeting of the Triune God in their face to face meeting before there is anything created in the cosmos. Genesis 1:26-27. "Let us make man in our image." We know from what we just read in Ephesians 1 that this determination to make man in the image of God occurred BEFORE the creation of the world. So, what we read in Genesis 1:26-27 is simply a repeat of what the Triune God had originally said in His purpose for man's creation.

So why create man in the first place? The Triune God who had always existed in three persons as One God decided to share the wonderful love that they shared with each other with a human family who would be taken up into the life of the Eternal God and thereby God would have this expanded family to share in His life forever. When God created Adam and Eve this was on His mind—to share His life and love with them forever. The original purpose He had in mind for all of mankind.

Note: IF Adam and Eve had NOT sinned and NOT eaten of the Tree of the Knowledge of Good and Evil, then the Incarnation of Jesus Christ STILL would have been necessary to CONNECT THE UNION between the Triune God and humanity. There simply would have been no need for 'Atonement' one way or the other.

BUT, Adam DID sin. And that sin and fallenness passed on to all of his descendents—all humans.

Now the incarnation takes on new meaning and the mission of Jesus takes on the need for the Atoning Sacrifice of the Son of God. Jesus now must be the Sacrifice for the sins of the whole world as John says in John 1:29, "The Lamb of God who takes away the sin of the world."

The incarnation now takes on a dual meaning with the sin of Adam putting all of humanity in a fallen state and death. ( In Adam all die. I Cor.15:22). The Incarnation will accomplish TWO things.

1. The Incarnation through the life, death, resurrection and ascension of Jesus Christ will be the Sacrifice and Propitiation for all sin.( I John 2:2)
2. The Incarnation through the life, death, resurrection and ascension will create the UNION between Triune God and humanity thereby LIFTING all to the Father in heaven and

seat humanity there WITH Jesus. Eph. 2:6. ( In Jesus ALL are made alive. I Cor.15:22)

This understanding tells all of us what God is up to. What His will is for mankind. What Jesus did. What Jesus IS still doing. It tells us that God so loved the world. It tells us that God loves YOU. It tells us that it has all been made possible by the Great SAVIOUR, Jesus Christ. **AMEN.**


# WHY MANKIND HATES THE TRUTH OF JESUS

(Preferring darkness to the light)


"It is not really fair and besides, God can not possibly be that good for this to be true.!"

Why humans hate the truth of Jesus. Man lives in darkness as the Gospel of John tells us. Not only does man live in darkness he prefers darkness and when the illuminating light of Jesus shines upon man his immediate reaction is to reject that light.

There are other factors as well which influence this 'reject' mode of man. Satan is the 'god of this world' and the prince of the power of the air. ( II Cor.4:4; Ephesians 2:2). And, he does not want any of us to see it and understand it. Ephesians 6 tells us that spirit powers war against man's mind keeping us further in the darkness of this world.

Religion has told us that God really doesn't love us and that He is so holy as to be disconnected from His creation and not only does He not really love us He doesn't even like us. Where do you think that thinking comes from?

SO, when the illuminating light of Jesus who is the light of the world (John 8:12) shines on us our immediate reaction is to turn away and come up with all kinds of excuses as to why Jesus' truth is WRONG.

The Good News is not so good to the average person today. It is news that we 'might' make it, might be saved, might be loved, might be accepted, might be adopted, and might live eternally with God IF....... IF we DO all the right things and get God to love us and want to save us and not fling us into everlasting torture. This 'CONDITIONAL' Good News is anything but Good News!

But the Good News is the Best News EVER. God loves us all. He planned from the beginning to ADOPT us into His very life through Jesus. He planned to include us all into His very existence and joy in the loving relationship He wants to have with ALL of mankind. He sent Jesus to this earth through the incarnation to make this a rock solid REALITY. Jesus did His job. The sin of the world and our personal sins were taken away in Jesus. ( John 1:29; I John 2:2). Jesus became sin for us that we might be the righteousness of God. ( II Corinthians 5:19-21).

SO, what remains for us? God loves us all. He predetermined at the beginning, before the foundation of the world, to Adopt us and include us in His life in Jesus forever. ( Ephesians 1:3-14). He took care of our sin problem at the cross 2000 years ago. He has sent the Holy Spirit to reveal these truths to us as He chooses in His time to make this known to us individually.

John 1:8 tells us that John wrote these things about Jesus that "you might believe." When we know Who we are in Jesus and believe it we can then live and experience the abundant life Jesus gives all of us. BUT, here again 'men's deeds were/are evil and man in his darkness wants to keep it that way. And, surely God can not be THAT Good!!!

Well, He is that GOOD!!! He is that much LOVE. He does Love you and me. He likes His children and wants to be with us FOREVER. And get this, He has the power to make all of this happen in Jesus. ( I Peter 1:3-6). We are destined by God to be with Him ( and each other ) forever in joy and pleasure and peace and beauty in the Father's home. The sad truth is that some won't believe this and not experience it with the Father but remain in misery and suffering!

The Good News is just that. GOOD NEWS. And it is Good News for EVERYONE.

But in order to experience this Good News personally, we MUST believe it. Without belief there is no way we can experience this joyful and abundant life Jesus gives.

Just because we may not understand some things does not make them not true!

Will we wipe away the darkness, which covers our spiritual eyes, and see Jesus Christ and the Father He came to reveal and the LOVE God has for us personally and BELIEVE.

# WHY TELL SOMEONE THE GOOD NEWS ?

How do you tell someone about the Good News? What do you say? What approach do you use? How do you broach the subject? And, WHY even tell them in the first place?

Look at people in general in our society. They are lonely. They don't feel valued. They feel inferior. Rejected. Unloved. Not belonging. Fearful of many different things—diseases, dying, and the afterlife. They feel insecure, unassured, confused, misdirected with feelings of no goals in life and just floating along like everybody else. They lack real Joy, peace, happiness, and hope. Does this picture look bleak to you? It does to me.

These are the people Jesus loves. He wants them to be connected to Him so that the ABUNDANT LIFE He gives can become a reality for all of these little ones who are His children.

In truth people are living out the life of a fallen nature and humanity bequeathed on them by Adam. The result of which are suffering, misery, angst, unhappiness and death. ( I Cor.15:22). In this heritage of Adam all are dying and death is the end result. But LIFE is the result IN Jesus.

Jesus has much to offer. He says that he came to bring LIFE and not just life but ABUNDANT Life. He states that " He is the way the truth and THE LIFE." He asserts that whoever believes in Him has passed from Death into LIFE. And that whoever believes in Him will NEVER DIE. (John 10:10; John 14:6; John 5:24; John 11:26).

Everything a human could possibly want is freely offered and given to all of us IN , BY, and THROUGH Jesus Christ. (James 1:17).

When we share the Good News with the unchurched or unbelievers or when we just share more of the Good News with anyone we are doing them the greatest favor anyone could ever do for them. Sharing the Good News is a joy and blessing to give out to these people. It is not a chore to feel failure in if they don't "accept Jesus" and get saved. They already are Saved and Adopted. They just need to be told the TRUTH !

# WILL GOD PUNISH THE WICKED FOREVER?

Western Christianity has been heavily influenced by Roman civil law and the laws of the Old Covenant both with their attendant requirements for PUNISHMENT for certain acts which judicially speaking were fitting for the crimes committed. We carry this concept with us as we approach an understanding of life after death for those who refuse to accept and believe their inclusion in the life of Jesus. We see these "wicked" as having to serve out an eternal condemnation by God to "pay" for their sinful lifestyle on this earth.

Justice DEMANDS punishment. All judicial systems have various sentences for certain crimes which the defendant must pay by serving due time-- up to life in prison.

Since we come at an understanding of how God deals with the wicked after death based on Roman civil law and Old Covenant judgements we understand from a law, punishment, judgement, and payment approach.

When we look at all humans—us included—we see humanity subject to DISOBEDIENCE and in total rebellion against God's laws and principles. Actually God made us this way subject to disobedience so that He could have MERCY on ALL.( ROM.11:32).

The good news is that while we ALL were ungodly sinners in rebellion and hatred against God Christ died for US ALL.(Rom.5:6-8). Christ PAID the Eternal price for all of our sins and wickedness and evilness and ungodliness and suffered all the suffering that is eternally needed or required for all humans. There does NOT REMAIN any more suffering or punishment or sacrifice that is required by any of us. Christ paid it ALL for ALL for ALL time!

When we come to the question will the wicked be tormented and or punished by God eternally in a state or condition or a place called "Hell", the answer should be OBVIOUS to all of us which is : NO, they will not be dealt with by God since God has already dealt with the Ungodly in the suffering and Death of JESUS CHRIST.

What we are talking about here is the EXTREME Grace of God extended to all of His children from the creation of the world. God has taken up all of humanity to His side in Jesus Christ. There is no longer any payment for the sins and wickedness and ungodliness of mankind due. It has been paid in FULL by Jesus Christ.

We need to come to a greater understanding of God's LIMITLESS Grace and Total Love demonstrated to us in that while were "yet ungodly sinners" Christ died for us ALL.

Now the only question remains: Will individuals believe this TRUTH? To those who do believe they will spend an eternal life in the most joyous fashion possible.

For those, however, who do NOT believe this TRUTH they will spend that same eternal life in a very different manner. One that the Bible calls Hell!! Misery, suffering, weeping and gnashing of teeth, in darkness and very extreme unhappiness. Notice: This will be by their CHOICE due to their choosing NOT to BELIEVE!!!!!!!!! Note: God is not the one putting them in Hell. They by their own choice put themselves in that state.

So belief becomes of paramount importance. Our future is secured in Jesus Christ and IN the life of the Great Triune God. Will YOU believe it?

God wants to know if YOU will believe it or not?

# WITH ADAM'S SIN, WHAT WAS GOD TO DO?

God created a perfect creation. God created the world and created Adam and Eve and placed them in a perfect environment. God desired to be with Adam (the name means mankind) forever in a continual state of happiness and bliss. God wanted to be in Adam's life and joy in His love for His children.

God's eternal purpose was not to be denied when Adam sinned by eating of the tree of the knowledge of good and evil. Jesus was coming to the earth to unite God with man and to Adopt man and include all of humanity in the life of God. This was God's purpose in creating man originally. (Ephesians 1:3-14). God simply wanted to share His abundant love with His children—forever.

When Adam sinned he brought the death penalty on himself and all of his offspring in human history. ( I Corinthians 15:22). Not only did he bring death on all of humanity, but untold misery and suffering we see in the human experience.

With Adam sinning now God is faced with a situation which needed to be reversed or "undone". Jesus' coming now would accomplish several things. It would allow for man to be UNITED with God in Union through His life, death, resurrection and ascension--the first purpose of Jesus' coming. Second, Jesus' suffering and death would now become payment for the sins of Adam and all of mankind bringing FORGIVENESS for ALL sins of ALL humans for ALL time. The Atonement. The life God originally gave to Adam and his descendents is now restored IN Jesus.( I Corinthians 15:22). "As in Adam ALL die, in Christ ALL are made alive." And Jesus coming provided for the Holy Spirit to be given to man to go along side us in our human walk and comfort us. Jesus coming would UNDO what Adam did.

However, from Adam on throughout human history mankind will face an existence influenced by the evil of another powerful spirit called the Adversary—Satan the Devil. Human history will be short lived with Satan as the "god of this world" with his defeat by Jesus (Matthew 4). However long man's human experience on this earth is it is still SHORT.

The good news is that God has not left us to the complete control and influence of Satan the Devil during this human stay on the earth. Jesus in the abundance of His love sent and poured out His Spirit on all humans thereby sharing his love with all mankind.

By and large man has NOT known all of this. When man lives his life NOT knowing who he is IN Jesus then the primary way he lives is in the influence of the Adversary and in the nature of his fallen mind. All sorts of evil, suffering and misery are the natural course of his life. His not knowing who he is in Jesus does not make him NOT in Jesus, but it prevents him from experiencing the real abundant life that Jesus gives.

Remember all things are created by, through, and for Jesus and He sustains ALL of creation. ( Colossians 1:16-17). And also that we live and move and have our being in Jesus. (Acts 17:28). And, that Christ is our LIFE. (Colossians 3:4).

So the main point here is in KNOWING. Knowing Who We Are In Jesus and believing it and thereby living in this knowledge. And, yet with this knowledge and belief we still sin but those sins are taken by Jesus and forgiven thereby allowing us to be continually declared righteous by Jesus.

God created a perfect world and cosmos. He has desired from the 'beginning' to live with man forever. His purpose was not thwarted and will never be thwarted since He has all power and will accomplish what

He desires. Nothing can ever separate us from the love of God which is in Christ Jesus. ( Romans 8:28-39).

God's purpose in creating originally was to have a FAMILY living with Him and IN Him forever. You are included in that family. And nothing is going to stop God from sharing that eternal life with us. Jesus saw to that!

# "WORK OUT YOUR OWN SALVATION"?

The question comes up from time to time, as it did just this past Sunday during a Q & A session at services, concerning what Paul meant in Philippians 2:12-13. Specifically, "...work out your own salvation with fear and trembling."

Let's remember that Paul is in prison in Rome as he writes this book. ( Ephesians and Colossians are the other two prison epistles from Paul's first imprisonment.) It is against the law for anyone to be a Christian at this time of around 60 A.D. Paul knows well the implications of carrying the Gospel message and being thrown into prison because of doing so.

In the 300 or so years following the life and death of Jesus it was a crime punishable by horrible death to be associated with Jesus or to claim to be a follower of Jesus or a Christian. At times this persecution was more severe than it was at other times. Martyrs were continually being unmercifully killed in public arenas to entertain the masses. Christians had to be very careful how they practiced their faith and how they presented the Gospel to those with whom they came in contact. FOXES BOOK OF MARTYRS is filled with the stories of these early Christians who gave their life for the truth.

From prison Paul wants to encourage those in Philippi to continue to put their faith into action, to allow God to work through them, and to work whatever good work their salvation inspires them to do in the world **even if** they must do so with the fear hanging over their head of being thrown into jail over doing God's work and possibly even being martyred. And, even in the face of immediate repercussions causing fear and trembling on their part, that God is with them and that he, Paul, wishes for them to continue on with the spreading of the Gospel message no matter what!

What these verses are **not** saying. They are not saying for anyone to work **for** their salvation, or to work **out** whatever is necessary to attain their salvation, or to work to **maintain** their salvation. Paul had just written in the previous book, of Ephesians, chapter 2:5-8, that—" it is by Grace that you **have been saved** through faith and this **not** from yourselves, it is the **gift** of God." Paul is not undoing in Philippians what he had just written in Ephesians.

# WORSHIPPING GOD AS THE PAGANS DID?

In Deuteronomy 12:29-32, God said not to worship Him the way the pagans worshipped their gods. True enough. Fundamentalists have used this scripture for years to uphold whatever aberrant "truth" they may hold to in order to stand alone as the sole beacon of light on said subject.

When the LORD made this statement in Deuteronomy 12 it was at a time when He was bringing the Israelites into pagan lands where they would set up His way of life based on His 613 rules and regulations—laws. These Israelites would be replacing people who practiced every conceivable manner of wickedness involving their "worship" of their gods imaginable. Much of their worship included indiscriminate sex worship of the pagan gods. He lists various things in a few scriptures near. Dt.14:1, " don't CUT yourselves or shave the front of your heads—resembling a male organ". Dt. 18:10, " don't sacrifice your children in FIRE , or seek DIVINATION, or, SORCERY, or, INTERPRETERS OF OMENS, or , engage in WITCHCRAFT, or, CAST SPELLS, or, seek a SPIRITIST, or , one who CONSULTS THE DEAD. God wanted Israel to be separate from these practices and gave them the law which would do this. The heathen's superstitious practices could not be included in this God given new way of life.

In John 4:21-24, Jesus talks with the Samaritan woman at the well and tells her that her past forms of worship and even what was practiced in Jerusalem would pass and indeed had passed as correct ways to worship God. Jesus clearly says that not the physical or superstitious practices would be acceptable, but that true worshippers would worship God in "Spirit and in Truth."

What Jesus is saying is that no legally formatted worship or superstitious worship would be of value. But, that worshipping God in Spirit and in Truth involved an intimate, personal RELATIONSHIP with the Father.

When we see in Colossians 1:20 that ALL things have been reconciled in Jesus Christ, all things take on new meaning for us. Activities take on new meaning. Practices take on new meaning. We see through the "eyes of faith" now. And live through the eyes of faith as well.

We obviously do many things the pagans did due to the fact that they were human and lived on this earth. Those things are not wrong for us to do! The pagans married, had children, wore rings, ate food, sang songs, played music, danced, laughed, loved art, built houses, had places of worship, kept harvest festivals, used greenery, holly berries, crosses, candles, bells and other things in their worship, and the list goes on and on. Just because the heathen or pagans did something or used something does not make it wrong for us to do or to use the exact same things!!! After all there are only so many things humans can use in our physical existence.

The Great Triune God wants us to realize who we are. We are His kids. He created us and Adopted us INTO His very life through the life, death, resurrection, and ascension of Jesus Christ. He wants us to know it and believe it and live it in RELATIONSHIP with Him.

In all honesty, however, I am sure this little paper will not convince some people that some things are still wrong for Christians to do today. I can only say that their "Spirit and Truth" has not grown to maturity just yet. But, then again, we have an eternity to grow inside of God's great love for us.

# YOU CAN'T HAVE IT BOTH WAYS !

You have heard the saying, "You can't have it both ways". When we consider TRUE Theological concepts this saying plays out with more impact than ever. Consider:

Either God, Father, Son and Holy Spirit Loves humanity ( all humans) or He doesn't.

Either Triune God is distant and disconnected from creation or He is present and involved.

Either God is INSIDE of His creation and INSIDE of humans or He isn't.

Either God's Glorious Plan applies to ALL things, ALL humanity, or it doesn't.

Either Christ Redeemed the Creation or He didn't.

Either Christ Reconciled all things to Himself or He didn't.

Either God so loved the (Entire) World that He gave His only Son for it or He didn't.

Either Christ's sacrifice was payment (propitiation) for ALL sins or it wasn't.

Either All died in Adam and All are made alive in Christ or they aren't.

Either all are buried with Christ in HIS baptism or all are not

Either all are crucified with Christ or all are not.

Either All are resurrected in Jesus or All are not.

Either All are seated at the right hand of the Father or they are not.

Either God's purpose is to save man and not condemn him or it isn't

Either we were chosen in Christ before the foundation of the world or we were not

Either Grace was given to us before time or it wasn't

Either God is the beginner and finisher of our faith or He isn't

Either we can be separated from God or we can not.

Either we are presented by Jesus without fault or we are not.

Either we live, move, and have our being in Jesus NOW or we do not

Either we are Adopted by God in Christ or we are not.

Either we are included IN the life of God or we are not.

Either the Kingdom was prepared for us before the foundation of the world or it wasn't

Either all died when Christ died or all did not.

Either we are all IN Jesus' hands or we are not

Either Humanity is the Elect of God or it is not.

Either we believe or we do not believe.

YOU CAN'T HAVE IT BOTH WAYS

PS Every "either" listed above carries scriptural proof in the affirmative of what is stated . That is another paper.


# YOUR INCLUSION IN THE LIFE OF GOD

What if ? What if you were informed by a really good source that there is a God and that He created the cosmos and humans originally to be His children in order to share His love with them, and He made all arrangements to provide for their physical life AND their eternal life forever. And you were informed that Nothing, absolutely nothing, could change that decision and reality which the Great God has brought about.

What if you were informed that this reality has Nothing to do with whether or not you believe it. That your belief or non-belief does not make it so or not so. It is so because the ALL-POWERFUL Father of all creation has made it so!

What if you were informed that this God- Father, Son, and Holy Spirit- the ONE Triune God- Loves YOU and sees you as His beloved child who He loves with complete and total Unconditional Love.

What if you were informed that there is not one single person on this earth that is MORE valuable to God than YOU!!! Actually ALL human beings are equally valuable to God.

What if you were informed that The Three in One , Triune God, Father, Son and Holy Spirit completely SAVED YOU with His Salvation by His Grace and Gift of Love BEFORE you were even born into this physical world.

And this Great God wants you to know it. He is not Hoping you will by any means MAKE it so, He informs us all by His Powerful

Declaration that this is the way it is and it is going to STAY this way!!!!!!!!!!!!

Would this information be GOOD NEWS to you? Well that is exactly what the Triune God calls it!! GOOD NEWS!!! And it is the BEST NEWS you or anyone else will ever hear. And, I know that this sounds simple and "too good to be true"!! And that it sounds too "easy" to our doubting minds. But that is just the point! God has made it simple so we CAN understand it and believe it. And, that is what Jesus Christ asks us to do—BELIEVE.

Just to get us started in a little examination of this, I am listing some Scriptures here for your inspection. They support what was said in the first part of this paper. So here we go:

Colossians 1:16-17—ALL things were created by the Word/Jesus and FOR Him, and that INCLUDES YOU.

Ephesians 1:3-14—YOU were chosen in by God BEFORE the creation of the world, by name, personally, and REDEEMED for God by the Blood of Christ. ( Jesus was even Slain before the foundation of the World—Revelation 13:8 ).

Romans 5:18—The One act / Life of Righteousness of Jesus brought Life to ALL Humans—YOU included!

I Corinthians 15:22-23—Adam passed the Death Penalty on to all of his descendents therefore All die, BUT, in Jesus ALL are made alive—not LATER—but NOW. ( See Acts 17:28—In Jesus we live and move and have our BEING!"—NOW.)

II Corinthians 5:14-19—Jesus Died for ALL . And, God has not counted our sins against us, but reconciling us to Himself in Christ.

I Timothy 2:6—Christ gave Himself a Ransom for ALL—You !

I John 2:2—He is the atoning sacrifice for the sins of the whole world.

I Timothy 4:10 – Our hope is in the living God, who is the Savior of ALL men/women, especially of those who believe.

Hebrews 10:10—We have ALL been made Holy through the sacrifice of the body of Jesus Christ one time for ALL !!!

Romans 8:15-16—We received the Spirit of sonship (Adoption) …we are the Children of God.

The GOSPEL OF JESUS CHRIST is simply this. God Loves us and has saved His creation in Jesus Christ—You included. What He wants is

227

for that Truth of this GOOD NEWS to be told to individuals who do not know that their Life is IN Jesus AND that His Life is IN them. They are Children of God. When they know this truth, then they can begin to live like it and begin to EXPERIENCE the Abundant Life that Jesus wants them to have in Him—John 10:10 " I came that they may have life and have it more abundantly."

We are not just saved FROM something, we are saved FOR something and that something is to share in the life of the Living God—Father, Son, and Holy Spirit.

REPENTANCE (Gk.Metanoia, or a change of mind) is simply coming to BELIEVE this truth and understanding just WHO we really are IN Jesus. Colossians 3:4 tells us that Jesus IS our Life. Our Real Life. And, He is our real Life FOREVER.!!!

What Jesus Christ has done For us and To us is truly Amazing. He has raised us up with Him and seated us with Him in the Heavenly realm. Ephesians 2:6.

Jesus speaks to all of us in John 14:20 when He says, " ...you will realize that I am in my Father and you are IN me, and I am IN you." This is something we DO NOT MAKE HAPPEN, it is something we come to BELIEVE. Jesus even says again in John 17:20-21, that we are IN Him and the Father ( by the Holy Spirit which God has placed in the heart of ALL Humans who have ever lived.) This is an inescapable Truth. And, God wants the world to know it!!! Sadly, some will NOT believe it. But, whether or not they believe it has nothing to do with whether or not it is SO. It is the TRUTH OF GOD. He wants you to know it and BELIEVE IT.

There are numerous other scriptures we could have included here on this subject, but for the sake of time and space we did not. Please feel free to discuss this further with the person who gave you this paper, they are most desirous of helping you understand more of just how much our Great God Loves you and has included you in His life FOREVER.

# JESUS ACCEPTED US INTO HIS LIFE
# ORIGINALLY

A common concept in Western Christian doctrine is that humanity is SEPARATED from God and that man must accept Jesus into his life after repenting and that this moves the believer from the state of 'lost' to saved and 'unseparates' him from God.

Often a verse such as Colossians 1:21 is used to show this separation. But is this actually the case? Is man lost until he 'accepts' Jesus into his life? Is man 'made right' with God when he—man—believes that Jesus died for his sins by shedding His blood? In other words, is the salvation of humans left up to their 'making' it happen by what they do or don't do, believe or don't believe? Who is the author and finisher or perfector of man's faith anyway?

Before we go further in this, let's look at Colossians 1:21 and see what it really says. " Once you were "ApallotrioO" in the Greek.. It means 'estranged' or 'alienated' in our language. It does not mean separated and can not mean separated here. Acts 17:28 says that mankind lives, moves, and has his being in Jesus Christ. If one were to be separated from Jesus totally, he or she would cease to exist at all !!!

This kind of thinking is really backwards. The truth is that Jesus from before the creation of the world ADOPTED humans into the life and family of God, INCLUDED man into the life of God, REDEEMED, RECONCILED, SAVED HUMANITY and ACCEPTED man INTO His life originally. This is the starting point. See: Ephesians 1:3-14.

Adam side tracked the plan of God by sinning and introducing sin into man's world. That sin brought death on all humans. ( I Cor.15:22 ). With Jesus' perfect ATONING Sacrifice man was forgiven all of his sins and made alive with Christ and declared to be RIGHTEOUS through Jesus Christ. ( Romans 5:18-20 ).

In reality Adam LOST the human race by sinning. But the Good News is that Jesus Christ came to 'seek and to save WHAT WAS LOST.!!!' (Luke 19:10). Jesus came and accomplished what He set out to do by becoming the 'Propitiation' for the sins of ALL THE WORLD. ( I Jn.2:2). No one escapes the 'Propitiatory' act of Jesus' saving work. Absolutely NO ONE!

When we use terminology such as 'one must accept Jesus into our life', what we really should be saying is acknowledging that Jesus has already accepted us into His life from the beginning and that we NOW have come to believe this FACT of ADOPTION AND INCLUSION AND SALVATION. We need to keep the "horse before the cart'—so to speak.

Sin has done a serious detrimental number on mankind. Sin has brought untold suffering, misery and pain on humanity. Through sin we have alienated and estranged ourselves from God—but we have NOT SEPARATED ourselves from Him. We have broken fellowship with Him. But we have never broken our RELATIONSHIP with Him. We are His Children—FOREVER. He is our FATHER forever.

Our Triune God has always purposed to have us in His life forever and He in our life forever as well. ( Jn.14:20 ; Jn.17:20-26). All the plans and preparations were designed by our God ORIGINALLY since before anything was ever created in the first place.

God's FINISHED PLAN does not depend on the puny efforts of weak, sinful, puny, mortal, human beings. It all depended on and depends on JESUS CHRIST. And He finished it. ( Jn.19:30). " IT IS FINISHED!"

The problem most of us have in explaining all of this comes from past misunderstandings stemming from wrong Western Christian Theological errors which have focused on the cross only and Atonement.

God is not mad at ANYBODY. God LOVES everyone. YOU too. God is not OUT TO GET anyone. God is not out to condemn anyone. God's plan has been perfect from the beginning in ETERNALLY SHARING HIS LIFE WITH HUMANITY. He wanted it to work. Imagine that!!! And the GOOD NEWS is that He HAS MADE IT WORK in, by, and through JESUS CHRIST's life, death, resurrection and ascension.

AMEN


# YOUR PERSONAL GOOD NEWS


Let's just cut to the chase. What you may have heard concerning Christianity, religion, and Theology aside we will look at some astoundingly good news most have never dreamed of.

The great Triune Creator God created human kind in order to share His LIFE of total love with that human family. God adopted humankind into his very life from the very beginning even before the foundation of the world ! (Eph.1:3-14). Jesus Christ created everything that exists FOR Himself and He sustains that creation. ( Col.1:14-17).

Triune God was so full of love and LIFE that it was bursting to overflow into "something" and that something was the human family God created and started with Adam.

The only way God could experience human life was to become human and in so doing was able to carry humanity into the very heart of Himself. But this union was not one sided. As humanity was carried into the heart of the Triune God, the LIFE, heart, essence, existence, spirit, being of God was imported into humankind by the Spirit of God making the connection, the union between God and man complete. All this was done through Jesus Christ's life, death, resurrection and ascension to the Father.

The GOOD NEWS of the Bible is simply this. We are God's children, with God's Life living in us by His Spirit and loved by our Father. We have an eternal future planned for us in our Father's house with the rest of our brothers and sisters. We can share in the abundance of that life now by knowing about it, knowing where it comes from in Jesus Christ, and believing it.

This is not an "IF" proposition. This is not something "to be" acquired. This is the TRUTH OF GOD. This is an ETERNAL DECLARATION AND PROCLAMATION of the WAY IT IS.

Adam's sin brought untold suffering and death into the human family. But in Jesus Christ abundant JOY and LIFE has replaced that suffering and death.

( I Cor. 15:22).

The KEY is just understanding what The Triune God's original purpose was and His POWER to bring it all about. ( I Peter 1:3-6). And He has! In JESUS CHRIST.

The really good news NOW is that....... YOU ARE INCLUDED .....in the whole plan and you have been since before the foundation of the world. (Eph.1:3-14). God has ALWAYS loved YOU!

Many QUESTIONS arise over this brief explanation of the Gospel. Some may call it an over simplification. What about this and what about that? What about sin? What about works? What about bad people? What about "Hell"? The "what abouts' are almost endless. But the Good News is Jesus. God With us. God WITHIN us. Immanuel. The answers are to be found to be sure. But they are ONLY found in Jesus. The place to start with any question is, " WHO is JESUS?" When we start there at the

231

correct starting place the beauty of the PLAN OF GOD opens up to our understanding like a beautiful flower on a spring morning.

GOD is LOVE. He loves YOU. You are the SON or DAUGHTER God has always loved and wanted. YOU are SPECIAL to God. How good is that?

And our future as Psalm 16:11 says will be filled " with pleasures forevermore at God's right hand." FOREVER.

You are loved, liked, wanted, adopted and included in the life of God. Jesus made it happen for all of us. Believe it !

AMEN AND AMEN

# RESOURCES AND RECOMMENDED READING LIST

( For Trinitarian Adoption and Inclusion Theology)

DANCING IN THE DARK, By  Graham Buxton

DOGMATICS IN OUTLINE, By Karl Barth

INVITATION TO THEOLOGY, By Michael Jinkins

PARABLE OF THE DANCING GOD, By C. Baxter Kruger

PARTICIPATION IN GOD: A PASTORAL DOCTRINE OF THE TRINITY , By Paul S. Fiddes

THE HUMANITY OF GOD, By Karl Barth

THE MEDIATION OF CHRIST, By Thomas F. Torrance

THE MYSTERY OF CHRIST AND WHY WE DON'T GET IT,

By Robert F. Capon

THE PARABLES OF JUDGEMENT, By Robert F. Capon

THE CHRISTIAN DOCTRINE OF GOD, ONE BEING THREE PERSONS, By Thomas F. Torrance

THE TRINITARIAN FAITH,  By Thomas F. Torrance

THE HOLY SPIRIT,  By Donald G. Bloesch

GOD IN THREE PERSONS, By Millard Erickson

LIFE IN THE SPIRIT, By Thomas C. Oden

THE GREAT DANCE, By C. Baxter Kruger

GOD IS FOR US, By C.  Baxter Kruger

Trinitarian Letters may be ordered from any book store. On line from Barnes and Noble, Books-a-Million, Amazon.com. They may be ordered from the author by sending $25, which includes shipping and handling to:

TRINITARIAN LETTERS
% PAUL KURTS
243 RAINBOW DR.
MADISON, ALABAMA 35758

E:Mail me personally at:

Paul.Kurts@gci.org


Check out the web site and blog for TRINITARIAN LETTERS  at www.trinitarianletters.com